Pharmaceutical and Medical Devices Manufacturing Computer Systems Validation

Pharmaceutical and Medical Devices Manufacturing Computer Systems Validation

By

Orlando López

Routledge
Taylor & Francis Group
A PRODUCTIVITY PRESS BOOK

First edition published in 2018
by Routledge/Productivity Press
711 Third Avenue New York, NY 10017, USA
2 Park Square, Milton Park, Abingdon, Oxon OX14 4RN, UK

Printed on acid-free paper

International Standard Book Number-13: 978-1-138-04118-9 (Hardback)
International Standard Book Number-13: 978-1-315-17461-7 (eBook)

Library of Congress Cataloging-in-Publication Data

Names: López, Orlando, author.
Title: Pharmaceutical and medical devices manufacturing computer systems validation / Orlando López.
Description: Boca Raton : Taylor & Francis, [2018] | Includes bibliographical references and index.
Identifiers: LCCN 2018020239 (print) | LCCN 2018021977 (ebook) | ISBN 9781315174617 (e-Book) | ISBN 9781138041189 (hardback : alk. paper)
Subjects: | MESH: Equipment and Supplies | Computer Systems | Computer Security | Technology, Pharmaceutical--methods
Classification: LCC RS122.2 (ebook) | LCC RS122.2 (print) | NLM W 26.55.C7 | DDC 615.10285--dc23
LC record available at https://lccn.loc.gov/2018020239

Visit the Taylor & Francis Web site at
http://www.taylorandfrancis.com

For Lizette,

Mikhail Sr., István, Christian, and

Mikhail Jr.

Contents

Preface

This is the second edition of my first book about computer systems validation (CSV). This edition is relevant to computer systems performing activities covered by the medicines' manufacturing practices regulation, including pharmaceutical, biologicals, medical devices, food, and blood related production systems and quality control systems performing current good manufacturing practices (CGMP*) quality control testing.

The first edition was published in 2004,[†] covering US FDA 21 CFR Part 11 and CSV.

This second edition provides updated and practical information. At the same time, it highlights and efficiently integrates Regulatory Authorities[‡] CGMP.

CSV is the process that assures the formal assessment and reporting of quality and performance measures for all the life cycle stages of computer system development,[§] its implementation, qualification and acceptance, operation, modification, requalification, maintenance, and retirement.[¶]

---

* Good Manufacturing Practices (GMPs) mean the part of the quality assurance process which ensures that products are consistently produced and controlled in accordance with the quality standards appropriate to their intended use (Commission Directive 2003/94/EC). GMPs are contained in regulations that describe the methods, equipment, facilities, and controls required for producing human and veterinary products, medical devices, and processed food.

† López, O. *21 CFR Part 11: Complete Guide to International Computer Validation Compliance for the Pharmaceutical Industry*. Boca Raton, FL: CRC Press, 2004.

‡ Bodies having the statutory power to regulate. The expression "regulatory authorities" includes the authorities that review submitted products data and consult inspections. These bodies are sometimes referred to as competent authorities.

§ Note: In this book a "developer" can either be an external company or an in-house software development group.

¶ Pharmaceutical Inspection Cooperation Scheme (PIC/S). *Good Practices for Computerised Systems in Regulated "GxP" Environments*, PI 011-3, September 2007.

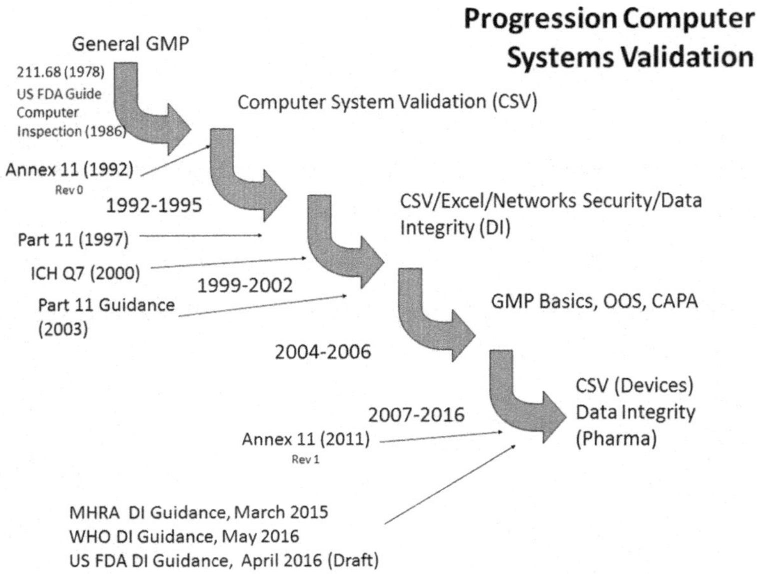

A practical approach will be presented to increase efficiency and to ensure that the validation of computer systems is correctly achieved.

Since writing my first book about CSV in 2004, computer validation practices have progressed. Many international guidelines and regulations have been written since 2004.* All of these guidelines and regulations have added value to the knowledge of computer validation practices and e-compliance.

As an example, the second revision of the EMA Annex 11 was published in 2011 providing a rich picture of computer e-compliance, including e-records integrity.

Another great shift since 2004, by the regulated entities, is the use of service providers (including Software as a Service [SaaS], Infrastructure as a Service [IaaS], and/or Platform as a Service [PaaS]) reducing the regulated entity information systems budget in the development, maintenance, and supporting of computer systems.

Over the past three years alone, several major regulatory authorities have published six new guidance documents addressing data management and data integrity in the pharmaceutical industry: United States (US) Food and Drugs Administration (FDA), World Health Organization (WHO), European Medicines Agency (EMA), United Kingdom (UK) Medicines and Healthcare Products Regulatory Agency (MHRA), Pharmaceutical Inspection

* López, O. "Regulations and Regulatory Guidelines of Computer Systems in Drug Manufacturing 25 Years Later." *Pharmaceutical Engineering,* 33(4) 2013.

Cooperation Scheme (PIC/S), China Food and Drugs Administration (CFDA), and Australia's Therapeutic Goods Administration (TGA). These guidance documents make available comprehensive expectations by the regulators about the management of regulated records and added regulatory expectations to be considered during the design of the application and the validation. These expectations are converted to requirements with the associated workflows. Each workflow needs to be validated.

This 2018 edition of my book covers CSV and e-compliance applicable to worldwide regulations.

Big Data and Internet of Things (IoT) are new technologies presenting current e-compliance understanding with new challenges.

As in my first book, my vision for this second edition is to make known my views on how to perform CSV, and to provide readers with information on how they should work successfully in an e-compliance role in today's high-pressure, regulated environment.

Control programs for pharmaceutical, medical devices, diagnostics and food production, and quality control systems relevant to the manufacture of products must be well documented and thoroughly specified. Computer systems must only change after careful control since the e-records associated within these systems are now highly relevant to the e-records integrity expectations. If manufacturing systems fail, the quality of the product and associated e-records are in question.

With the expectations about data integrity by all worldwide regulatory agencies or competent authorities, CSV practitioners are encountering a new wave of controls that must be added to e-compliance programs. Any data created as part of a CGMP record must be retained so that it can be evaluated by the quality unit as part of release criteria and maintained for CGMP purposes.

This book emphasizes the promotion of a conceptual understanding of e-compliance in the context of computer systems under the relevant CGMP regulation.

It initiates with a discussion of the CSV concepts, prerequisites and the regulatory requirements associated with the computer systems in the main regulatory agencies or competent authorities.

It follows with the review of key relevant processes and related documentation supporting the CSV process.

In addition, this book covers e-records integrity controls and explains how technologies such as hashing, encryption, and digital signatures can support e-records integrity in the applicable medicines' manufacturing practices regulation.

It is not the intention of this book to develop a paradigm or model for the regulated industry.

Enjoy reading!

Orlando López
E-records Integrity and E-compliance SME
olopez6102@gmail.com

Chapter 1

Introduction

Regulatory authorities acknowledge the use of computer systems* performing operations covered by the medicines' manufacturing practices regulation, and the applicable controls that must be in place to ensure that such computer systems are trustworthy. The essentials of complying with these regulations are outlined in Chapter 14.

To demonstrate that a computer system is trustworthy, the Development Period needs to follow a documented system life cycle (SLC) (Chapters 6 and 7) and, during the operational life period the system needs to be subjected to the Current Good Manufacturing Practice (CGMP) controls associated with the Operational Life (Chapter 12).

This book complements the basic features referenced above. A computer system performing operations covered by the medicines' manufacturing practices regulation and the applicable controls must be developed following software engineering and operational current practices. The output of these two key processes will provide a trustworthy system.

Chapter 2 contains a high-level description of the validation process applicable to computer systems to achieve and maintain proper performance, correct operation, system integrity and product quality by computer systems in a manufacturing environment.

The key required expectation of regulatory authorities and competent authorities covering medicine manufacturing practices are discussed in Chapter 3. This chapter considers expectations by regulatory authorities from the US, Australia, Brazil, Canada, China, United Kingdom, and Japan. In addition, it covers expectations by worldwide healthcare-related

* System: A group of related objects designed to perform or control a set of specified actions.

entities such as the Pharmaceutical Inspection Cooperation/Scheme (PIC/S), the World Health Organization (WHO) and the International Conference on Harmonization (ICH).

Chapters 4 and 5 cover common factors and e-compliance practices followed in computer systems validation (CSV). In case of new technologies, these common practices can be used during implementation and operation.

A typical SLC is described in Chapter 6. The SLC comprises the framework and activities to develop a system and operate a computer system.

Chapter 7 discusses the SLC documentation and its relationship with CSV and e-compliance.

The management of requirements is discussed in Chapter 8. This is an important element in the CSV. The success or failure of a project is based on the correct definition and the attributes of requirements. Key issues in the implementation and maintenance of the requirements are discussed as well.

The concept of risk based validation was introduced in the regulated industry back in the early 2000s. The extent of the software validation effort should be commensurate with the associated risk. This practice is introduced in Chapter 9.

For complex systems, the validation plan should be developed after establishing the validation approach. The approach should be based on a risk assessment. validation plans are discussed in Chapter 10.

The integration of project management, SLC and production CSV processes managing the validation of a computer system is discussed in Chapter 11. The focus is on production systems.

After the deployment of computer systems, the validation activities are not over. Chapter 12 gives details of the procedural control during the Operational Life.

Since I wrote the first revision of this book in 2004, one big shift in the information technology (IT) sector is the use of service providers (including Software as a Service [SaaS], Infrastructure as a Service [IaaS] and/or Platform as a Service [PaaS]) by regulated entities. This shift reduces the regulated entity IT budget. The IT Department should be considered a service provider. Suppliers and service providers are discussed in Chapter 13. A key instrument to establish the roles and responsibilities of the suppliers and service providers is the service level agreement (SLA). This tool is discussed in Chapter 22.

A key chapter in this book is Chapter 14, Trustworthy Computer Systems. Trustworthy computer systems consist of computer infrastructure, applications, and procedures that:

- Are reasonably suited to performing their intended functions
- Provide a reasonably reliable level of availability, reliability and correct operation
- Are reasonably secure from intrusion and misuse
- Adhere to generally accepted security principles

The above key items are summarized in the quality-related attributes at the end of the development and during the operational processes of computer systems.

In computer systems, electronic records' integrity is a critical element of an organization's quality program, and recently oversights have been brought to the forefront by regulatory agencies citing violations and inadequacies in findings from inspections, audits, and warning letters. Based on ISO/IEC 17025, the integrity requirements for electronic records are reviewed in Chapter 15. In addition, Chapter 16 compliments Chapter 15 by providing cryptographic-based technologies supporting the integrity of electronic records.

CGMP applications in the manufacturing operating environment must run in qualified infrastructure. The infrastructure is basically a transport means that is used to move information from one location to another. This information may establish the quality of a product. Chapter 17 provides the concepts for the qualification of infrastructure.

As a result of not following good configuration management practices, new expectations from the regulatory agency/competent authority, outdated technologies, and so on, computer systems fall out of CGMP compliance. For reasons explained before, systems need from time to time be remediated. Chapter 18 is dedicated to remediation related activities.

Chapter 19 suggests an organization structure supporting CSV programs.

Chapter 20 recommends an approach to the correlation between the system life cycle (SLC) and e-records life cycle using the EU Annex 11 SLC.

One of the most important services in e-records integrity and e-signatures – digital date and time stamps – is described in Chapter 21.

Access Management, Big Data, Clouds Environments, Internet of Things (IoT), SLAs, and Wireless are areas in e-compliance that are, at present, under regulated user and regulatory agencies attention. Chapter 22 reviews these technologies and critical processes.

Based on the earlier revision of the ISO 12207 (1995), Chapter 23 guides the reader on how to put together all the elements discussed in this book.

As stated in the first edition of this book (2004), quality is built into a computer system during its conceptualization, development, and operational life periods. The validation of computer systems cannot be tested into the system. The validation of computer systems is an ongoing process that it is integrated into the entire SLC. The intention of this book is to provide the key processes to build quality into computer systems performing operations covered by medicine manufacturing practices regulation.

The recommendations of the controls, as described in this book, are purely from the standpoint and opinion of the author, and should serve as a suggestion only. They are not intended to serve as the regulators' official implementation process.

Chapter 2

What Is a Computer Systems Validation (CSV)?

In the context of the regulated users* and Regulatory Authorities, computer systems used in the manufacturing of regulated products should be developed and operated to assure proper performance, correct operation, system integrity, and product quality.

Computer systems provide an effective method to perform routine and repetitive tasks. Although generally more reliable than manual equivalents, such systems demand adequate controls for equipment setup and programming/configuration.

All regulatory authorities call for manufacturers† to implement quality systems to ensure the correctness and appropriateness of the computer systems functionality based on the intended use, changes, interfaces, data inputs/outputs, and data processing, as applicable. This "ensures accurate results and reduces the risk of failure of the system."‡ The validation process is ensured by following "appropriate development methodology using a quality system approach."§

---

* Regulated user: The Regulated Good Practice entity, that is responsible for the operation of a computerized system and the applications, files and data held thereon. (PIC/S PI 011-3).

† Manufacturer: An entity that engages in CGMP activities, including implementation of oversight and controls over the manufacture of drugs to ensure quality.

‡ OMCL Network of the Council of Europe Quality Assurance Document. *Validation of Computerised Systems*, July 2009.

§ TGA. *Australian Code of Good Manufacturing Practice for human blood and blood components, human tissues and human cellular therapy products*, April 2013.

Specifically to ensure accurate functionality and the protection of e-records, certain controls must be in place*:

- Access to the system by authorized personnel only
- Use of passwords
- Creation of backup copies
- Independent checking of critical e-records
- Safe storage of e-records for the required time
- The systematic use of an accurate, secure, audit trail (where appropriate)

The controls referenced above are specified, implemented, tested, and maintained during the SLC.

The SLC is based upon good engineering practices that have been in existence for many years. In addition, it is expected that documented evidence will be produced and maintained during the SLC.

The deliverables that are natural byproducts of the SLC are very closely aligned with the "documented evidence" that is required in the CSV to ensure a high degree of assurance that the computer system will consistently meet its predetermined specifications and quality attributes†.

CORE PRINCIPLE

The computer systems validation process incorporates "planning, verification, testing, traceability, configuration management, and many other aspects of good software engineering that together help to support a final conclusion that software is validated."

– PIC/S CSV PI 011-3, September 2007

PI 011-3‡ defines CSV as the "formal assessment and reporting of quality and performance measures for all the lifecycle stages of software and system development, its implementation, qualification and acceptance, operation, modification, re-qualification, maintenance and retirement. This should enable both the regulated user, and competent authority to have a high level of confidence in the integrity of both the processes executed within the controlling computer system(s) and in those processes controlled by

* EU Commission Directive 2003/94/EC, October 2003.

† Herr, R. R. and Wyrick, M. L. "A Globally Harmonized Glossary of Terms for Communicating Computer Validation Key Practices." *PDA Journal of Pharmaceutical Science and Technology*, 53(2) 1999; 97–103.

‡ Pharmaceutical Inspection Cooperation Scheme (PIC/S). *Good Practices for Computerized Systems in "GxP" Regulated Environments*, PI 011-3, September 2007.

and/or linked to the computer system(s), within the prescribed operating environment(s)."

The purpose of CSV is to ensure an acceptable degree of evidence (documented, raw data), confidence (dependable and thorough, rigorous achievement of predetermined specifications), intended use, accuracy, consistency, and reliability*. Furthermore, for systems using automated data inputs and outputs (I/Os), the CSV ensures the accuracy and efficiency of the e-records inputs, outputs, and processing.

If the above criteria are met, it indicates that a system or software complies with applicable CGMP requirements and the system can be considered validated.

In the pharmaceutical and biotechnology context, the CSV process† is applicable to computer systems used in the production of a medicinal product and computer systems used in the implementation of the medicinal product quality system.

In the medical device context, these areas are applicable to computer systems used in the production of a device; computer systems used in the implementation of the medical device quality system; software used as a component, part, or accessory of a medical device; and software that is itself a medical device.

The CSV process, an element of the applicable computer systems development and maintenance methodology, integrates applicable regulatory compliance throughout the full SLC. Refer to Chapter 6.

> "FDA has maintained the requirement for validation because the agency believes that it is necessary that software be validated to the extent possible to adequately ensure performance."
>
> *US FDA CDRH, General Principles of Software Validation; Guidance for Industry and FDA Staff*

Quality needs to be built into computer systems starting in the requirements definition, specification of the design, and building. Quality cannot be generated retroactively. The validation of new computer systems planning shall start during the project planning. Assuring the quality of computer systems must be considered as part of the ongoing business activity and part of the general quality processes.

* WHO. "Validation of Computerized Systems." *WHO Technical Report Series* No. 937, Annex 4, Appendix 5, 2006.

† Process: A set of specified, ordered actions required to achieve a defined results.

The CSV, when established properly, provides the repeatable process that assures a computer system's consistent performance within pre-established operational limits and intended use.

The CSV process is implemented through the use of procedures. These procedures establish "how" to conduct the CSV effort. The procedures should identify the specific actions or sequence of actions that must be taken to complete individual validation activities, tasks, and work items*. Refer to Chapter 12.

Even if in the applicable predicate rule there is no implicit requirement related with a CSV, any computer system performing regulated operation(s)† must be validated for its intended use. This requirement applies to any computer system used to automate the design, testing, manufacturing, labeling, packaging, distribution, complaint handling, or to automate any other aspect of a regulated function.

CSV is a valuable process assuring the quality of computer systems and the associated processing and outputs. It can increase the reliability of computer systems, resulting in decreased failure rates, fewer recalls, e-records integrity issues, and corrective actions. CSV can also reduce long-term costs by making it easier to modify computer systems and re-validate as a result of changes.

SIPOCs

As specified above, the CSV process can be defined as the "formal assessment and reporting of quality and performance measures for all the lifecycle stages" of the computer system. In this book, the life cycle periods of computer systems are: Conceptualization, Development, Early Operational Life, Maturity and Aging. Refer to Chapter 6.

The two SIPOCs depicted in this section represent high-level process maps of the CSV process. One SIPOC represents the system development life cycle (SDLC) process (see Figure 2.1) and the second SIPOC represents the maintenance processes (see Figure 2.2).

---

* US FDA. *General Principles of Software Validation; Final Guidance for Industry and FDA Staff*, January 2002.

† Regulated operation: Process/business operations carried out on a regulated agency product that is covered in a predicated rule. In the context of this book the referenced predicate rule is the Good Manufacturing Practice (GMP).

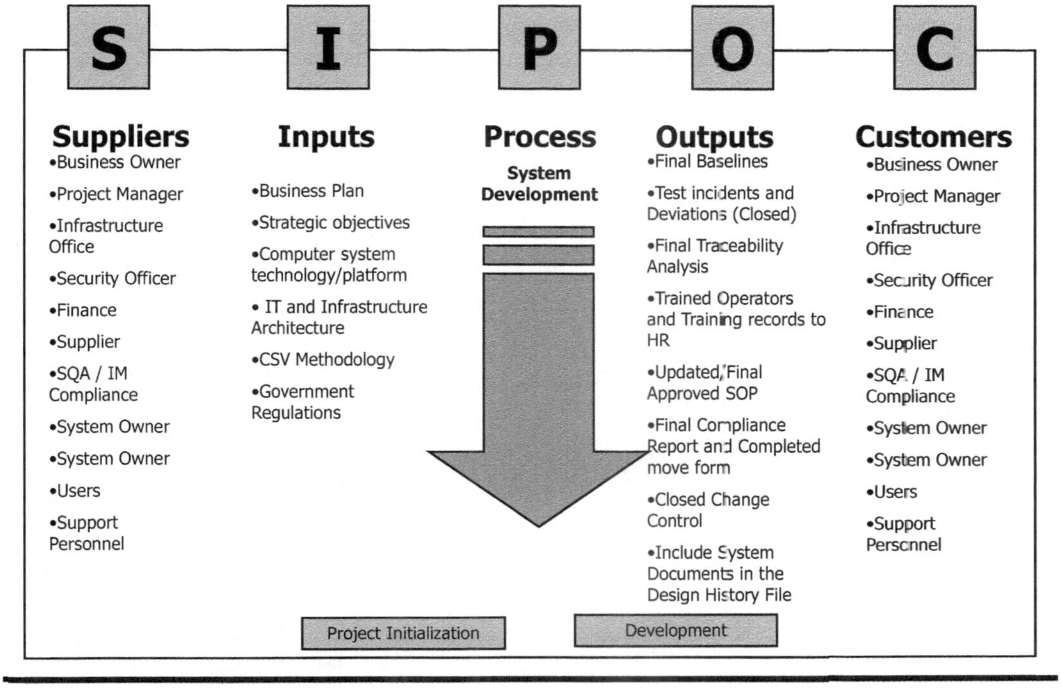

Figure 2.1 System Development.

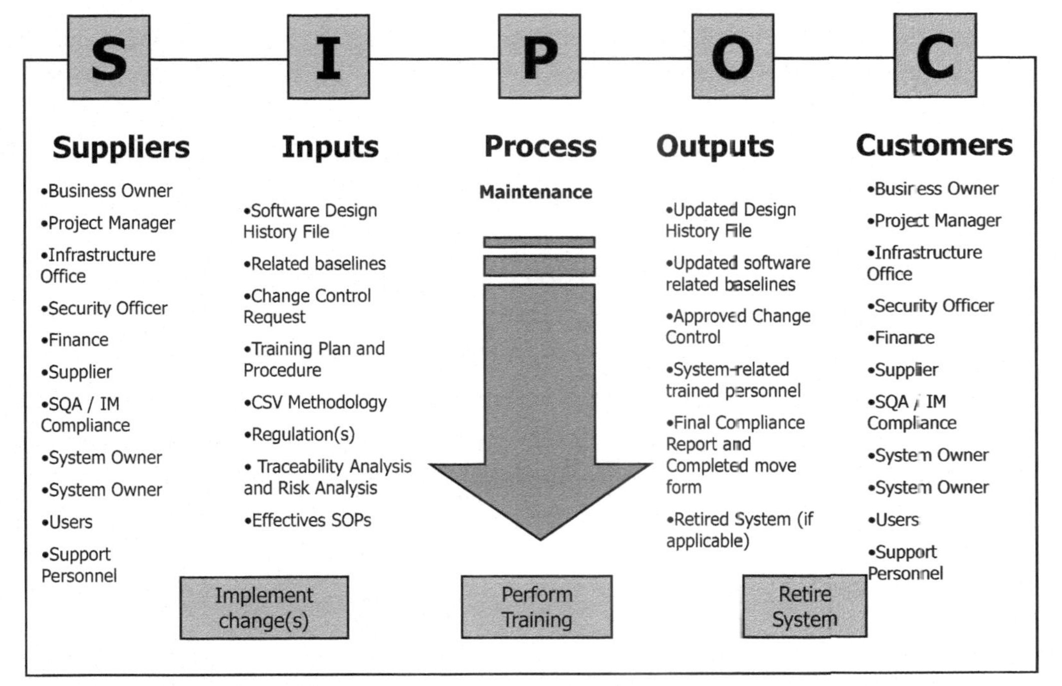

Figure 2.2 System Maintenance. Note: "Implement Change(s)" requires to start all over the system life cycle, from concept to go live.

When Are Computer Systems Validated?

A computer system is considered CGMP if the system or any output of the system is used in conjunction with the activities defined in the applicable CGMPs regulation.

CGMP computer systems used in production quality systems, whether in the production and process controls, distributing, laboratory testing and analysis, and many other aspects of the quality system associated with manufacturing, must be prospectively validated.

Sample Related Regulations/Guidance

The following are worldwide regulations and guidance linked with computer systems validation. Chapter 3 expands on many of the following regulations.

- *21 CFR Part 11.10(a)*: Validation of systems to ensure accuracy, reliability, consistent intended performance, and the ability to discern invalid or altered records. (US FDA)
- *21 CFR Part 211.68(a)*: Automatic, mechanical, or electronic equipment or other types of equipment, including computers, or related systems that will perform a function satisfactorily, may be used in the manufacture, processing, packing, and holding of a drug product. If such equipment is so used, it shall be routinely calibrated, inspected, or checked according to a written program designed to assure proper performance*. (US FDA)
- *21 CFR Part 820 and 61 FR 52602*: Software validation is a requirement of the quality system regulation. (US FDA)
- *Annex 2, Article 6*: Computerized system verification shall include the validation of the application program and the confirmation of the infrastructure, the scope and extent of which shall be based on scientific risk assessment. The risk assessment should take full account of the scope and use of the computerized system. The verification state should be maintained during the life of the computerized system. (SFDA)

* While not explicitly stated, the phrase in Section 211.68(a) "according to a written program designed to assure proper performance" is generally taken to mean that written validation procedure and the associated maintenance procedures are established.

- *Annex 11, Principle*: The application should be validated; IT infrastructure should be qualified. (EMA)
- *General Principles of Software Validation; Final Guidance for Industry and FDA Staff* (January 11, 2002): Software validation is the confirmation by examination and provision of objective evidence that software specifications conform to user needs and intended uses, and that the particular requirements implemented through software can be consistently fulfilled. (US FDA)
- *GUI-0104-12*: GMP related computerized systems should be validated. The depth and scope of validation depends on the diversity, complexity and criticality of the computerized application. (Canada)
- *ICH Q7a*: Computerized systems used in the manufacture of APIs should be properly developed, validated and maintained to assure data and product integrity. Section 5.4 covers the computer systems validation requirements. (ICH Q7a)
- *OMLC*: The purpose of the validation is to guarantee the confidence in scientific results obtained with each computerized system. (Official Medicines Control Laboratories [OMCL] Network of the Council of Europe Quality Assurance Document, *Validation of Computerised Systems*, July 2009).
- *RDC No. 17 – Article 573*: Validation shall be considered part of the lifecycle of a computerized system, comprising the steps of planning, specifying, programming, testing, documentation, operation, monitoring, maintenance and change. (ANVISA)
- *TRS No. 937 – Appendix 5, Annex 4*: 1.1 Computer systems should be validated at the level appropriate for their use and application. This is of importance in production as well as in quality control. (WHO)

Core Principles

The following core principles associated with the validation of computer systems.

General Principles

- The general principles related with computer systems validation are discussed in Chapter 5.

Life Cycle Principles

- The core principles related with the system life cycle are discussed in Chapter 6.

Access Authorization Principles

- Computer systems should have sufficient controls to prevent unauthorized access or changes to data. There should be controls to prevent omissions in data (e.g. system turned off and data not captured). There should be a record of any data change made, the previous entry, who made the change, and when the change was made. (ICH Q7)

Data I/O Principles

- Input to and output from the computer or other records or data must be checked for accuracy. (21 CFR Part 211.68(b))
- In the context of data integrity, computer systems used to create, modify, and maintain electronic records and to manage electronic signatures in scope of Part 11 are also subject to the validation requirements. (See 21 CFR 11.10(a).) Such computer systems must be validated to ensure accuracy, reliability, consistent intended performance, and the ability to discern invalid or altered records.*

Data Storage and Backup Principles

- Regular back-ups of all files and data should be made and stored in a secure location to prevent intentional or accidental damage. (*WHO Technical Report Series*, No. 937, Annex 4, Appendix 5, Section 5.1, 2006.)
- A backup file of data entered into the computer or related system shall be maintained. (21 CFR Part 211.68(b))
- Data should be checked periodically to confirm that they have been accurately and reliably transferred. (*WHO Technical Report Series*, No. 937, Annex 4, Appendix 5, Section 3.3, 2006.)

* US FDA, *General Principles of Software Validation; Final Guidance for Industry and FDA Staff*, January 2002.

- If system breakdowns or failures would result in the permanent loss of records, a back-up system should be provided. A means of ensuring data protection should be established for all computerized systems. (ICH Q7)

Error Handling and System Failure Principles

- Incidents related to computerized systems that could affect the quality of products or the reliability of records or test results should be recorded and investigated. (ICH Q7)

Additional Readings

López, O. "Computer Systems Validation" in *Encyclopedia of Pharmaceutical Science and Technology*. 4th ed. New York: Taylor & Francis, 2013; 615–619.

López, O. "Computer Systems Validation" in *Encyclopedia of Pharmaceutical Technology*, 2nd ed. New York: Mercel Dekker, 2003

Chapter 3

CGMP Regulatory Requirements for Production Computer Systems

Introduction

A critical expectation pertinent to the computer systems performing activities covered by the medicines' manufacturing practices regulation is the validation of such systems.* After reading this chapter and the materials listed as references, the reader may agree that the principles of CSV (Chapter 5) are contained in all major worldwide regulations and guidelines. This is consistent with the globalization of the manufacture of medicinal products for the healthcare industry.

The accurate validation process is ensured by following "appropriate development methodology using a quality system approach."† The accurate validation process "ensures accurate results and reduces the risk of failure of the system".‡

Consistent with the SLC, the computer validation process incorporates "planning, verification, testing, traceability, configuration management, and many other aspects of good software engineering that together help to

* Argentina's *General Guidelines of Good Manufacturing Practices for Processors, Importers/Exporters of Medicines*, ANMAT N° 2819/2004 (Section 4.11), May 2004.

† TGA. *Australian Code of Good Manufacturing Practice for Human Blood and Blood Components, Human Tissues and Human Cellular Therapy Products*, April 2013.

‡ OMCL Network of the Council of Europe Quality Assurance Document. *Validation of Computerized Systems*, July 2009.

support a final conclusion that software is validated." (PIC/S CSV PI 011-3, September 2007).

The extent of the computer validation must be based on a justified and documented risk assessment (Chapter 9). The risk assessment should take into account the intended use of the system, product quality, the complexity of the system, and the impact of the system on the reliability of drugs CGMP records (EU Annex 11-1 and ICH Q9).

This chapter is organized by expectations by key regulatory agencies, expectation by worldwide entities, e-records integrity, and a summary.

Expectations by Key Regulatory Authorities

Australia

Applicable computer systems regulations and guidelines in the Therapeutic Goods Administration (TGA) are:

- *Medical Products*: Chapter 4, Section 4.9 in the TGA Code of GMP and its Annex 11.
- *APIs*: Q7A Good Manufacturing Practice Guidance for API, Part II, Section 5.4.
- *Medical devices*: IEC 62304: Medical device software—Software life cycle processes.
- *CGMP Human Blood Tissues*, April 2013.

Of great relevance is Section 4.9 in the TGA Code of GMPs. It provides the expectations of TGA's inspectors on electronic records:

> Data may be recorded by electronic data processing systems, photographic or other reliable means, but detailed procedures relating to the system in use should be available and the accuracy of the records should be checked. If documentation is handled by electronic data processing methods, only authorised persons should be able to enter or modify data in the computer and there should be a record of changes and deletions; access should be restricted by passwords or other means and the result of entry of critical data should be independently checked. Batch records electronically stored should be protected by backup transfer on magnetic tape, microfilm, paper

or other means. It is particularly important that the data are readily available throughout the period of retention.*

Brazil

Applicable computer systems regulations in the Brazil's National Health Surveillance Agency† is Title VII Resolution of the Executive Board No. 17, Computerized Information Systems. This can be found on page 109, www.in.gov.br/imprensa/visualiza/index.jsp?jornal=1&pagina=94&data=19/04/2010.

These regulations, from April 2010, are very comprehensive and similar to the recent EU Annex 11 (Rev 1).

At the same time, on April 2010, Anvisa published the "Guia De Validação De Sistemas Computadorizados" or Computerized Systems Guideline.

This guide was developed to assist in the management and validation of computerized systems which have an impact on GxP. The accuracy and integrity of data records are essential to the life cycle of the product, from the area of research, through pre-clinical and clinical studies, quality control, and production to distribution and storage area.

As with all current computer systems validation methodologies, this guideline provides a risk based approach to validate computer systems.

Part 11 and the Part 11 Guidance are referenced in this document.

Canada

In Health Canada, Canadian GMPs (GUI-0001, February 2018) applies to pharmaceutical, radiopharmaceutical, biological, and veterinary drugs.

Regarding computer systems, the main guideline is the PIC/S Annex 11: Computerized Systems, in the PE 009-6(Annexes) from April 2007. This is revision 0 (1992) of the EU Annex 11.

As evidence of compliance to the appropriate regulatory quality system, Health Canada requires medical device manufacturers to be certified in a quality system. ISO 13485 is the Health Canada standard providing a comprehensive management system for the design and manufacture of medical devices.

---

* Therapeutic Goods Administration. *Australian Code of GMPs for Medicinal Products*, Section 4.9, August 2002. Note: On July 2010, the TGA GMPs were replaced by *PICS Guide for GMP for Medicinal Products 2009*.

† Anvisa, Brazilian Agência Nacional de Vigilância Sanitária (National Health Surveillance Agency), http://portal.anvisa.gov.br/wps/portal/anvisa/home.

The provisions in Section 7.5.2 in ISO 13485 (*Validation of processes for production and service provision*) specify that regulated organizations shall establish documented procedures for the validation of the application of computer software (and changes to such software and/or its application) for production and service provision that affect the ability of the product to conform to specified requirements. Such software applications shall be validated prior to initial use.

The specifics related with Section 7.5.2 in ISO 13485 are contained in ISO 62304 and ISO 12007.

ISO 12207 *Systems and software engineering – Software life cycle processes* is an international standard for software life cycle processes. It aims to be the standard that defines all the tasks required for developing and maintaining software.

ISO 62304 *Medical device software – Software life cycle processes* is an international standard which specifies life cycle requirements for the development of medical software and software within medical devices.

China

The most recent Chinese GMP applicable to computer systems is defined in the China FDA GMP Annex 2 Computerized System. It is effective since December 2015. The context of this Annex, is very similar to the 1992 revision of the EU Annex 11.*

Europe

The European Medicine Agency (EMA/EMEA)† sets legislation in the European Union (EU) applicable to the computer systems performing functions established‡ in the GMP§ for medicinal products for human use, investigational medicinal products for human use, and veterinary medicinal products.

* http://eng.sfda.gov.cn/WS03/CL0768/65113.html.

† Mc Cormick, K. "Overview: Regulatory Framework – EMEA." ISPE Knowledge Break – EMEA, 2009.

‡ "Establish" means define, document (in writing or electronically), and implement.

§ In the EU context, "GMP regulated activities" is defined as the manufacturing-related activities established in the basic legislation compiled in Volume 1 and Volume 5 of the publication *The Rules Governing Medicinal Products in the European Union*, http://ec.europa.eu/health/documents/eudralex/index_en.htm.

The legislation associated with computer systems for medicinal products for human use and investigational medicinal products for human use is delimited in Article 9-2 as part of the Commission Directive 2003/94/EC*:

> When electronic, photographic or other data processing systems are used instead of written documents, the manufacturer shall first validate the systems by showing that the data will be appropriately stored during the anticipated period of storage. Data stored by those systems shall be made readily available in legible form and shall be provided to the competent authorities at their request. The electronically stored data shall be protected, by methods such as duplication or back-up and transfer on to another storage system, against loss or damage of data, and audit trails shall be maintained.

Similar requirements applicable to veterinary medicinal products can be found in 91/412/EEC.†

The above Directives were expanded via a guidance document, EU Annex 11.

The Eudralex Volume 4, Annex 11, which refers specifically to computer systems and IT infrastructure, provides guidance for the interpretation of the above requirement to all EU Member States, the three European Economic Area (EEA) states and Switzerland. Annex 11 can be found in Volume 4 of *The Rules Governing Medicinal Products in the European Union*. Volume 4 includes the EU Guidelines to Good Manufacturing Practice Medicinal Products for Human and Veterinary Use, Parts I, II, and III and the Annexes.

Eudralex Volume 4, Annex 11 (EU Annex 11‡) which pertains to computer systems, provides guidance for the interpretation of the GMP for all European Union (EU) members. EU Annex 11 can be found in Volume 4 of *The Rules Governing Medicinal Products in the European Union*. Volume 4 covers the interpretation of the principles and guidelines of GMP regulated activities.

---

* Commission Directive 2003/94/EC Laying Down the Principles and Guidelines of Good Manufacturing Practice in Respect of Medicinal Products for Human Use and Investigational Medicinal Products for Human Use, October 1994.

† Commission Directive 91/412/EEC Laying Down the Principles and Guidelines of Good Manufacturing Practice for Veterinary Medicinal Products, July 1991.

‡ Annex 11 to Volume 4 of the "Rules Governing Medicinal Products in the European Community, Computerized Systems." http://ec.europa.eu/health/files/eudralex/vol-4/annex11_01-2011_en.pdf.

The first edition dates back to the 1992. In January 2011 the EMA announced the new revision of this EU Annex 11. This revision came into effect in June 2011.

EU Annex 11 is strictly applicable to the EU GMP/GDP on electronic systems used in regulated manufacturing processes, although any manufacturer in the world who wishes EU market approval need to take it into account as an applicable requirement.

The main principle of the EU Annex 11 states that: "The application should be validated; IT infrastructure should be qualified."

This document then continues on with two additional principles and 17 specific recommendations for computer operations. Paragraph 4 of the annex specifically refers to the need to ensure that the software has been under an appropriate quality management system which incorporates a system development life cycle.

Annex 11 has a much broader scope than Part 11. Speaking strictly about e-records and electronic signatures (e-signatures), Part 11 goes beyond Annex 11. Annex 11 complements Part 11 very well providing some specificity in areas that are left vague in Part 11.

The European Compliance Academy (www.gmp-compliance.org/eca_news_kat_3.html) published answers to questions concerning the first four items of the Annex 11. They were provided by inspectors and industry experts during the Conference on Computer Validation, held 8–9 June 2011 in Mannheim, Germany.

During the subsequent Pharmaceutical Inspection Cooperation Scheme (PIC/S) events in Kiev, Ukraine, 30 September to 5 October 2012, members reviewed the revision of several PIC/S GMP Guides and Annexes based on the revisions of the EU GMP Guides and Annexes. The updated EU Annex 11 on Computerized Systems was adopted and, based on the revisions, the PIC/S also adopted the revision of its associated guide, PIC/S PI 011-3.*

Appendix III provides a cross reference between Annex 11 and many other regulations and guidelines, including 21 CFR Part 211.

Japan

Japan's GMP requirements are defined by the Pharmaceuticals and Medical Devices Agency (PMDA).

---

* Pharmaceutical Inspection Cooperation Scheme (PIC/S). *Good Practices for Computerized Systems in "GxP" Regulated Environments*, PI 011-3, September 2007.

Similar to PIC/S PI 011-3, the Japanese requirements on computer systems in the area of GMP are established in the *Guideline on Management of Computerized Systems for Marketing Authorization Holders and Manufacturers of Drugs and Quasi-Drugs.*

This guideline and a related Q&A can be downloaded from http://academy.gmp-compliance.org/guidemgr/files/COMPUTERIZED_SYSTEMS_JAPAN.PDF.

United Kingdom

The Medicines and Healthcare Regulatory Agency (MHRA) in the United Kingdom is responsible for ensuring that medicines and medical devices work and are acceptably safe.

The MHRA is very influential in e-compliance. One of the main contributions of the MHRA to e-compliance is the recent guidance about data integrity, *MHRA GxP Data Integrity Guidance and Definitions* (March 2018).

United States

CGMP Applicability to Hardware and Software

By 1983 the "Guide to Inspection of Computerized Systems in Drug Processing" addressed the applicability of the CGMP computer hardware and software. Computer hardware and software are considered to be equipment and records or standard operating procedures (instructions), respectively, within the context of the CGMP regulations.

One year later the US FDA Compliance Policy Guide (CPG) 7132a.11, "CGMP Applicability to Hardware and Software", was issued confirming the connection between the CGMP regulations to the computer hardware and computer software. In the absent of an FDA reference on a computer-related topic, the CGMP regulation provides the guideline to comply with the FDA.

The current equivalence of software and records in this CPG has been superseded by the approach taken in the Guidance on Part 11, Scope and Application. Actually, software is considered standard operating procedures (instructions).

By means of CPG 7132a.11 each predicate regulation* in the US FDA provides implicitly computer systems-related requirements. The same model is applicable to other medicines' manufacturing regulatory agencies. As an

* Predicate regulations address the research, production, and control of FDA regulated articles.

example, the WHO* considers the computer hardware and software to be equipment and standard operating procedures, respectively, within the context of the CGMP regulations.

21 CFR Part 211.68†

As an example of the application of CPG 7132a.11 in a predicate rule, 211.68 is an element of 21 CRF Part 211, the CGMPs applicable to medicinal products in the US FDA.

The updated 2008 CGMP, effective since December 4, 2008,‡ defines the applicable regulations to the computer systems and associated CGMP e-records as follows:

- Computer systems can be used to perform operations covered by the drugs CGMP regulation. These computer systems require a written validation process.
- Computers systems documentation and validation documentation shall be maintained.
- There must be procedural controls for managing changes to infrastructure and application software, including documentation.
- Computer systems' electronic records must be controlled including records retention, backup, and security.
- Based on the complexity and reliability of computer systems there must be procedural controls and technologies to ensure the accuracy and security of computer systems I/Os electronic records and data.
- Computer systems must have adequate controls to prevent unauthorized access or changes to data, inadvertent erasures, or loss.
- There must be written procedural controls describing the maintenance of the computer system, including an ongoing performance evaluation and periodic reviews.§
- Specifically, for Sections 211.101(c), 211.103, 211.182, and 211.188(b)(11), verification by a second individual may not be necessary when automated equipment is used as described under Section 211.68.

In addition to the above, the following US Drug CGMP sections are also applicable to the hardware, software and/or CGMP e-records (Table 3.1).

* *WHO Technical Report Series*, No. 937, Annex 4, 2006.

† López, O. "A Historical View of 21 CFR Part 211.68." *Journal of GXP Compliance,* 15(2) 2011.

‡ 73 FR 51932, September 8, 2008.

§ Review: Checking of the suitability of a document.

Table 3.1 CGMP Regulations Applicable to Computer Hardware, Software, and/or CGMP E-Records

US Drugs CGMP	*Description*
211.22	Responsibilities of QC Unit, including evaluation of CGMP records.
211.22(a)	Accuracy and review of records.
211.25	Personnel Qualifications.
211.42	Design and Construction.
211.63	Equipment design, size, and location.
211.67	Cleaning and Maintenance.
211.68	Accurate records.
211.68(b)	Computer systems validation (CSV); control of records, attributable records.
211.100	Written Procedures, Deviations and documentation controls.
211.100(a)	Process control (e.g. computer systems) properly designed.
211.100(b)	Records recorded contemporaneously.
211.101(c) 211.103 211.182 211.188(b)(11)	Double Check on Computers.
211.101(c)	Review of records.
211.101(d)	Attributable record.
211.105(b)	Infrastructure hardware identification.
211.110(a)	CSV.
211.122	Attributable record.
211.160(a)	Document controls.
211.180	General (Records and Reports) including determination of original or a true copy; maintaining records for CGMP purposes.
211.180(a)	Records retention.
211.180(c)	Storage and record access.
211.180(d)	Records medium, including retaining original records or true copies.

(*Continued*)

Table 3.1 (Continued) CGMP Regulations Applicable to Computer Hardware, Software, and/or CGMP E-Records

US Drugs CGMP	*Description*
211.182	Use of log(s).
211.186	Attributable record and document controls.
211.188	Attributable record.
211.188(a)	Reproduction accuracy.
211.188(b)	Documentation and operational checks.
211.188(b)(11)	Attributable record.
211.189(e)	Records review and legible record.
211.192	QC record review. Audit trails related with production and control records must be reviewed and approved by the QC unit.
211.194(a)	Original or a true copy; review of records,
211.194(a)(7)	Attributable records.
211.194(a)(8)	Attributable records and second-person records review.

Source: Blood Establishment Computer System Validation in the User's Facility. http://www.fda.gov/downloads/BiologicsBloodVaccines/GuidanceComplianceRegulatoryInformation/Guidances/Blood/UCM078815.pdf.

This guidance document was originally written in 1993, revised as a draft again in 2007, and finalized in April 2013.

Since blood and blood components are defined as drugs in the FD&C Act, the CGMP in 21 CFR, Parts 210 and 211, are applicable. This guidance document is intended to be used in conjunction with the applicable federal standards in 21 CFR, Parts 600 through 680, and Parts 210 and 211, as they pertain to biological products for human use.

In addition, blood bank software products are medical devices. Then, the medical devices 21 CFR 820 regulatory requirements for software that is itself a medical device are applicable.

As in many US FDA computer systems validation guidance documents, the component highlighted in this blood establishment guidance document is the computer systems validation program. The program, when executed correctly, establishes and demonstrates:

- Proper performance
- Proper implementation of the functions to be performed
- The way in which it will interact with both manual and automated operations
- Data integrity

Irrespective of the source of the software model (acquirer,* supplier,† or developer‡) the development of the computer system should follow accepted standards for the SLC including, but not limited to, proper design, software validation and verification procedures, change control, and detailed documentation.

Regulated users must ensure that the computer systems are either assessed for compliance to the applicable regulatory requirements or that compliance is built into the system during its development and implementation.

The 1993 draft version of this guidance document makes reference to the implementation of audit trails as part of the functionality of blood bank software:

> An audit trail documents changes made to the data. Audit trail records are part of the system's documentation and should only be accessible or reviewed by authorized persons (e.g., identified establishment personnel, FDA Investigators). Audit trails can be used to record access to the system. Each time an authorized or unauthorized user tries or gains access to the system there should be a log entry. At a minimum, an audit trail should include:
>
> - the name of the person making the change
> - date
> - time
> - field name
> - previous data
> - current data

* Acquirer: An organization that acquires or procures a system, software product or software service from a supplier (ISO 12207:1995. Note: most recent revision is ISO/IEC 12207:2008).

† Supplier: An organization that enters into a contract with the acquirer for the supply of a system, software product or software service under the terms of the contract (ISO 12207:1995. Note: most recent revision is ISO/IEC 12207:2008).

‡ Developer: An organization that performs development activities (including requirements analysis, design, testing through acceptance) during the software life cycle process (ISO 12207:1995. Note: most recent revision is ISO/IEC 12207:2008).

A similar note can be found in the 2007 draft version.

> PIC/S PE-005-3 establishes guidelines to the GMP inspectors to use during inspections of blood establishments' computer systems. These guidelines can be found from Sections 9.8 through 9.13.
>
> - The hardware and software of the computers should be checked regularly to ensure reliability. The software (program) should be validated before use.
> - Computer hardware and software should be protected against use by unauthorized persons. The users of computers should be trained and should be authorised only to handle data required for the task(s) they perform.
> - There should be documented procedures for backup protection against loss of records in the event of planned and unplanned function failures.
> - A procedure should define the routine action taken in the event of breakdown. Checks of these actions should be performed at least once a year.
> - Changes to computerized systems (hardware, software or communication) should be validated, applicable documentation revised (if appropriate) and personnel trained before the change is introduced into routine use. Only authorised persons should make changes to software.
> - Records of the changes to computerized systems (hardware, software or communications) should be retained for at least ten years.

Note that records retention schedules for blood establishments mentioned in the PIC/S PE-005-3 may vary in the FDA applicable regulations. Refer to 21 CFR Part 606.

Expectation by Worldwide Entities

ICH Q7

Computer systems used in the manufacture of active pharmaceutical ingredients (APIs) should be accurately developed, validated and maintained to assure data and product integrity.

Section 5.4 of the International Conference on Harmonization (ICH) of Technical Requirements for Registration of Pharmaceuticals for Human Uses Q7, Good Manufacturing Practice Guide for Active Pharmaceutical

Ingredients (APIs), covers the requirements associated with computer validations of systems manufacturing APIs.

5.40. GMP related computerized systems should be validated. The depth and scope of validation depends on the diversity, complexity and criticality of the computerized application.

5.41. Appropriate installation qualification and operational qualification should demonstrate the suitability of computer hardware and software to perform assigned tasks.

5.42. Commercially available software that has been qualified does not require the same level of testing. If an existing system was not validated at time of installation, a retrospective validation could be conducted if appropriate documentation is available.

5.43. Computerized systems should have sufficient controls to prevent unauthorized access or changes to data. There should be controls to prevent omissions in data (e.g. system turned off and data not captured). There should be a record of any data change made, the previous entry, who made the change, and when the change was made.

5.44. Written procedures should be available for the operation and maintenance of computerized systems.

5.45. Where critical data are being entered manually, there should be an additional check on the accuracy of the entry. This can be done by a second operator or by the system itself.

5.46. Incidents related to computerized systems that could affect the quality of intermediates or APIs or the reliability of records or test results should be recorded and investigated.

5.47. Changes to the computerized system should be made according to a change procedure and should be formally authorized, documented and tested. Records should be kept of all changes, including modifications and enhancements made to the hardware, software and any other critical component of the system. These records should demonstrate that the system is maintained in a validated state.

5.48. If system breakdowns or failures would result in the permanent loss of records, a backup system should be provided. A means of ensuring data protection should be established for all computerized systems.

5.49. Data can be recorded by a second means in addition to the computer system.

Based on the ICH Q7, the European Chemical Industry Council or CEFIC (from its French name *Conseil Européen des Fédérations de l'Industrie Chimique*) Task Force Computer Validation published a CSV best practice document on December 2002. The guidelines expanded the specific issues addressed above and applicable to computer systems in the API production control and data handling situations. This best practice document can be found at http://apic.cefic.org/pub/compvalfinaldraftDecember2002.pdf.

The Canadian GUI-0104 Health Products and Food Branch Inspectorate, harmonizes APIs standards from Pharmaceutical Inspection Cooperation/ Scheme (PIC/S) and ICH. GUI-0104 was published in November 2013 and incorporate the computer-related concepts of PIC/S Annex 11. This document be found at www.canada.ca/en/health-canada/services/drugs-health-products/compliance-enforcement/information-health-product/drugs/guidelines-active-pharmaceutical-ingredients-0104.html.

Similar to the EU Annex 11, the Brazilian RDC Resolution #69, dated on December 2014, provides the provisions on CGMP for APIs. Chapter VI (Documentation and Records) covers the subject of the chapter when recorded through electronic processing. Article 106, put emphasis on the reliability of the e-records.

Paragraph 2 in chapter VI provides the typical e-records integrity controls:

> If the data recording is done through electronic processing, it should be ensured that:
>
> - only authorized people can modify the data stored on computers;
> - there is a record of changes made;
> - computer access is restricted by passwords or other means;
> - entry of data considered critical is checked by a designated person other than the one who made the records or is checked by the system itself; and
> - electronic records of the batch data are protected by transferring copies on magnetic tape, microfilm, paper printing or other means.

Section VI in chapter XII refers to the validation of computerized systems.

The International Pharmaceutical Excipients Council (IPEC) published in 2008 an Audit Guideline designed as a tool to assist in evaluating the manufacturing practices and quality systems of excipient manufacturers.*

* www.ipec-europe.org/UPLOADS/GMP_Audit_Guidelines__2008Final(1).pdf.

This guideline is also a reference to assist excipient manufacturers in meeting appropriate good manufacturing practice (GMP) requirements to assure consistent product quality.

Section 6.3.2.3 in the Audit Guideline refers to computers. The questions in the Audit Guideline related to computers are:

- If computerized systems are used in a manner that can impact excipient quality, have they been demonstrated to consistently function as expected?
- What process is used to control changes to systems and programs that can have an effect on the quality of the product to assure that changes receive the proper review and approval with regard to potential effects before being instituted and that only authorized personnel can make such changes? Are personnel trained subsequent to changes?
- How is access to computerized systems limited in order to protect records from tampering, and prevent data alteration?
- If passwords are used as a security measure, are there provisions for periodic changing of passwords? Are there designees for all critical system operations and emergencies?
- What is the procedure for reviewing and updating security access when a person leaves the department or company? Is their access to the system or their access codes to the system revoked in a timely fashion?
- What backup systems are in place, such as copies of programs and files, duplicate tapes, or microfilm, and has retrievability of information from master tapes and backup tapes been verified? Are there procedures in place for disaster recovery, in the event of a power outage, loss of server and computerized systems, and so on?

ICH Q9

Section II.4 of the ICH of Technical Requirements for Registration of Pharmaceuticals for Human Uses Q9, Quality Risk Management, contains the guidelines associated with an approach to quality risk management regarding the quality of drug substances and drug (medicinal) products across the product life cycle.

The risk assessment should be used:

- To select the design of computer hardware and software (e.g. modular, structured, fault tolerance);

- To determine the extent of validation, as an example,
  - identification of critical performance parameters;
  - selection of the requirements and design;
  - code review;
  - the extent of testing and test methods; and
  - reliability of electronic records and signatures.

This approach is consistent with Volume 4 EU Guidelines to Good Manufacturing Practice Medicinal Products for Human and Veterinary Use, Annex 20 – Quality Risk Management.

OMCL Network of the Council of Europe

Under the auspices of the European Directorate for the Quality of Medicines and Healthcare it has published the Validation of Computerized Systems, Core Document and three Annexes, defining the basic principles for the validation of computer systems used within the Official Medicines Control Laboratories (OMCL) with impact on quality of results.

These four documents cover in-house and commercial software for calculation, database computer systems, Laboratory Information Management Systems (LIMS), Electronic Laboratory Notebooks (ELN), and computers as part of test equipment.

Like much other guidance, it establishes that "validation is to guarantee the confidence in scientific results obtained with each computerized system. A validated system ensures accurate results and reduces the risk of failure of the system."

*Validation of Computerized Systems**

- Annex 1: Validation of computerized calculation systems: example of validation of in-house software (Spreadsheet/Microsoft Excel). (www.edqm.eu/sites/default/files/guidelines-omcl-computerised-systems-annex1-march2018.pdf)
- Annex 2: Validation of computerised systems Annex 2: Validation of complex computerised systems. (www.edqm.eu/sites/default/files/guidelines-omcl-computerised-systems-annex2-march2018.pdf)
- Annex 3: Validation of computers as part of test equipment. (www.edqm.eu/medias/fichiers/NEW_Annex_3_Validation_of_computers_as_part_of_tes.pdf)

* www.edqm.eu/sites/default/files/guidelines-omcl-computerised_systems-core_document-march2018.pdf.

PIC/S

Good Practices for Computerized Systems in Regulated GxP Environments (PI 011-3, September 2007) is the basis for computer-related GMP inspections applicable to the members of PIC/S organizations. In particular its Annex 11, "Computerized Systems" (Rev 0) is the reference document when inspecting such systems.

It provides recommendations and background information concerning computer systems that will be of assistance to inspectors for training purposes and during the inspection of computer systems.

The PIC/S organization develops and promotes guidance documents for regulatory inspectors. These guides are very valuable for the industry too because they represent the inspector's perspective by regulatory inspection. These guides could be considered as a kind of "common denominator" in order to enable mutual recognition agreements (MRA) between the regulatory agencies of the PIC/S country members.*

WHO†

As part of GMP guidelines on validation, the World Health Organization (WHO) published in 2006 Technical Report 937, Annex 4 in Appendix 5 covering computer systems validation.

In addition to the maxims provided by similar guidelines on computer systems validations, this particular guideline provides in Section 3.3 "general good manufacturing practice (GMP) requirements" applicable to computer systems in a post-validation program:

- Verification and revalidation: After a suitable period of running a new system it should be independently reviewed and compared with the system specification and functional specification.
- Change control: Alterations should only be made in accordance with a defined procedure which should include provision for checking, approving and implementing the change.
- Checks: Data should be checked periodically to confirm that they have been accurately and reliably transferred.

* http://academy.gmp-compliance.org/guidemgr/files/PICS/PI%20011-3%20RECOMMENDATION%20ON%20COMPUTERISED%20SYSTEMS.PDF.

† http://whqlibdoc.who.int/trs/WHO_TRS_937_eng.pdf.

E-Records Integrity

Data integrity is a fundamental requirement of the pharmaceutical quality system. It applies equally to manual (paper) records and electronic records (e-records).

As the result of the relevance to demonstrate the quality of drug products, the following guidance documents were written, between 2015 and 2018, by regulatory agencies or competent authorities:

- China FDA Standard on Drug Data Management (Draft October 2016)
- EMA Questions and Answers on Data Integrity (August 2016)
- EU OMLC Quality Management Guideline on Management of Documents and Records (January 2016)
- *MHRA GxP Data Integrity Guidance and Definitions* (March 2018)
- PIC/S *Good Practices for Data Management and Integrity in Regulated GMP/GDP Environments* (Draft August 2016)
- TGA Data Management and Data Integrity (April 2017)
- US FDA Data Integrity Guidance (Draft April 2016)
- WHO Guidance on Good Data Management Practices (Draft September 2015)

Each data integrity-related guidance document calls for the relevant CGMPs applicable to computer systems managing CGMP records. The integrity of e-records is ensured by implementing the applicable guidance during the life cycle of CGMP e-records.

All guidance documents call for the reliability of CGMP records from the framework of the regulatory agencies or competent authorities. Some of the guidance content is typical data integrity guidance. Other guidance documents are more inclusive, covering data quality and/or data management.

Department of Defense (DoD) 501.2-STD, *Design Criteria Standard for Electronic Records Management Software Applications*, provides software engineering practices to manage e-records from the context of computer applications.

Final Note

Since 1988, the attention by the FDA and other worldwide regulatory authorities to computer systems has increased in tandem with the use of computers as part of the manufacturing of drug products and the impact of computers controlling the manufacturing process in drug quality. The records created and maintained by such computer systems are used to demonstrate the quality of the products.

The objective of this chapter is to present and briefly discuss the latest regulations and guideline documents impacting the current requirements applicable to computer systems in the manufacturing environment. There is a notable amount and quality of the regulatory requirements and regulatory guidelines provided by the worldwide regulatory authorities.

One of the significant differences between computer systems validation regulations and regulatory guidelines of 2002 and 2018 is that today's regulatory methodologies and guidelines requires a risk based approach throughout the life cycle of the computer system taking into account patient safety, data integrity and product quality (Figure 3.1).

The two most influential guidelines applicable to production systems and quality control systems relevant to the manufacture of medicinal products are FDA Data Integrity (Draft) and the EU Annex 11. The ultimate purpose of these guidelines is to provide reliable CGMP records. The reliability of e-records is the foundation of the CGMPs. The electronic information properly

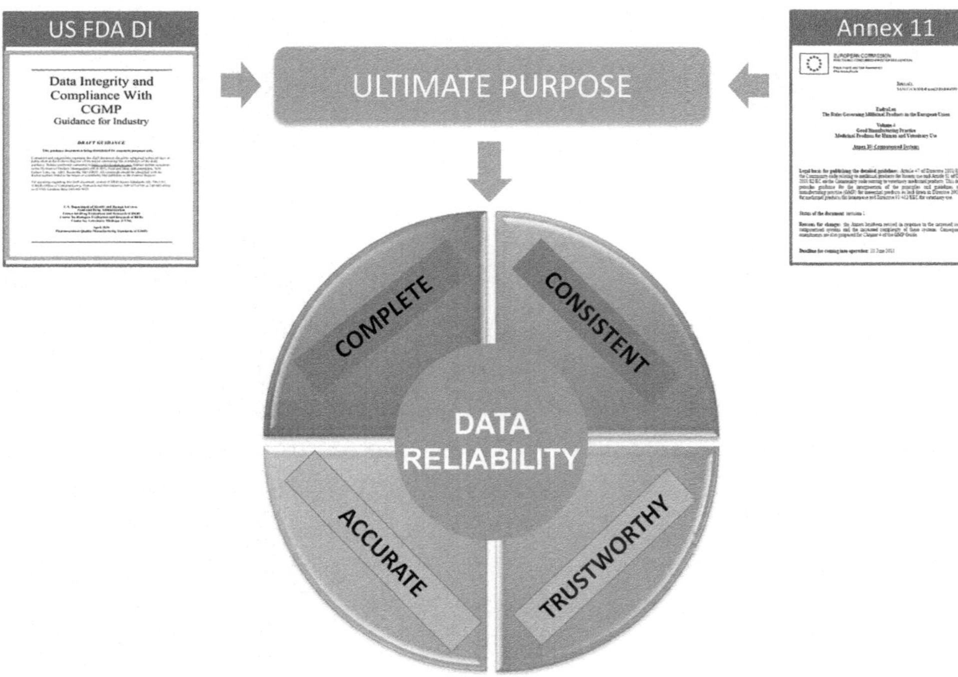

Figure 3.1 Data reliability.

recorded is the basis for manufacturers to assure product identity, strengths, purity, and safety.* The e-records also demonstrate that the manufacturer process adheres to the GMPs, including instructions.

Common factors in many of the current computer-related regulations and guidelines are:

- EU Annex 11 is a source to the majority of the current regulations and/or guidelines.
- Computer systems performing a regulated function must be suitable for its intended purpose, maintained appropriately and technically applicable for use, to give assurance that the product is manufactured to required specifications.
- Comprehensive procedures relating to the operation of the computer system in use should be available.
- The validation of a computer system is based on the applicable SLC.
- All changes to computer systems and electronic records must only be made in a controlled manner in accordance with a defined procedure.
- Regular backups of all relevant electronic records (e.g. electronically stored batch records) should be done.
- The management of e-records (e-records, e-signatures and associated metadata) must be performed in a trustworthy approach during processing, while in transit, and in computer storage.
- E-records are readily available throughout the period of retention.
- The accuracy of the e-records in storage must be checked periodically.
- Physical and/or logical controls must be in place to restrict access to computer systems and e-records to authorized persons.

The above items are important activities that together help to support a final conclusion that software is validated and the integrity of the e-records.

The regulations and guidelines assist the regulated user to develop a computer system validation program consistent with current recognized principles of the applicable system development methodology and quality assurance that are current good practices. It is very important that the regulated user keep track of updates to the applicable regulations and guidelines.

---

* Wechsler, J. "Data Integrity Key to GMP Compliance." *Pharmaceutical Technology*, September 2014.

Core Principle

> For computer systems performing activities covered by the medicines' manufacturing practices regulation it is required that general CGMP principles be considered.
>
> *(APV Guideline Computerized Systems, Version 1.0, April 1996)*

Additional Reading

López, O. "Regulations and Regulatory Guidelines of Computer Systems in Drug Manufacturing – 25 Years Later." *Pharmaceutical Engineering*, 33(4) 2013.

Chapter 4

Maxims* in CSV

The development of business requirements, objective evidence, intended use, proper performance, and operating environment are maxims† or general rules in an effective CSV program.

Business Requirements

To be able to develop a computer system, the reason to undertake the computer system implementation is needed. The business requirements provide this information. In addition, the business requirements make available the benefits that the developing organization or its customers expect to receive from the system. Business requirements may be outlined in several documents such as a project charter, business case, or in a project vision and scope statement.

Business requirements bring the project owner, stakeholders and the project team on the same page.

The following business requirements should be considered:‡

- Problem statement
- Project vision

---

* López, O. "Computer Systems Validation" in *Encyclopedia of Pharmaceutical Science and Technology*, 4th ed. New York: Taylor & Francis, 2013: 615–619.

† Axiom: A statement or proposition which is regarded as being established, accepted, or self-evidently true.

‡ Parker, J. "Business, User, and System Requirements." http://enfocussolutions.com/business-user-and-system-requirements/, February 2012.

- Project constraints (budget, schedule, and resources)
- Project objectives
- Project scope statements
- Business process analysis
- Stakeholder analysis

The results from the business process analysis and stakeholder analysis activities are also considered business requirements. The purpose of the business process analysis is to determine how the business process will work. It is often necessary to resolve deficiencies in the business process before trying to automate it.

Objective Evidence

The US Food and Drug Administration (FDA) considers software validation as the "confirmation by examination and provision of objective evidence that software specifications conform to user needs and intended uses, and that the particular requirements implemented through software can be consistently fulfilled."*

The key concepts in the preceding definition are "objective evidence" and "intended use."

Objective evidence is produced after a number of formal and informal activities, many of which must be completed in a pre-defined order. All these activities are delimited as part of the SLC. The working products produced after each phase in the SLC provide the objective evidence that is required to demonstrate that the computer system conforms to the needs of the user, intended use and that all requirements can be consistently achieved.

Intended Use

Computer systems used in the manufacturing of regulated products, either control the quality of a product during testing, manufacturing, and handling processes; manage information business operations; manage data used to

* US FDA. *General Principles of Software Validation; Final Guidance for Industry and FDA Staff*, January 2002.

prove the safety; efficacy and quality of the product and formulation; and provide data for drug submissions.

The intended use concept can be found in the majority of the applicable regulations and guidelines.

The regulated user shall establish the intended use of the computer system, including the proper performance within the intended use. The intended use and proper performance are established by:

- Selection by the design team of the computer infrastructure based on capacity and functionality requirements
- Identification and implementation of the operational functions associated with the users, sequencing, regulatory, security, company (e.g. standards), safety requirements, and so on
- Identification and implementation of the operational limits in support to the operational and controls
- Identification and implementation of "worst case" operational or production conditions

Proper Performance

The phrase "proper performance" relates to one of the general principles of CSV. The computer systems must be validated to the possible level to effectively ensure proper performance. Planned and expected performance is based upon predetermined design specifications.

The same exact computer system used in two different facilities will have different validation requirements based on the intended use, operating environment, and proper performance.

Operating Environment

Another key concept in the definition of CSV is the intended use of the computer system within the operating environment.

In the regulatory context, computer systems apply not just to the computer system (i.e. software and hardware), but to the combination of:

- The computer system
- The process being controlled or monitored by the system

- The people
- The documentation (including standard operating procedures) required to use, operate, and support the system
- Any equipment or instruments being controlled or monitored by the system

All the above elements are called the operating environment (Figure 4.1).

The terms automated systems, computerized system, and computer-related system were coined to emphasize this concept.

The "operating environment" impacts the "intended use." Establishing the intended use of a computer system is essential at the beginning of a computer system's life cycle.

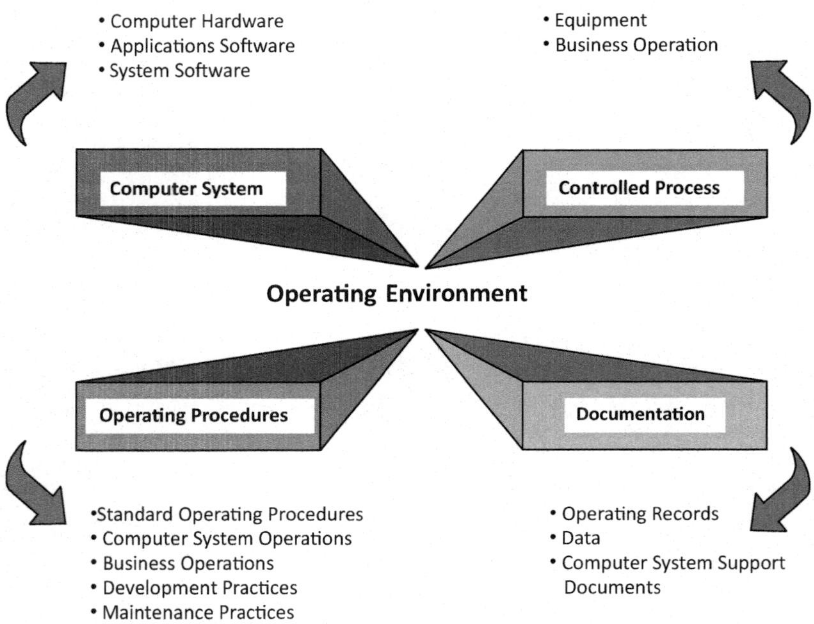

Figure 4.1 Operational environment. (From Herr, R. R. and Wyrick, M. L. "A Globally Harmonized Glossary of Terms for Communicating Computer Validation Key Practices." *PDA Journal of Pharmaceutical Science and Technology*, 53(2) 1999; 97–103.)

Chapter 5

General CSV Principles[*]

Core Principle

> The computer systems validation process incorporates "planning, verification, testing, traceability, configuration management, and many other aspects of good software engineering that together help to support a final conclusion that software is validated."
>
> *(PIC/S CSV PI 011-3, September 2007)*

Principle 1

> The regulated user should take all reasonable steps, to ensure that the system has been developed in accordance with an appropriate quality management system.
>
> *(EU Annex 11-4.5, <https://www.linkedin.com/pulse/eudralex-volume-4-pharmaceutical-quality-system-ruddy-msc-?published=u&trk=hp-feed-article-title-share>)*

A quality management system (QMS) defines all activities of the management function which influence the quality of a product. It is the total of the organized arrangements made with the objective of ensuring that medicinal products are of the quality required for their intended use.

The QMS determines the quality policy, objectives, and responsibilities, and implements them by such means as quality planning, quality

* Principle: A basic foundation of beliefs, truths, and so on, upon which others are based.

control, quality assurance, and quality improvement within the quality system.

Applicable to computer systems, software quality management is presented in the following areas: "Goals and Objectives" and "Methodologies".

The Goals and Objectives cover the following areas: Quality Goals and Objectives, Outsourced Services, Planning, Tracking, Software Quality Management System Documentation, and Customer Requirements.

Methodologies cover the following areas: Review, Inspection, and Testing; Change Management Methods; Cost of Quality; Quality Data Tracking; Problem Reporting, and Corrective Action Procedures; and Quality Improvement Processes.

Principle 2

> Computer systems performing regulated operations "should be validated. The depth and scope of validation depends on the diversity, complexity, and criticality of the computerized application."*
>
> *(see Chapter 2)*

Principle 3

> The computer system owner has the ultimate responsibility for ensuring that documented validation evidence is available to GxP inspectors for review.
>
> *(PIC/S PI 011-3)*

The system owner is the person responsible for the availability, validation state, and maintenance of a computer system and for the security of the data residing on that system.†

* ICH. *Guidance for Industry Q7A Good Manufacturing Practice Guidance for Active Pharmaceutical Ingredients*, August 2001.

† EudraLex. "EU Guidelines to Good Manufacturing Practice, Medicinal Products for Human and Veterinary Use Part 1, Annex 11 – Computerized Systems." *The Rules Governing Medicinal Products in the European Union*, Volume 4. June 2011.

Principle 4

> Validation shall demonstrate that the parameters defined as critical for its operation and maintenance are properly (adequately) controlled/managed. In addition, validation assures data and product integrity.

One of the objectives of the validation is to establish the correctness and accuracy of the inputs and outputs e-records from the computer systems. Input/output miscalculations can result in severe production errors and distribution of adulterated products.

In addition, security measures must be implemented, verified, tested and maintained to support the life cycle of the critical process parameters. These security measures assure that only authorized personnel institute changes in the process parameters.

An element in the e-records governance is the computer validation process. This process provides the initial assurance of the successful implementation of the e-records integrity controls. These controls are to be maintained through the operation, maintenance, and retirement of the computer system.*

The Heads of Medicines Agencies (HMA) and the European Medicines Agency (EMA) had determined early in 2015 "the need to ensure the integrity of the data on which regulatory decisions about medicines are based. Concerns about data integrity may arise for many reasons, e.g. poor training, inadequate implementation, or occasionally due to suspicions of falsification. The integrity of the data in the studies used to support market authorization is fundamental to trust and confidence in the products themselves."†

Principle 5

When planning the validation, the following points should be considered:

- Development of business requirements
- Objective evidence
- Intended use

---

* López, O. "Computer Systems Validation" in *EU Annex 11 Guide to Computer Validation Compliance for the Worldwide Health Agency GMP*. Boca Raton, FL: CRC Press, 2017; 121–132.

† HMA and EMA. "EU Medicines Agencies Network Strategy to 2020." March 2015.

- Proper performance
- Operating environment

(see Chapter 4)

Principle 6

> After a suitable period of running a new system it should be independently reviewed and compared with the system specification and functional specification.
>
> *(WHO Technical Report Series, No. 937, 2006. Annex 4. Appendix 5, Section 3.3)*

Computer systems should be periodically evaluated to confirm that they remain in a validated state and are compliant with the applicable GMP regulation(s). Such evaluations should include, where appropriate, the current range of functionality, deviation records, incidents, problems, upgrade history, performance, reliability, security and validation status reports.*

In the context of Annex 11, any periodic review should fall under self-inspections described in Chapter 9 of EU GMP.†

Principle 7

> Changes to the computer system, including migration of data, should be made according to a change procedure and should be formally authorized, documented and tested. Records should be kept of all changes, including modifications and enhancements made to the hardware, software and any other critical component of the system. These records should demonstrate that the system is maintained in a validated state.
>
> *(ICH Q7)*

---

* EudraLex. "EU Guidelines to Good Manufacturing Practice, Medicinal Products for Human and Veterinary Use Part 1, Annex 11 – Computerized Systems." *The Rules Governing Medicinal Products in the European Union*, Volume 4. June 2011. http://ec.europa.eu/health/files/eudralex/vol-4/annex11_01-2011_en.pdf.

† McDowall, R.D. "Periodic Evaluation" in *EU Annex 11 Guide to Computer Validation Compliance for the Worldwide Health Agency GMP*, Orlando Lópezed. Boca Raton, FL: CRC Press, 2015; 91–110.

Modifications and adjustments to computer systems shall only be made in accordance with a defined procedural control which includes provision for defining, documenting, and implementing the modification and/or adjustment.

Any modification to computer software (system and applications), infrastructure hardware, configuration files, e-records and process equipment are verified and documented and only made by authorized personnel.

The above referenced verification ensures the integrity of the data including any data that describes the context, content, and structure.

Principle 8

> There should be written procedures for performance monitoring, change control, program and data security, calibration and maintenance, personnel training, emergency recovery and periodic re-evaluation.
>
> *(WHO Technical Report Series, No. 937, 2006. Annex 4. Appendix 5, Section 1.6)*

After a computer system has been deployed and released for use, the system enters the Operational Periods: early operational; maturity, and aging. Each of these periods is discussed in Chapter 6.

During the Operational Periods a computer system performing manufacturing-related operations is employed in its operational environment, monitored for satisfactory performance, and modified, as necessary, to correct problems or to respond to changing requirements.*

Since computer systems likely contain errors, and for the reason that users will probable request improvements, procedural controls must exist for monitoring the performance of a computer system in its operational environment.

On computer systems controlling a manufacturing process, its quality can progress with time and the level of confidence in its performance can also consistently increase with time.

* US FDA. *Glossary of Computerized System and Software Development Terminology*, Division of Field Investigations, Office of Regional Operations, Office of Regulatory Affairs, Food and Drug Administration, August 1995.

A monitoring procedural control includes methods for:

- Identifying and documenting incidents, errors, and improvements requests
- Validity assessment
- Response priority assignment
- Defining the scope and frequency of monitoring

Computer systems changes are habitually part of a configuration management. Change requests for computer systems maintenance can take many forms. These can be corrections, adaptive, and perfective changes.

In any case, the change request must be reviewed and approved before its implementation.

For each computer systems change made in the operational environment, all the life cycle development phase activities are considered and possibly repeated to confirm that nothing is overlooked.

Computer system security relates to personnel, data, communications, and the physical protection of computer infrastructure. It includes the protection of computer infrastructure and applications from accidental or malicious access, use, modification, destruction, or disclosure (IEEE). The subject of computer system security and trustworthiness is addressed in Chapter 14.

Personnel operating, maintaining, and programming computer systems should have adequate training and experience to perform the assigned duties. One aspect to consider is the extent of operation and system management. Training should include not only the intended use and the system operation but also cover the implication of system faults, system changes, security procedures, manual operation of the system, and documentation of system errors. The organization must record the training of computer system-related personnel.

Training records are managed and retained by either the department providing the training or by another designated department. The project leader for new systems, or the system administrator for existing systems should coordinate the training. The system administrator may maintain a copy of the training records throughout the life of the computer system.

For the readiness of computer systems, the continuity of support for those processes in the event of a system breakdown must be established. These arrangements should be adequately documented and tested (EU Annex 11-16).

Computer systems should be periodically evaluated to confirm that they remain in a validated state and are compliant with GMP. Such evaluations should include, where appropriate, the current range of functionality, deviation records, incidents, problems, upgrade history, performance, reliability, security, and validation status reports (EU Annex 11-11).

Principle 9

The following procedures and controls must be adopted for records retained by computer storage in a typical manufacturing environment (e.g. supervisory control and data acquisition [SCADA]):

- Records should be regularly and progressively backed up, and the backup retained at a location remote from the active file (EU Annex 11-7.2; ICH Q7 5.48, PIC/S PI 011-3 19.5 and 211.68(b)).
- Data collected directly from equipment and control signals between computers and equipment should be checked by verification circuits/ software to confirm accuracy and reliability (211.68(b) – I/Os verification and EU Annex 11-5).
- Interfaces between computers and equipment should be checked to ensure accuracy and reliability (211.68(b) and EU Annex 11-5).
- There should be documented contingency plans and recovery procedures in the event of a breakdown. The recovery procedures should be periodically checked for the return of the system to its previous state (EU Annex 11-13).
- The system should be able to provide accurate printed copies of relevant data and information stored within. Printed matter produced by computer peripherals should be clearly legible and, in the case of printing onto forms, should be properly aligned onto the forms (EU Annex 11-8.1).

The above items can be found in the Australia TGA "CGMP Human Blood Tissues" (April 2013).

Principle 10

At a certain point during the Operational Life, the computer system is to be retired. This decision will initiate the Retirement Phase and, probably, a Conceptualization Period for system replacement.

In case of computer system retirement, the following steps should be taken:

- Set up a data preservation plan which could include one of the following options:
  - the new system will be able to retrieve data from previous systems.
  - preserve previous applications.
- Archive hard copies (when allowed).
- Completion of system documentation and validation records.
- Execution of the data preservation plan.
- QA audit on the preservation documentation.

The above items can be found in the CEFIC's "Computer Validation Guide", January 2003.

Chapter 6

System Life Cycle

Introduction

A high level of assurance of quality and reliability cannot be attributed to a computer system based basically on a series of tests exclusively designed to confirm the correct function of the application software and its interaction with the infrastructure.*

> **LIFE CYCLE MODEL**
>
> "Framework of processes and activities concerned with the life cycle that may be organized into stages, which also acts as a common reference for communication and understanding."
>
> *ISO/IEC 12207:2008, Definition 4.17*

The system life cycle (SLC) is comprised of a sequence of periods that may overlap and/or iterate, as appropriate for the project's scope, magnitude, complexity, changing needs and opportunities. Each period is described with a statement of purpose and outcomes. The system life cycle processes and activities are selected and employed in a period to fulfill the purpose and outcomes of that period.

The SLC is the "period of time that begins when a product is conceived and ends when the product is no longer available for use".†

The SLC comprises the system development life cycle (SDLC) and, the computer systems operational and maintenance processes.

The development life cycle methodology (e.g. waterfall, spiral, Agile software development, rapid prototyping, incremental, and synchronize and

* PIC/S. *Guide to Good Manufacturing Practice for Medicinal Products,* PE 009-5, September 2007.

† ANSI/IEEE Std 610.12-1990. *Standard Glossary of Software Engineering Terminology. Institute of Electrical and Electronic Engineers,* New York: Institute of Electrical and Electronic Engineers, 1990.

stabilize) associated with the SLC contains the software engineering tasks and associated work products necessary for supporting the computer system validation effort. The SLC breaks the systems development process down into sub-periods during which discrete work products are developed. This approach leads to well-documented systems that are easier to test and maintain, and for which an organization can have confidence that the system's functions will be fulfilled with a minimum of unforeseen problems.

The development life cycle methodology contains specific verification, analysis, and/or test activities that are performed based on the type of software, complexity, and intended use of the computer system. These activities in turn help build quality into the computer system and also provide for the collection of data to measure that quality.

During the computer system's Operational Life, a computer system performing manufacturing-related functions is employed in its operational environment, monitored for satisfactory performance, and modified, as necessary, to correct problems or to respond to changing requirements.*

The System Life Cycle

Figure 6.1† depicts an SLC adapted to different system acquisition strategies and software development models. It is focused on software engineering key practices. It does not specify or discourage the use of any particular software development method. The acquirer determines which of the activities outlined by the standard will be conducted, and the developer is responsible for selecting methods that support the achievement of the requirements. A modifiable framework must be tailored to the unique characteristics of each project.

While a consensus has not developed as to the naming of the SLC periods, the SLC includes at least the following periods:

- Conceptualization
- Development

* US FDA. *Glossary of Computerized System and Software Development Terminology*, Division of Field Investigations, Office of Regional Operations, Office of Regulatory Affairs, Food and Drug Administration, August 1995.

† Herr, R. R. and Wyrick, M. L. "A Globally Harmonized Glossary of Terms for Communicating Computer Validation Key Practices." *PDA Journal of Pharmaceutical Science and Technology,* 53(2) 1999; 97–103.

- Early operational life
- Maturity
- Aging

Based on Figure 6.1, Project Recommendation, Project Initiation, Release for Use, and Retirement are events. These events are considered phase gates or major decision points, which include formal approvals before the development can proceed to the next period.

Certain discrete work products are expected when evidencing the development and maintenance work of computer systems compliance to regulatory requirements. The selected SLC should specify the overall periods, and the associated events dictate the minimum requirements regardless of the chosen development method. These development methods and deliverables are also known as the development methodology. The development methodology establishes the detailed discrete work products by phases and events and by associated activities. The computer systems development approach must be consistent with the selected SLC. The most common development methodologies are the Waterfall Model, the Incremental Development Model, the Evolutionary Model, Object-Oriented approach, and the Spiral Model.

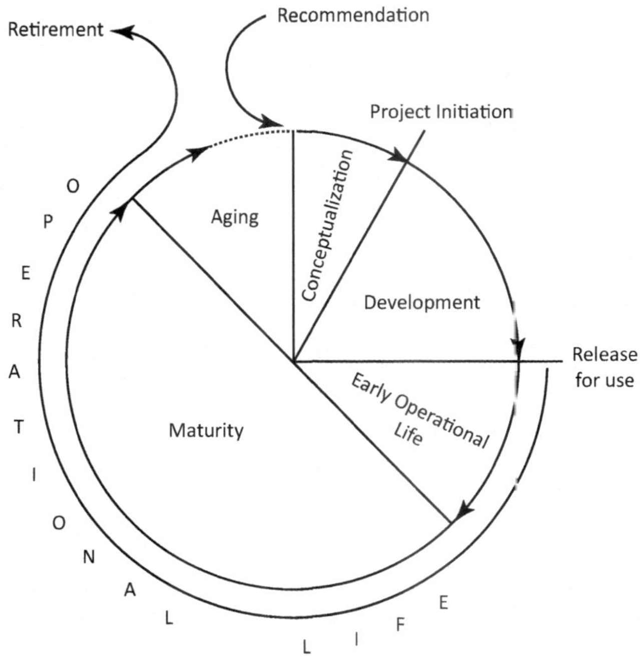

Figure 6.1 SLC.

A critical function of the validation process is to provide assurance that the development and operational life methodologies are consistent and followed. The SLC and the associated development and operational life methodologies applicable to computer systems performing regulated operations shall be described in procedural control(s). The project team may have the authority to select developmental and operational life methodologies that best suit the nature of the system under development and operational life methodologies different from the one included in the related procedural control. If this is the case, the selected development or operational life methodologies must be explained in the validation plan or equivalent document.

In general, it is the objective of the regulated companies to select the appropriate SLC and the associated development methodologies applicable to their development environment. Development and maintenance teams shall receive adequate training in the use of the chosen methodologies.

To evaluate adherence to the selected methodology, quality checkpoints (e.g. verifications) are conducted during the project. Considering Figure 6.1 as an example, each event associated when the SLC is a checkpoint when quality checks can be conducted.

Applicable Quality Principles to the SLC

The following quality-related principles are implemented during the manufacturing-related computer systems SLC.

- Quality, safety, and effectiveness must be designed and built into the system.
- Quality cannot be inspected or tested into the finished system.
- Each period of the SLC must be controlled to maximize the probability the finished system meets all design specifications.

Implementing the above principles as part of an SDLC and, the computer systems operational and maintenance processes, provides value in preventing software defects. Errors become costlier as they move through the SDLC, and it's more cost effective to fix bugs earlier than later.

The Systems Sciences Institute at IBM has reported that the cost to fix an error found after product release was four to five times as much as one uncovered during design, and up to 100 times more than one identified in the maintenance phase. Refer to Figure 6.2.

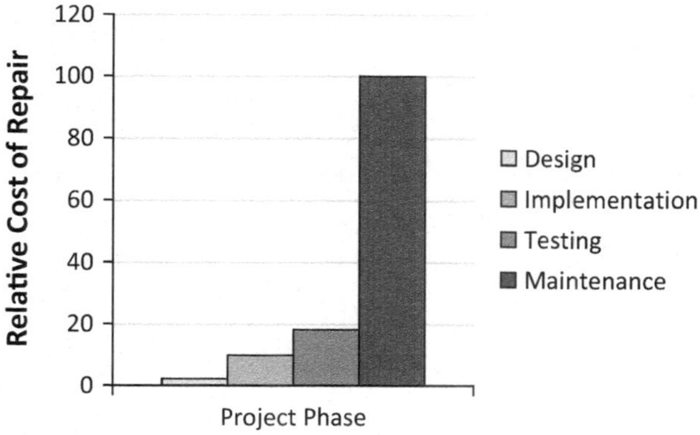

Figure 6.2 Relative cost of fixing an error.

Life Cycle Principles

1. There needs to be a formal planned approach by the developer and integrator to assure that quality is built into the product. ISO 12207 provides a quality system model for quality assurance in design, development, production, installation, and servicing, a.k.a SLC. (PIC/S PE 009-5)
2. The SLC is independent of any specific development and maintenance methodologies. It includes the following periods: Conceptualization, Development, Early Operational Life, Maturity and Aging; and the following events: Project Recommendations, Project Initiation, Release for Use and Retirement.
3. "The validation documentation and reports should cover the relevant steps of the life cycle." (EU Annex 11-4.1)
4. Requirements specifications should describe the required functions of the computer system and be based on documented risk assessment and GMP impact. User requirements should be traceable throughout the life cycle.* (EU Annex 11-4.4)
5. Risk management should be applied throughout the life cycle of the computer system taking into account patient safety, data integrity and product quality. As part of a risk management system, decisions on the extent of validation and data integrity controls should be based on a justified and documented risk assessment of the computer system. (EU Annex 11-1)

* López, O. "Requirements management." *Journal of Validation Technology*, 17(2) 2011.

Sample Related Regulations/Guidance/Standards

- ISO 12207, *Systems and Software Engineering – Software Life Cycle*, 2008.
- ISO/IEC 62304, *Medical device software – Software life cycle processes*, 2006.
- ISO/IEC 90003, *Software engineering – Guidelines for the application of ISO 9001:2000 to computer software*, 2004.
- PIC/S, *Guide to Good Manufacturing Practice for Medicinal Products. PE 009-5*, September 2007.
- US FDA, *General Principles of Software Validation; Final Guidance for Industry and FDA Staff*, January 2002.

Core Principle

> Validation should be considered as a part of the complete life cycle of a computerized system, which should include the stages of planning, specification, programming, acceptance testing, documentation, operation, monitoring, modification and discontinuation.
>
> *(Brazilian RDC Resolution #69, CGMP for APIs)*

Additional Readings

ISPE/PDA. Good Practice and Compliance for Electronic Records and Signatures. Part 1 Good Electronic Records Management (GERM)." July 2002.

Grigonis, G. J., Subak, and Wyrick M. L. "Validation Key Practices for Computer Systems Used in Regulated Operations." *Pharmaceutical Technology*, June 1997; 74–98.

Chapter 7

SLC Documentation

In the context of computers, SLC documentation means records that provide information about development, configuration, operation and maintenance, from high-level design documents to end-user manuals. The computer system documentation covers the relevant steps of the lifecycle,* related Standard Operating Procedures (SOPs), hardware, and the software (application and system).

The complexity and amount of the documentation that are typically needed to support a validated computer system may vary from system to system depending on the regulated company validation strategies.

As a record, the documentation will be governed by how the document is used in the manufacture of the healthcare product. Its exact use will then be taken into consideration to define and apply the appropriate sections of the applicable regulations that address records.

Good documentation constitutes an essential part of the quality assurance system and is key to operating in compliance with the regulated environment. But more importantly, the documentation is a key element during the operational life of the computer system. During this period, the documentation is used by the maintainer to modify, migrate, and/or retire the computer system. The documentation is the first tool in which the maintainer can learn from the developers' knowledge of the computer system.

All necessary controls for good documentation to support the integrity of the documentation must be in place. These controls may require software

* EU Annex 11-4.1.

development/configuration, and confirmation of the correct implementation as part of the validation of computer systems.*

The documentation retention requirements are the same as the record retention requirements applicable to the healthcare product.

Attributes of documents in compliance with GMP requirements include being written, clear, free from error, appropriate, verified, approved, and kept up-to-date.†

As expected in any GMP-related record, the process of SLC documentation authoring, reviewing, approving, distributing, retention, and periodic reviewing of documentation must adhere to the document control related policies and procedures concerned.

Types of Documents

Among the many documents that are used to outline systems and validation activities there are five that deserve emphasis:

- Specifications
- Plans
- Protocols
- SOPs
- Reports

Specifications

These are the written documents that define what the computer systems are supposed to do, including their functions, requirements, and configuration. The specifications serve as a basis for quality evaluation.

Plans

Studies such as validation should be conducted in accordance with written documents that describe overall objectives, approaches and procedures to be used.

Planning documents may use various formats and styles, and different descriptive terms may be used such as Master Validation Plans, project plans,

---

* WHO. "Guidance on Good Data and Record Management Practices." QAS/15.624, September 2015 (Draft).

† EU Commission Directive 2003/94/EC, October 2003.

study plans, research plans, development plans, and others. Regardless of terminology, it is important that suitable documents denote intentions in sufficient detail.

Protocols

Protocols are documents prepared before conducting the software testing. Protocols commonly define test methods and for conduct of the study, and list acceptance. Written protocols give instructions for performing and recording certain discreet operations for a particular application. Protocols are often more specific or limited in scope than planning documents.

Protocols may be cited in validation planning documents, and/or may be prepared for individual validation studies. In order to be objective (nonbiased) it is important that protocols be written and approved prior to initiating the testing.

An important element of protocols is to establish written acceptance criteria. Protocols should also specify who is responsible for conducting testing, what methods are to be used, how data are to be collected and reported. They should also indicate expected review and evaluation procedures to determine if acceptance criteria were met. In the context of software engineering, a protocol is equivalent to a test procedure.

Executed protocols and other relevant information need to be formally evaluated with applicable findings in approved summary reports. The results and discussions need to be presented clearly in a manner that can be readily understood. It must demonstrate which criteria and data were used in the decision-making process, and conclusions should be supported adequately.

In relation to the integrity of the executed protocols, Section 1.8 in the EMA Annex 15, establishes that the "appropriate checks should be incorporated into qualification and validation work to ensure the integrity of all data obtained."*

PRINCIPLE

"Good documentation constitutes an essential part of the quality assurance system and is key to operating in compliance with GMP requirements."

Volume 4, EU GMP Medicinal Products for Human and Veterinary Use, chapter 4: Documentation

* EudraLex. "EU Guidelines for Good Manufacturing Practice for Medicinal Products for Human and Veterinary Use, Annex 15: Qualification and Validation." *The Rules Governing Medicinal Products in the European Union*, Volume 4. March 2015.

Note that there is no difference in requirements on documentation whether in paper form or electronic form.

SOPs

Many records need to be established to describe validation procedures and techniques, and to define the control or production systems. The number and type of SOPs or procedural controls needed will vary with each application, but it is important that procedures be written, appropriate, clear, accurate and be approved by designated individuals.

Refer to Chapter 12 related to operational and maintenance procedures.

Reports

Reports record the conduct of particular exercises, projects or investigations, together with results, conclusions and recommendations.

As stated in Chapter 6, the SLC "breaks the systems development process down into sub-periods during which discrete work products are developed." For each SLC period and event, the computer systems validation process is documented. Certain discrete work products are expected when evidencing the validation state of the computer systems. These verified work products establish the compliance to the user's needs, quality, and applicable regulatory requirements.

In the software engineering context, computer systems documentation is regarded as software. All regulatory provisions applicable to software are also applicable to its documentation.

Computer system documents are generated during the conceptualization and development periods. They are updated during the Early Operational Life, Maturity and Aging Periods. The documents are finally retired as part of the Retirement Event.

The above is the typical documentation of organizations that define and develop software products.

Obsolete information must be archived or destroyed in accordance with a written record retention plan.

Typical Documentation for the Acquisition Process

The assumption in the acquisition process is that the software product to be acquired meets the intended use of the regulated entity. There are other processes, out of the scope of this section, to determine the fitness for purpose of the software to be acquired.

As part of acquiring software, the typical SLC documents that the regulated entity should have in their files are those related to the agreements and audits results around the software provider's quality system and particular SDLC methodology.

Where the regulated entity chooses to acquire software, which can affect product conformity with requirements and/or manage regulated e-records, the regulated entity shall hold responsibility for the suitability and maintenance, if applicable, of the application software.

The suitability of the software is evaluated by the implementation of a reliable development life cycle (e.g. compliance audit) and the fulfillment to the intended use (e.g. product audit).

If maintenance is to be provided by the software developer, a clear statement covering the associated developer's responsibilities must be defined in a formal quality agreement (e.g. service level agreement [SLA]).

TYPICAL SLC DOCUMENTATION

- Project and validation plans
- Risk analysis
- System requirements specification deliverable(s)
- System specification deliverable(s)
- Technical design specification deliverable(s)
- Source code/configurable code/scripts
- Quality audit and technical review reports
- Testing plans and reports
  - unit
  - integration
  - functional
- Factory Acceptance Test (FAT) and Site Acceptance Test (SAT) plans and results
- Qualification plans
- Validation/qualification results and summaries
- Traceability analysis
- User manuals
- Configuration management records

Note that during the operation of the system, the interface between the regulated entity and the supplier are the periodic audits to the supplier by the regulated entity. These system audits are performed to verify the application and effectiveness of the maintenance-related controls as defined in the SLA.

This typical documentation for the acquisition process, referenced above, may be pertinent to the software portion in a typical software as a service (SaaS) environment.

ASTM E 2500-13

ASTM E 2500-13 (Standard Guide for Specification, Design, and Verification of Pharmaceutical and Biopharmaceutical Manufacturing Systems and Equipment) is a risk based approach industry standard applicable to automated control systems.

This was the first standard that formalized the use of vendor documentation, including a test document, supporting the verification* of the manufacturing system.

The fundamental element to use vendor documentation to support the manufacturing system verification, including the software controlling the manufacturing system, is an acceptable quality system by the vendor. These vendor documents must be reviewed by the subject matter experts and quality unit representative.

The intended use of the system is, as an element in validation, a critical component.

In addition, it is stressed that the subject matter experts (SMEs) should drive the specification, design, and verification of the manufacturing-related software.

Test Scripts and Test Results

Test cases should include worst case conditions and confirmation of consistent functionality.†

Worst Case Conditions

After understanding the intended use of the computer system and the process the manufacturing computer system is to be managed with, then worst case conditions are better understood.

Worst case conditions testing encompasses the most appropriate challenge conditions and circumstances which have the greatest chance of finding errors, such as speed, data volume, and frequency.‡

These are test cases which expose program behavior at the boundaries of its input and output domains; program responses to invalid, unexpected, and

* Verification: The process of determining whether or not the products of a given phase of the SLC fulfills the requirements established during the previous phase.

† *WHO Technical Report Series*, No. 937, Annex 4, Appendix 5, Section 7.2.5, 2006.

‡ FDA. *Glossary of Computerized System and Software Development Terminology*, Division of Field Investigations, Office of Regional Operations, Office of Regulatory Affairs, August 1995.

special inputs are confirmed; the program's actions are revealed when given combinations of inputs, unexpected sequences of inputs, or when defined timing requirements are violated.

Worst case condition test cases are executed as part of the functional testing.

Confirmation of Consistent Functionality

The level of testing replication to a computer system should be sufficient to confirm consistent functionality as expected in the requirements.

Test scripts and test results which are part of a testing activity, should contain appropriate information that clearly identifies them. This information may include: an identification number which is traceable to a requirement identification number, the revision number of the document, the test execution or review date, the executed test outcome, and the name and signature of the person who conducted the test or review.

The completion of executed test outcomes in a paper-based environment should follow a set of pre-defined good documentation practices as follows:

- Always use water insoluble ink of suitable darkness to ensure copying will accurately transcribe the numbers.
- Pencils, white-out or erasable pen must never be used.
- Corrections should be made with a single line through the error followed by the initials and date of the person making the correction.
- Blanks, lines or spaces for recording data or comments which were not used when the document was completed should be crossed through or otherwise indicated as not applicable.
- Another, independent, person should verify calculations, test script execution, and test results, as applicable.

One key project related document is the traceability analysis. The correct analysis provides evidence that the computer system matches the assigned operational function and suitable for its intended use or assigned operational function within the operating environment.

Core Principle

> The validation documentation and reports should cover the relevant steps of the life cycle. Manufacturers should be able to justify their

standards, protocols, acceptance criteria, procedures and records based on their risk assessment.

(EU Annex 11-4.1)

Additional Reading

EudraLex. "EU Guidelines to Good Manufacturing Practice, Medicinal Products for Human and Veterinary Use, Chapter 4: Documentation." Volume 4, June 2011, https://ec.europa.eu/health/documents/eudralex/vol-4_en.

Chapter 8

Management of the Computer System Requirements*

Introduction

A requirement is a need or expectation that is stated, generally implied or obligatory. "Generally implied" means that it is common practice for the relevant stakeholder such that its absence would be deemed an obvious shortcoming.

The term "requirement" defines a bounded characterization of the system scope that can be generated by different relevant stakeholders. It includes the information essential to communicate an understanding of the problem and to support relevant stakeholders in its resolution. Various types of requirements include product, functionality, performance, regulatory, legal, reliability, supportability, usability, security, and non-functional requirements.

The majority of computer system failures are due to poor requirements gathering and management. This includes not understanding the business impact, what the customer wants, and how the stakeholder is to interact with the computer system. This situation negatively affects subsequent development activities, associated work products, and quality.

Requirements management is the process of documenting, analyzing, assessing the risk, tracing, prioritizing and agreeing on requirements, and

---

* López, O., "Requirements management." *Journal of Validation Technology* 17(2) 2011.

then controlling change and communicating to relevant stakeholders.* It is a nonstop process throughout a project.

According to the ASTM E 2500-13, requirements come from four areas: product knowledge, process knowledge, regulatory agencies, and company quality standards.

Requirements may be captured as user scenarios, function and feature lists, analysis models or specifications. These work products are used as a framework to select the supplier/integrator, to develop other work products associated with the development of the computer system, to develop the user acceptance plan/test, and to develop the maintenance/operational procedural controls.

Requirements engineering strives to understand what the relevant stakeholders need and want before beginning to design and build a solution. Tools that software engineers can leverage include Six Sigma, voice of the customer (VOC), quality function deployment (QFD), failure mode and effect analysis (FMEA), requirements analysis matrix (RAM), orthogonal array (OA), cause and effect analysis (C-E), design structure matrix (DSM), Pugh matrix, and so on.

The requirements engineering tasks comprise:

- *Inception* – context-free questions are used to establish a basic understanding of the problem, the perspectives of relevant stakeholders who want a solution, the nature of the solution, and the effectiveness of the collaboration between the relevant stakeholders and developers.
- *Elicitation* – the product objectives are found out from the relevant stakeholders, as well as what is to be done, how the product fits into business needs, and how the product is used on a day to day basis.
- *Elaboration* – a refined technical model of software function, behavior, and information is developed.
- *Negotiation* – requirements are categorized and organized into subsets, relations among requirements identified, requirements reviewed for correctness, requirements prioritized based on the relevant stakeholder needs.
- *Specification* – requirements are derived from, or provided by the relevant stakeholders describing the function, performance, and development

* A stakeholder is anyone who has a stake in the successful outcome of the project – system owner(s), business managers, regulated end-users, quality assurance, software engineers, support people, and so forth.

constraints for a computer system. These work products should be in a form suitable for requirements management through the life cycle and beyond.

- *Requirements validation* – formal technical reviews are used to examine the specification work products to ensure requirement quality and that all work products conform to agree upon standards for the process, project, and products.
- *Requirements management* – are activities that help a project team to identify, control, and track requirements and requirement changes as the project proceeds.

Figure 8.1* depicts a typical systems development distribution showing the percentage of effort needed for each key developmental activity. Except for requirements management, front end activities, includes requirements engineering, should take between 40 and 50% system development life cycle (SDLC) distribution.

The importance of managing requirements is depicted in Figure 6.2. This figure correlates the cost to find and fix defects during the SLC. For example, in 1976, the cost to fix an error found after product release was up to 100 times more than one identified in the Design Phase.

This chapter covers the product requirements† activities only. Project requirements are out of the scope of this chapter.

- "Front end" Activities
  - Customer communication
  - Analysis
  - Design
  - Review and modification
- Construction
  - Coding or code generation
- Testing and Installation
  - Unit, integration
  - White-box, black-bix
  - regression

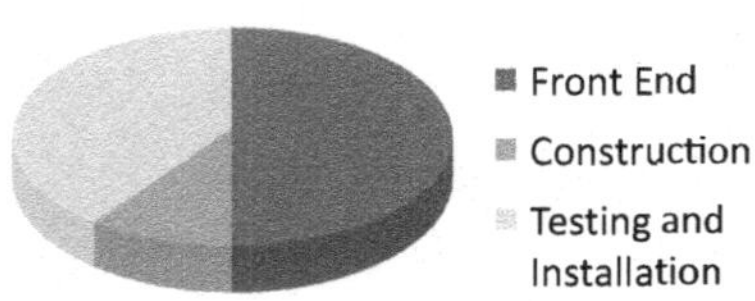

Figure 8.1 Systems development distribution.

---

* Pressman, R. S. *Software Engineering: A Practitioner's Approach*, 7th ed. New York: McGraw-Hill, 2009.

† Product requirements: Include high-level features or capabilities that the business team has committed to delivering to a customer. Product requirements do not specify how the features or the capabilities will be designed.

Requirements Management

> "A software requirements traceability analysis should be conducted to trace software requirements to (and from) system requirements and to risk analysis results."
>
> *US FDA General Principles of Software Validation*

The purpose of the Requirements Management process is to maintain and control a current, correct, and documented common understanding of the relevant stakeholders, intended product use, development resources, constraints, and needed computer system capabilities that were captured and baselined in the requirements documentation. It describes the tasks necessary to correct, update, and control a Requirements Specification* document (RS). Figure 8.2 depicts the key inputs to the requirements specification.

The result of the requirements management process is an updated organized set of documented requirements throughout the system life cycle that:

- Supports the relevant stakeholder's needs, goals, and objectives.
- Remains within a well-defined scope.
- Identifies and quantifies impacts of changes including those of scope, schedule, cost, hardware, and staffing.
- Controls the current, documented RS.

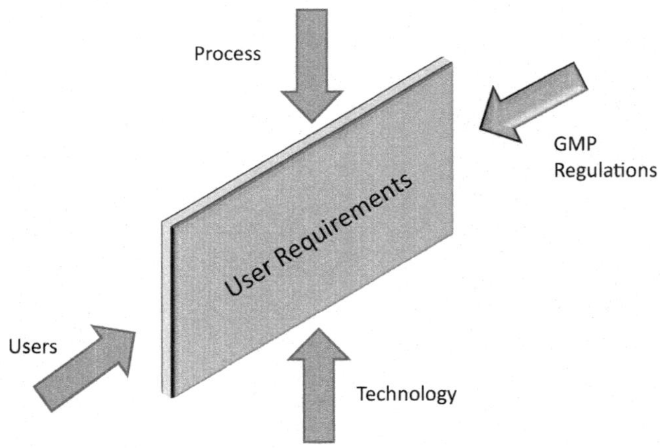

Figure 8.2 Inputs to the Requirements Specification.

* Specification: A document that specifies, in a complete, precise, verifiable manner, the requirements, design, behavior, or other characteristics of a system or component, and often, the procedures for determining whether these provisions have been satisfied. (IEEE)

A Requirement Management plan may be necessary for highly complex and highly critical projects. The Requirement Management plan is used to record the activities required to effectively establish* the project requirements from definition, through traceability, to delivery.

The Requirements Management plan is created during the early Development Period of the SLC (refer to Chapter 6). Its intended audience is the project manager, project team, project sponsor, and any senior leaders whose support is needed to carry out the plan.

According to the Capability Maturity Model Integration (CMMI)† activities as part of the requirements management and elements of the plan are:

- Obtaining an Understanding of Requirements.
- Obtaining Commitment to Requirements.
- Managing Requirements Changes.
- Maintaining Bidirectional Traceability of Requirements.
- Ensuring Alignment between Project Work and Requirements.

Figure 8.2 provides the relationships between these activities.

Obtaining an Understanding of Requirements

The intent is to establish project criteria to identify providers of appropriate requirements, criteria for the evaluation and acceptance of requirements, and to ensure through an analysis or review process that the established criteria are met.

Those who receive requirements, analyze them with the sources to ensure that a compatible, shared understanding is reached on the meaning of requirements. The result of these analyses and dialogs is

REGULATORY GUIDELINE

"The Quality System regulation requires a mechanism for addressing incomplete, ambiguous, or conflicting requirements. Each requirement (e.g. hardware, software, user, operator interface, and safety) identified in the software requirements specification should be evaluated for accuracy, completeness, consistency, testability, correctness, and clarity."

US FDA 21 CFR 820.30(c)

* Establish: Define, document and implement. (21 CFR 820.3[k])

† Carnegie Mellon University Software Engineering Institute. *Capability Maturity Model Integration for Development (CMMI-DEV)*, Version 1.3, November 2010.

Table 8.1 Attributes of Requirements

Attribute	*Definition*
Unambiguous	All requirements must have only one interpretation: • Clearly and properly stated. • Complete.
Verifiable	A human being or a machine must be able to verify that the system correctly enacts the stated requirements.
Traceable	The requirements must be traceable from other design and test documents. To facilitate the traceability, each requirement should be uniquely identified.
Modifiable	Unanticipated changes must be able to be made easily.
Usable	Each requirement must be tied to business values, identified as a priority for the customer, and appropriate to implement by the development team. The RS must be usable by not only the development team but also subsequent maintenance teams who will be called upon to modify and change the system.
Consistent	Individual requirements must not conflict with each other. Requirements must be consistent as well with overall architectural approach and quality attribute priorities.
Complete	It must contain clear descriptions of all features and functions of the system. It must clearly contain definitions of all known situations the system could encounter.

an approved requirements specification including the definition of the system boundaries.

Example work products for this practice include:

- Lists of criteria for distinguishing appropriate requirements providers.
- Criteria for evaluation and acceptance of requirement (refer to Table 8.1).
- Results of analyses against criteria.

Lack of evaluation and acceptance criteria often results in inadequate verification, costly rework or customer rejection.

Obtaining Commitment to Requirements

Once the understanding of the requirements is established, this practice deals with agreements and commitments among those who have to carry out the activities necessary to implement these requirements.

The main deliverable after getting the commitment of the relevant stakeholders is the requirements specification (RS). It is a document approved by all relevant stakeholders. The RS establishes the relevant stakeholders' requirements baseline, and retains changes of need and their origin throughout the SLC. It is the basis for traceability to the computer system requirements and forms the definitive source of information about requirements for subsequent systems and communications with stakeholders.

Later, in the thick of development, the RS will be critical in preventing scope creep or other unnecessary changes. As the system evolves, each new feature opens a world of new possibilities, so the RS anchors the team to the original vision and permits a controlled discussion of scope change.

While many organizations use only documents to manage requirements, others manage their requirements baselines using software tools. These tools allow requirements to be managed in a database, and usually have functions to automate traceability (e.g. by allowing electronic links to be created between parent and child requirements, or between test cases and requirements), electronic baseline creation, version control, and change management. Usually such tools contain an export function that allows a specification document to be created by exporting the requirements data into a standard document application.

The RS must include an overview of the process in order to familiarize the infrastructure and application developers with the regulated user, business process, regulatory and data acquisition requirements of the system, and any special considerations for the project. The system functionality must be well defined at the outset in order to provide the prospective supplier/integrator with enough information to provide a detailed and meaningful proposal. Specifically, on data acquisition systems, the RS must include data definitions; data usage information; data storage, retention, and security requirements; and operational requirements and constraints.

The RS addresses:

- The scope of the system and strategic objectives.
- Process overview, sequencing requirements, operational checks.
- Sufficient information to enable the supplier/integrator to work on a solution to the problem (e.g. device driven sequencing, the methods required of the presentation of data, data security, data backup, data and status reporting, and trending, etc.).
- Redundancy and error-detection protocol.
- Operating environment.

- Interfaces (e.g. to field devices, data acquisition systems, reports, and human machine interface), I/O lists, communications protocols and data link requirements.
- Information gained from operators and supervisors on the system design requirements and expectations in order to influence how the system is designed and operated.
- Type of control and process operations to be performed.
- Data storage requirements.
- Transaction/data timing requirements and considerations.
- Regulatory requirements.
- Preliminary evaluation of the technology.
- Feasibility study and preliminary risk assessment.
- Safety and security considerations.
- Security, other requirements.
- Non-functional requirements (e.g. SLC development standards, programming language standards, program naming convention standards, etc.).

Each requirement in the RS should have the attributes depicted in Table 8.1.

The requirements should be verified during each phase of the SDLC. In a classic "V" model, the requirements are tested during the user acceptance testing, a.k.a the performance qualification (PQ) in the US FDA regulated industries context. This testing should include the verification of the procedural controls associated with the system which were identifies in the RS.

Managing Requirements Changes

Once commitments to the requirements are established and plans have been made, the project will transform from planning mode to execution mode. During the project execution phase, possible conditions precipitating a change are:

- A new requirement is identified.
- The software project is re-scoped (requirements added, dropped, or modified).

- An inconsistency is identified between the capabilities of the developed product and the documented requirements.

Figure 8.3 depicts that inputs and outputs of the management of requirements changes.

The entry criterion to this process is:

- A requirement change request has been submitted.

The tasks associated with this process include:

- Analysis of change request for impact and feasibility.
- Preparation of an impact analysis statement.
- Determination of the disposition of the change request (e.g. accept, reject, defer).

If the change request is accepted, then:

- Generate changed RS and change requests for other controlled products as applicable and necessary.

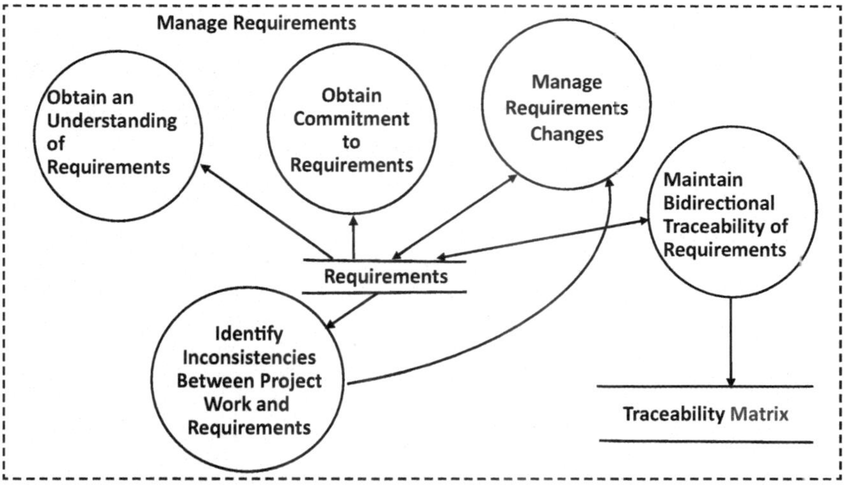

Figure 8.3 Requirements Management.

- Implement the change. Also, make the necessary modifications to related artifacts: RS, modeling diagrams, quality function deployment, generic specifications, and so on.
- Verify and validate changed RS.
- Update and distribute updated documentation as necessary.

The exit criteria to this process are:

- Decision was made through the applicable process not to proceed with the change.

  or
- Updates to requirements made, distributed and controlled.
- Other work product change requests have been generated as required.

The impact analysis process, as part of the Management of Requirement changes, by itself has multiple steps. This process must be clearly defined and communicated to the customer as well as to the project team. The high-level steps of the change impact analysis process include:

1. Get change request.
2. Expand the demand statement using Voice of the Customer (VOC) analysis (who, what, when, where, why, and how).
3. Analyze engineering impacts:
   a. The "hows" yield clues around impacted features.
   b. Identify, using for example quality function deployment (QFD), associated functionality and design parameters. These design parameters are the engineering items to be scrutinized to determine their impact.
4. In review meeting(s), analyze if a problem requires only a hardware/machine "tweak" or if it requires a software change.
5. Analyze software impacts:
   a. Using the QFD, identify all the functionalities (use cases) that are impacted.
   b. For each use case, analyze graphical user interface (GUI) and controller change required using the traceability analysis.
   c. Conduct risk analysis, for example based on failure mode and effect analysis (FMEA), so the potential regressive damage due to the change is minimized.
6. Create the change request impact analysis document and review with customer.

Maintaining Bidirectional Traceability of Requirements

> Traceability is an essential aspect of verification, and it is an important input into design reviews.

Requirements traceability (Figure 8.4) is concerned with documenting the origin of a requirement as well as the relationships between requirements and other development artifacts, such as designs, models, analysis results, code and test plans/cases/procedures/results (Figure 8.5).

The purpose of requirements traceability is to facilitate:

- Overall quality.
- Understanding of the product.
- Tests necessary to verify.
- Ability to manage change.

The intent of this practice is to maintain the bidirectional traceability of requirements for each level of product decomposition. Refer to Figure 8.6.

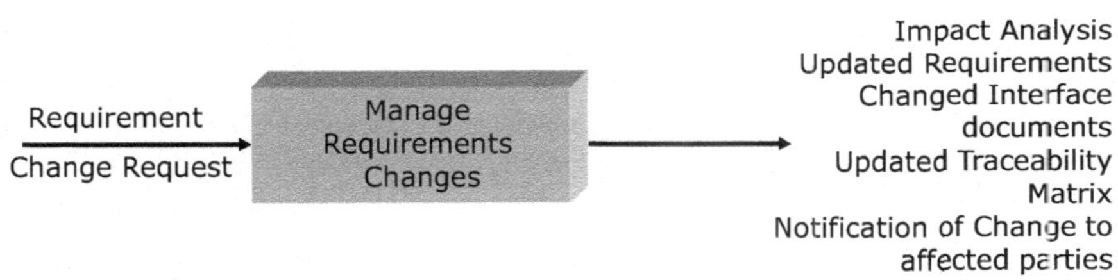

Figure 8.4 Manage requirements changes.

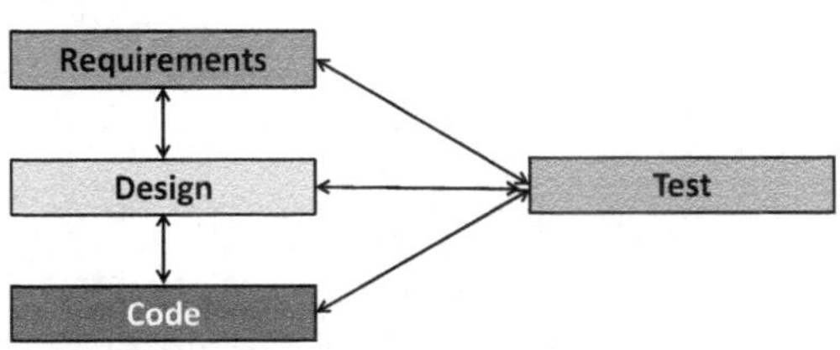

Figure 8.5 Requirements traceability.

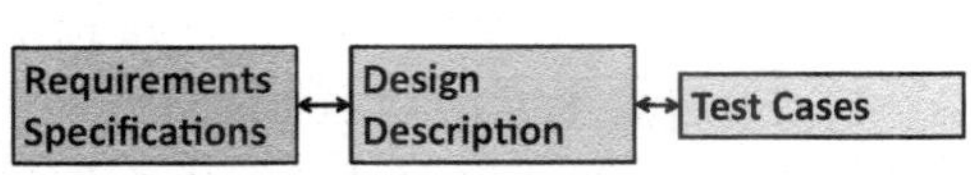

Figure 8.6 Forward_Backward traceability.

The following two types of traceability are recommended:

1. Forward traceability (i.e. to all documents spawned by the System Requirements Specification [SRS]). This depends upon each requirement in the SRS having a unique name or reference number.
2. Backward traceability (i.e. to previous stages of development). This depends upon each requirement explicitly referencing its source in earlier documents.

The forward traceability of the RS is especially important when the software product enters the operation and maintenance phase. As code and design documents are modified, it is essential to ascertain the complete set of requirements that may be affected by those modifications.

It should be possible to trace back to the origin of each requirement and every change made to the requirement should therefore be documented in order to achieve traceability.

Requirements traceability is also useful when conducting impact assessments of changes to requirements, design or other configured items.

When the requirements are managed well, traceability can be established from the source requirement to its lower level requirements and from the lower level requirements back to their source. Such bidirectional traceability helps determine that all source requirements have been completely addressed and that all lower level requirements can be traced to a valid source.

The example below shows the links that are to be maintained. To demonstrate how bidirectional traceability evidence of sorting (and use) by each column is to be captured.

Traceability is an essential aspect during the verification activities in the SLC, and it is an important input into design reviews. A formal design review is recommended to confirm that requirements are fully specified and appropriate before extensive software design efforts begin.

Table 8.2 depicts the traceability activities during a typical SLC.

The practice of requirements traceability is iterative. It is conducted throughout the SLC and involves the following activities:

- *Functionality* – Defining functional requirements based on technical assumptions and/or client needs.
- *Traceability* – Setting up and maintaining a requirements traceability system.

Table 8.2 Inputs to the Requirements Specification

Unique Requirement ID	*Requirement Description*	*Design Reference*	*Module / Configured Item Reference*	*Release Reference*	*Test Script Name / Step Number Reference*

- *Log* – Updating regularly (at least weekly) the traceability matrix with new information.
- *Communicating* – Communicating regularly (at least weekly) with stakeholders about the status of requirements.
- *Log* – Recording data used to track the requirements in the traceability matrix.
- *Communication* – Communicating to stakeholders that a particular requirement has been completed.

The traceability of requirements can be built into documentation and code without having to have a separate traceability document. Three common approaches are: traceability matrix, using computer databases to evaluate traceability, and building inherent traceability into the structure of the documentation and code. Software developers have flexibility in how they want to implement traceability (Table 8.3).

Note that the correct traceability analysis provides evidence that the computer system matches the assigned operational function and is suitable for its intended use or assigned operational function within the operating environment.

Ensuring Alignment Between Project Work and Requirements

This practice focuses on maintaining consistency between requirements, project plans, work products, and, in case of inconsistencies, initiates corrective actions to resolve them. For example, the project plan should be revised if changes to the requirements are identified as impacting the schedule.

Table 8.3 Traceability Activities and SLC

SLC Phase	*Typical Traceability Task(s)*	*Comment*
Requirements	• Software requirements to system requirements (and vice versa) • Software requirements to risk analysis	A traceability analysis should be conducted to verify that the software design implements all of the software requirements. As a technique for identifying where requirements are not sufficient, the traceability analysis should also verify that all aspects of the design are traceable to software requirements.
Design	• Design specification to software requirements (and vice versa)	A traceability analysis should be conducted to verify that the software design implements all of the software requirements. As a technique for identifying where requirements are not sufficient, the traceability analysis should also verify that all aspects of the design are traceable to software requirements. An analysis of communication links should be conducted to evaluate the proposed design with respect to hardware, user, and related software requirements.
Construction/ source code/ configuration	• Source code to design specification (and vice versa) • Test cases to source code and to design specification	A source code traceability analysis is an important tool to verify that all code is linked to established specifications and established test procedures. A source code traceability analysis should be conducted and documented to verify that: • Each element of the software design specification has been implemented in code; • Modules and functions implemented in code can be traced back to an element in the software design specification and to the risk analysis; • Tests for modules and functions can be traced back to an element in the software design specification and to the risk analysis; and

(*Continued*)

Table 8.3 (Continued) Traceability Activities and SLC

SLC Phase	*Typical Traceability Task(s)*	*Comment*
		• Tests for modules and functions can be traced to source code for the same modules and functions.
Developer's Software Testing	• Unit (module) tests to detailed design • Integration tests to high-level design • System tests to system requirements	Control measures, such as a traceability analysis, should be used to ensure that the intended coverage is achieved.
User acceptance testing	User acceptance test to system requirements	• In a typical "V" model this is the ultimate test. Each requirement must map to at least one test case. • Control measures, such as a traceability analysis, should be used to ensure that the intended coverage is achieved.
Maintenance		After the computer system has been delivered for operations, the forward traceability of the RS is especially important when the software product enters the maintenance phase. As part of the activities to conclude a project, the requirements traceability matrix must be updated with the as-built information. The objective is to have an up-to-date matrix describing how the system's final design satisfied the functional, business, security, and technical specifications in the requirements document. As code and design documents are modified, it is essential to be able to ascertain the complete set of requirements that may be affected by those modifications. With the new project, a new cycle begins to the requirements management process.

Corrective actions *taken by the project to resolve inconsistencies can also result in changes to project plans and supplier agreements.*

Summary

It is necessary to identify, control, and track requirements before design and construction of a computer system can begin.

The Requirements Management consists of five activities:

- Obtaining an Understanding of Requirements.
- Obtaining Commitment to Requirements.
- Managing Requirements Changes.
- Maintaining Bidirectional Traceability of Requirements.
- Ensuring Alignment between Project Work and Requirements.

The relevance of the Requirements Management to successfully manage a computer system implementation project is stressed by distributing over 40% of the SDLC on managing requirements.

The main activities of the Requirements Management are to meet the VOC and keep updated the Requirements Specification during the SDLC. The quality and completeness of the requirements contribute to the accuracy of the specification.

The success of computer systems implementation/maintenance depends on these three tasks. As depicted on Figure 8.2, a practical and accurate requirements specification will contribute to the successful implementation of the computer system, on time, within the budget, and on schedule.

Requirements Management can achieve the success described above if it is maintained throughout the system life cycle.

Tools

Cybernetic Intelligence GmbH – EasyRM, www.cybernetic.org/contents/en/easyrm.php.

IBM Rational® RequisitePro® – IBM tool used for Requirements Management, www.ibm.com/support/knowledgecenter/en/SSSHCT_7.1.0/com.ibm.reqpro.help/helpindex_rp.html.

Rational Software – Rational RequisitePro, ftp://ftp.software.ibm.com/software/rational/web/datasheets/reqpro.pdf.

Siemens – Systems Engineering and Requirements, www.plm.automation.siemens.com/en/products/teamcenter/requirements-management/.

Telelogic Inc. – tool used for requirements management www-01.ibm.com/software/awdtools/doors/?&ca=qapromo-s0swg-b0swg-l0-d0swgmer-n0363-o0doors-g0usen/.

Tools noted here do not represent an endorsement, but rather a sampling of tools in the category of requirements management. In most cases, tool names are trademarked by their respective developers.

Core Principle

> User RS should describe the required functions of the computerised system and be based on documented risk assessment and GMP impact. User requirements should be traceable throughout the life cycle.
>
> *(EU Annex 11-4.4)*

Additional Readings

ASTM E 2500-13. *Standard Guide for Specification, Design, and Verification of Pharmaceutical and Biopharmaceutical Manufacturing Systems and Equipment*, 2013.

Best Practices in Requirements Engineering, www.stickyminds.com/sitewide.asp?Function=edetail&ObjectType=ART&ObjectId=13169&tth=DYN&tt=siteemail&iDyn=37.

Carnegie Mellon University Software Engineering Institute. "Capability Maturity Model Integration for Development (CMMI-DEV)." Version 1.3, November 2010.

IEEE Std 1233. "Guide for Developing System Requirements Specifications." 1998.

ISO 9001. "Quality Management Systems – Requirements." 2008.

ISO/IEC 9126. "Software Engineering – Product Quality." 2001.

ISO/IEC 12207, "Systems and software engineering – Software life cycle processes." 2008.

ISPE/GAMP. "GAMP Traceability for GxP Regulated Application." *Pharmaceutical Engineering*, 26(1) 2006.

NASA. Software Engineering Documents, www.nasa.gov/offices/oce/functions/software/index.html.

US Center for Disease Control (CDC). *CDC Unified Process Practices Guide – Requirements Management.* 2007, www2.cdc.gov/cdcup/.

US Food and Drugs Administration (FDA). *General Principles of Software Validation; Final Guidance for Industry and FDA Staff*, June 2001.

Additional regulatory or guidance references associated with this topic can be found at: "PIC/S Guidance on Good Practices for Computerised Systems in Regulated 'GxP' Environments" (PI 011-3), US FDA 21 CFR 211.68; US FDA 21 CFR 820.30(g), 21 CFR 820.70(i) and 21 CFR 11.10(a). http://en.wikipedia.org/wiki/Requirements_traceability.

Chapter 9

Risk Based Validation

Introduction

> Risk Management is like project management for adults.

Risk management is the starting point of every project and involves a systematic application of policies, procedures, and practices to the analysis, evaluation, and control of risks. It is a key component of quality management systems.

Risks for a given hazard is a function of the relative likelihood of its occurrence and its consequence. Risk management includes the identification and description of hazards, how they might occur, their expected consequences, and an estimation or assessment of their relative likelihood. Following the estimation of risks, risk management focuses on controlling or mitigating the risks.

Thorough consideration of use-related hazards in risk management processes should include the following tasks:

- Identify and describe hazards related to device use through analysis of existing information.
- Apply empirical techniques, using representative users, to identify and describe hazards that do not lend themselves to identification through analytical techniques.
- Estimate the likelihood and consequences (risk) of use scenarios resulting in hazards.
- Develop strategies and controls to eliminate or reduce the likelihood, or mitigate the consequences, of use-related hazards scenarios.

- Select and implement control strategies.
- Ensure controls are appropriate and effective in reducing risk.
- Determine if new hazards have been introduced as a result of implementing control strategies.
- Verify that functional and operational requirements are met.
- Validate safe and effective device use.

Software development is one of the most risk prone management challenges. Risk factors are usually present that can negatively impact the development process and, if neglected, can lead to project failure. To counteract these factors, system risk must be actively assessed, controlled, and reduced on a routine basis.*

Risk is defined as the probability of an undesirable event occurring and the impact of that event if it does occur. The result of this analysis will influence the degree to which the system development, implementation, and maintenance activities are performed and documented. By evaluating the system risk analysis, the system owner may uncover potential problems that can be avoided during the development/implementation process. The chances of a successful, if not perfect, system implementation is improved.

Risk Assessment in Computer Validation, Where Does It Apply?

According to the FDA's General Principles of Software Validation[†] the extent of the software validation effort should be commensurate with the associated risk. In addition, the extent of validation, should take into account the impact the systems have on ability to meet predicate rule requirements.

The EU Annex 20[‡] provides a possible use on computer systems risk analysis to determine the extent of validation:

- Identification of critical performance parameters
- Selection of the requirements and design

* Software Technology Support Center, DAF. "Guidelines for Successful Acquisition and Management of Software Intensive Systems." Vol. 1, February 1995.

† US FDA. *General Principles of Software Validation; Final Guidance for Industry and FDA Staff*, January 2002, www.fda.gov/cdrh/comp/guidance/938.html.

‡ EU Annex 20 "The Rule Governing Medicinal Products in the European Union," EudraLex, "EU Guidelines for Good Manufacturing Practices for Medicinal Products for Human and Veterinary Use, Quality Risk Management," February 2008.

- Code review
- The extent of testing and test methods
- Trustworthiness of e-records and signatures

The extent of validation is based on a justified and documented risk assessment which should include a determination of the potential of the system to affect product* safety, product efficacy, product quality, patient safety, and record/data integrity, authenticity, and confidentiality.

Another criterion to account as part of the extent of validation is the system's complexity and the knowledge within the organization of the technology. The selection of validation activities, tasks, and work items should be commensurate with the complexity of the software design and the risk associated with the use of the software for the specified intended use.

As applicable, additional criteria to consider in the risk assessment include the level of standardization, configuration, customization, intended use, and vendor's quality system assessment results.

In those systems which manage GMP e-records and/or e-signatures, the validation efforts should take into account as well the impact those systems might have on the integrity of such records and/or e-signatures.

A risk based approach should be utilized with respect to systems validation, audit trails, and record copying. However, records must still be maintained or submitted in accordance with the underlying predicate rules.

If remediation is necessary for the applicable predicate rule and/or e-records integrity compliance, a remediation plan must be established† using a documented risk based approach (refer to Chapter 18).

The regulated user firm size or resource constraint are not criteria to consider on risk based validation.

For lower risk computer systems, only baseline validation activities or GMP controls may be conducted. As the risk increases, additional validation activities should be added to cover the additional risk. Validation documentation should be sufficient to demonstrate that all software validation plans and procedures have been completed successfully.

There are a variety of risk assessment and management strategies to assess impact on patient safety, product quality, and data integrity which assists the regulated users in allocating resources. In an effort to avoid redundancy it

---

* 'Product' in the context of the FDA means the FDA regulated article such as food, human or veterinary drug, biological product, medical device, or radiological product.

† Establish means define, document (in writing or electronically), and implement. (21 CFR 820.3(k)).

is recommended that risk assessment efforts be performed according to the regulated user standardized approach.

Risk Management

Risk management can be approached based on levels. Three levels can be acknowledged in computer systems environments: process, system, and function.

- *Process* – What processes to remediate and control?
  - Risks from critical processes.
  - e.g. clinical data management.
- *System* – What systems to remediate and control?
  - Risk from entire system supporting a critical process.
  - e.g. clinical data management system.
- *Function* – What functions require controls?
  - Risk from specific functions that a system performs – pieces and parts of systems need to be treated differently.
  - e.g. clinical data entry.

The process risk analysis is usually performed during the product/process/manufacturing development phase. The products of the process risk analysis are the inputs to the system risk analysis.

There are seven steps necessary for assessing and managing risks:

- A description of the risk.
- The cause(s) of the risk.
- The level of concern regarding the risk based on a qualitative estimate, including any definition of terms used.
- The likelihood of occurrence of the risk based on a qualitative estimate, including the definition of terms used.
- The method(s) of control used to eliminate or mitigate the risk, e.g. a change in the design specification, alarm warning and/or error messages, implementation of a manual process and/or workaround.
- The traceability of each method of control to the corresponding critical requirement specified in the requirements specification deliverable.
- Monitor and manage the implementation of the requirements identified during the risk analysis.

Some of the items to consider when conducting the risk analysis include:

- Regulatory areas of the system
- Size of the computer system and number of users
- Complexity of the system in terms of the design
- Type of data the system handles
- Functionality of the system
- Interaction with and impact on existing systems
- Vendor reliability
- Effect/impact of system non-compliance
- Safety to the customer, employee, and community
- Cost versus benefit of the system

The results of the risk analysis review must be documented. To adequately analyze the risks, a comprehensive requirements specification deliverable is required. The best time to perform an initial risk analysis is just after the project team has completed the review of the requirements specification deliverable. The review of the risk mitigation-related elements resulting of the risk analysis should be performed during a technical design review.

Risk management encompasses three processes: risk assessment, risk mitigation, and assessment. In Figure 9.1, reviewing the effects and assessing risks to the applied controls are considered elements of the assessment.

Risk Analysis

A detailed risk analysis should be performed, building on the initial risk analysis performed during the concept phase. The risk analysis process assesses

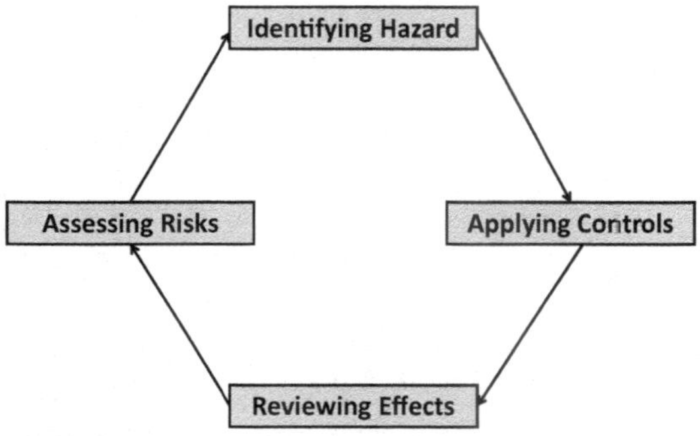

Figure 9.1 Risk management.

risks associated with processes and functions defined in the requirement specification deliverable and functional specification. The activities are:

- Identify processes/functions/transactions (as appropriate)
- Assess risk by analyzing:
  - Risk scenarios
  - Effects for each event
  - Likelihood of events
  - Severity of impact
  - Likelihood of detection
- Plan for reduction or elimination of those risks, based on the analysis

Risk Mitigation

Strategies for mitigation or applying controls of the identified risks may include modifying the process or system design, modification of project approach or structure, modifying the validation and testing approach, adding new features, apply external procedures, and/or more detailed rigorous specification and verifications.

When possible eliminate the risk by design. Appropriately designing the selected technology decreases or even eliminates the risk.

Risk Evaluation and Assessment

Verification activities should demonstrate that the controls are effective in performing the required risk reduction.

Some activities to assess the effectiveness of the implemented mitigation(s) to the risk uncovered are:

- Monitor the implemented controls.
- Periodic review—the frequency and extent should be based on the level of risk.
- Change management to apply risk management activities.

Integration Risk Management with SLC

The support of the risk management process during the life cycle includes:

Conceptualization

- Identified risks are used to support the development of the system requirements, including security requirements, e-records integrity requirements and so on.

  The risks to e-records are determined by the potential of the e-record to be deleted, amended or executed without authorization and the opportunity for detection of those activities and events.*

Development

- The risks identified during the Conceptualization and Development periods can be used to support the application analyses of the computer system. These analyses may lead to architecture and design trade-offs during the system development.
- The risk management process supports the assessment against its requirements and within its operational environment. Decisions regarding risks identified must be made prior to system operation.

Operational Life

- Risk management activities are performed for periodic reviews or whenever major changes are made to the computer system in its operational production environment (e.g. new system interfaces).

Retirement

- Risk management activities are performed for system components that will be disposed of or replaced to ensure that the hardware and the software are properly retired, that residual data is appropriately handled, and that system migration is conducted in a secure and systematic manner.

Tools

Tools associated with the risk analysis are:

- Failure Mode Effects Analysis (FMEA)
- Failure Mode, Effects and Criticality Analysis (FMECA)

---

* MHRA. *MHRA GxP Data Integrity Guidance and Definitions*, March 2018.

- Fault Tree Analysis (FTA)
- Hazard Operability Analysis (HAZOP)
- Preliminary Hazard Analysis (PHA)
- Risk ranking and filtering

Core Principles

- The focus is *de facto* on critical areas that could potentially compromise product quality, patient safety, and record/data integrity.
- The evaluation of the risk to quality should be based on scientific knowledge and, ultimately, link to the protection of the patient.
- The level of effort, formality and documentation of the quality risk management process should be commensurate with the level of risk.
- Risk management is the starting point of every project.
- Reevaluate the risk analysis from time to time throughout the project (e.g. project reviews and/or end of a development phase) and whenever major deviations from the project plan occur.

Regulatory Requirements/Guidance

> Risk management should be applied throughout the lifecycle of the computerised system taking into account patient safety, data integrity and product quality. As part of a risk management system, decisions on the extent of validation and data integrity controls should be based on a justified and documented risk assessment of the computerised system.
>
> *(EU Annex 11-1)*

SIPOC (Figure 9.2)

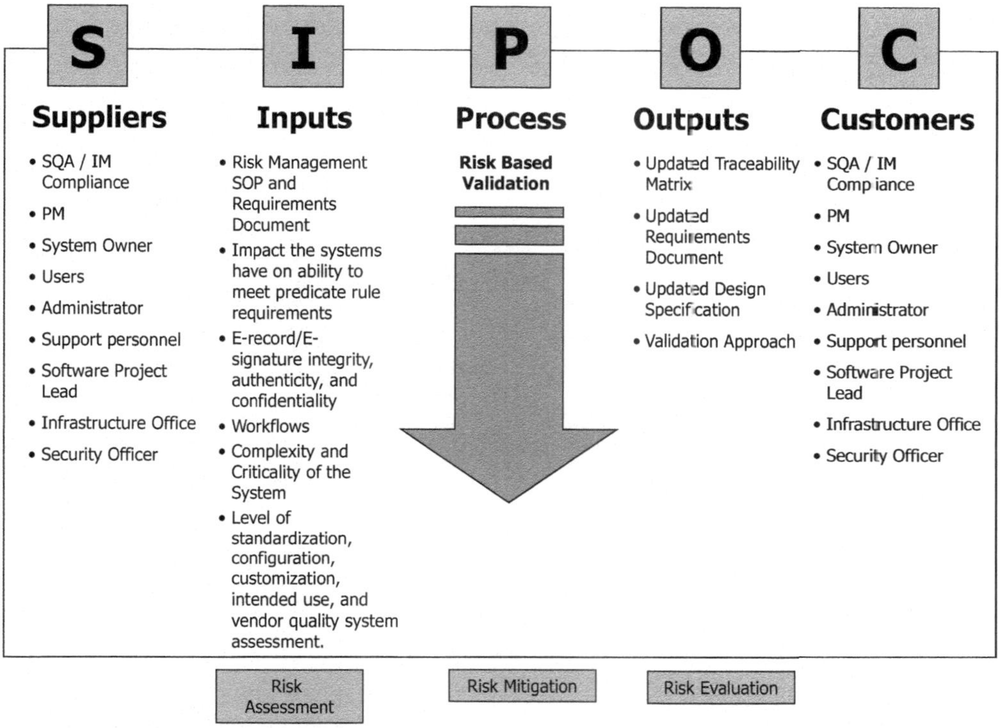

Figure 9.2 Risk based validation SIPOC.

Additional Readings

EudraLex. "EU Guidelines for Good Manufacturing Practices for Medicinal Products for Human and Veterinary Use, Annex 20 – Quality Risk Management." *The Rules Governing Medicinal Products in the European Union*, Volume 4. February 2008.

GAMP®/ISPE. "Risk Assessment for Use of Automated Systems Supporting Manufacturing Process – Risk to Record, Pharmaceutical Engineering." November/December 2002.

GAMP®/ISPE. "Risk Assessment for Use of Automated Systems Supporting Manufacturing Process – Functional Risk, Pharmaceutical Engineering." May/June 2003.

GHTF. "Implementation of Risk Management Principles and Activities Within a Quality Management System." May 2005.

IEC/ISO 31010. "Risk Management – Risk Assessment Techniques." 2009.

ICH Harmonized Tripartite Guideline. Quality Risk Management, Q9, November 2005.

NIST. "Computer Security Risk Management" in *An Introduction to Computer Security: The NIST Handbook*, Special Publication 800-12, 2007.

WHO. "WHO Guidelines on Quality Risk Management." *WHO Technical Report Series,* No. 981, Annex 2, 2013.

Chapter 10

CSV Plans and Schedules*

CSV Plans

Specifically for large and middle size complex systems, a validation project plan, also known as a CSV Plan, is developed to formalize the CSV process.

The CSV Plan is the center for the tracking the execution of a validation project. It is used throughout the life cycle of an implementation project and shall be kept up-to-date.

The CSV Plan describes the extent of system validation, i.e. scope, validation, qualification, revalidation, lists key steps, project organization, project members roles and responsibilities, step-by-step activities and their chronology, and provides the schedule of a computer implementation project and assigns responsibility for tasks. In addition, it addresses measures to control the quality of the project such as phase gates reviews and communications.

The CSV Plan is traceable to the final validation summary report.

The CSV Plan should include:

- Organizational structure of the computer system/automation project.
- Responsible departments and/or individuals.
- Resource availability.
- Time restrictions.
- Any project supporting process not covered in SOPs, e.g. Development Methodology, implementation project sign-off.

* López, O. *21 CFR Part 11: Complete Guide to International Computer Validation Compliance for the Pharmaceutical Industry*. Boca Raton, FL: CRC Press, 2004; 43–45.

- Work products or deliverables.
- Overall acceptance criteria.
- Sample format of key documentation.
- Schedule and timeline.

The CSV Plan ensures that the tools are in place to guide and control multiple parallel development activities and assures proper communications and documentation.

During the execution of a project, verifications and qualifications, the plan provides the criteria for the reliability of the work products, so that when the due dates for completion/hand-over arrive, a high degree of certainty exists that the system is validated.

When multiple departments are involved in a project, the system owner will take responsibility for the validation documentation. Other departments will provide documentation and personnel to support the development, validation and maintenance effort.

Validation plans are not required by any of the predicated regulations. However, this is considered to be a key project management practice. Validation plans are an essential document for the overall management of projects and are crucial for the success of the projects.

Managers, their peers, end-users and those responsible for delivering the system typically approve validation plans. Quality assurance may also sign the document. The validation project plan and the requirements specification deliverable, together outline all of the technical and regulatory requirements applicable for a project.

Project validation plans should be started during the early stages of a project. Initial project concepts and planning estimates should be elements in the creation of project validation plans. The initial project verification activities will assess the project team's capability to produce a validated system. This (e.g. risk assessments) provides inputs to define the level of testing effort expected. Project verifications and qualifications identify any critical deviations to the expected project timing and quality levels, as well as other issues that could affect the timely approval of the validation report.

An approved version of the validation plan should be available when a computer technology supplier or contract developer is being selected, and it should be updated whenever project events or verification and qualification results require a change. An example of a project event would be a change in project scope.

Documents which provide information to update the validation plans are:

- System requirements
- Risk analysis and its review during the project phases
- Criticality and complexity analysis
- Project verification and qualification results
- Other system descriptions

The format of validation project plans is flexible and may incorporate Gantt charts. The contents of the validation plan may include, but are not limited to, the following:

- Document control section:
  - System/installation name
  - Author(s)
  - Creation, save and print date
  - Version number
  - Document identification
  - Document history
    - Reviewer and the review date
    - External document references
    - Table of contents
  - Intended audience
  - Scope
  - Objective
  - System description
  - Validation acceptance criteria
  - Verification activities and deliverables
  - Qualification activities and deliverables
    - Qualification planning
    - Project verification
    - Installation qualification
    - Operational qualification
    - Performance qualification
    - Process validation
  - Roles and responsibilities
    - Application owner

- Project management
- Quality assurance
- Validation team
- Computer technology supplier or contract developer

– Document control

– Project schedule
  - Project activities
  - Project documentation and its delivery

Project Schedule

Validation plans should include a high-level project schedule which includes the identification of resources. As further project information is known, additional elements can be incorporated to the validation and project schedule process. Figure 10.1* depicts a typical systems development distribution showing the percentage of effort needed for each key developmental activity.

One key consideration in the project schedule is to provide adequate time for system analysis and preparation of specifications. Attempts to speed the development of specifications are the single largest contributing factor to poorly developed and poorly validated systems.

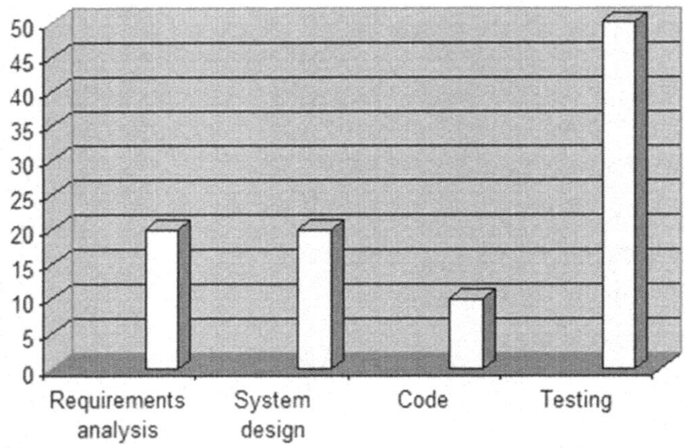

Figure 10.1 Systems development distribution.

* Pressman, R. S. *Software Engineering: A Practitioner's Approach*, 4th ed. New York: McGraw-Hill, 1997.

The following list includes examples of items which need to be tracked as part of the project schedule:

- Project kick off
- Validation plan preparation, review, and approval
- Training of the validation team
- Applicable SLC periods and events
- Review and/or development policies, guidelines, standards and procedural controls
- Quality checkpoints for reviews
- Project documentation due dates/reviews/approvals
- Qualify computer technologies suppliers and/or contract developers (if applicable)
- Development and approval of procedural controls
- Write specific plans and protocols for IQ, OQ, PQ
- Develop the traceability analysis and verify the traceability of the design and testing elements against user requirements
- Review/approve specific protocols
- Monitor the execution of specific protocols
- Assemblex, review and approve the results
- Assemble, review and approve the final validation report

Validation plans and their associated schedules are living documents that should be reviewed periodically. Phase gate verification activities, which are performed during each event, may be a perfect place to review the project plan and schedule.

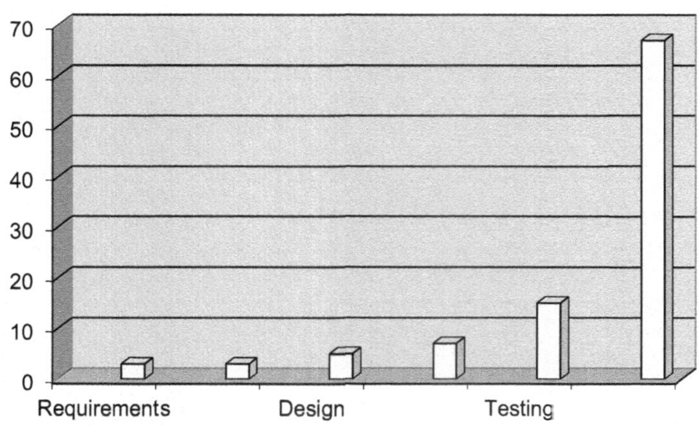

Figure 10.2 Software development stages relative costs.

As part of the Conceptualization period, project sponsors and others are presented with an estimate of the total effort to be expended, including maintenance for the system. The relative costs of each development stage are depicted in Figure 10.2.* Note that the maintenance of existing software can account for over 70% of all effort expended by a software organization and this cost will be passed on to the customer.

As part of the schedule, it should be considered that majority of the development of computer systems fails due to poor gathering of requirements. This situation leads to negatively affect subsequent development activities and associated work products. An investment up front yields savings (cost avoidance) later.

* Pressman, R. S. *Software Engineering: A Practitioner's Approach*, 4th ed. New York: McGraw-Hill, 1997.

Chapter 11

Project Management, SLC, Production CSV, ITIL

Introduction

Project Management (PM), SLC, Production CSV, and Information Technology Infrastructure Library (ITIL) are four processes interconnected and related with a typical computer system in a manufacturing facility.

The alignment between these four processes provides the smooth system development and, at the same time, the validation of the computer systems.

PM is the process that initiates, plans, executes, controls, and closes the work of a team to achieve specific goals and meet specific success criteria. It takes an individual project from the point it is approved to the point the project goal is achieved and the project is completed. In addition, the PM controls the common activities of the above processes during the development and operational life of the services/technologies.

Progression through the project is controlled through a series of reviews. These reviews ensure that the quality and value of each project is such that progression remains desirable.

SLC is the "period of time that begins when a product is conceived and ends when the product is no longer available for use".*

The SLC comprises the system development life cycle (SDLC) and, the computer systems operational and maintenance processes (Chapter 12). The SLC

* ANSI/IEEE Std 610.12-1990. *Standard Glossary of Software Engineering Terminology, Institute of Electrical and Electronic Engineers*, New York, 1990.

ensures that the software development and software maintenance are properly controlled and documented.

The SDLC methodology associated with the SLC contains the software engineering tasks and associated work products necessary to support the CSV effort.

The SLC and associated supporting processes (working methods) form the basis of the Quality Management System (QMS) that provides the stable working platform for any project.

The QMS in turn should be of an acceptable standard and must stand up to an audit by an outside party.

ITIL, in the past an acronym for "Information Technology Infrastructure Library," is a set of practices for IT service management (ITSM) that focuses on aligning IT services with the needs of business.

Note that all of these processes must reflect a logical and optimum sequence of events. Some activities simply cannot happen, or it would be less productive for them to happen, until the preceding one has been accomplished.

The alignment of the above four processes will result in integrated practices to properly assess and report the "quality and performance measures for all the lifecycle stages of software and system development, its implementation, qualification and acceptance, operation, modification, re-qualification, maintenance and retirement".*

The project management methodology should be the process that mixes the SLC, CSV, and ITIL processes. All the applicable CSV projected outputs should be consistent with the SLC outputs.

Lastly, CSV outputs are connected with the risk associated with the project.

The alignment of all these processes can be categorized in two groups: alignment as part of the life cycle of a new technology or service, and the alignment as part of a service delivery resulting from the addition or capacity expansion.

Alignment – New Technology/Service Life Cycle

PM takes an individual project from the point it is approved to the point the project is achieved, completed and implemented. As part of the PM, the CSV activities, defined through the SLC, provides procedures and practices supporting the quality of the work products applicable to the project.

* Pharmaceutical Inspection Cooperation Scheme (PIC/S). *Good Practices for Computerized Systems in "GxP" Regulated Environments*, PI 011-3, September 2007.

A project begins with an approved project/work request; and is completed with a solution designed, tested and deployed to address a specific set of customer needs. PM addresses the above activities during the Start-up, Development, and Implementation Phases. The equivalent activities are performed in the SLC during the Conceptualization and Development Periods.

After completing the implementation of the service based on the specific customer requirements, the Service Operations processes ensure that the customers have access to the appropriate service. Service Operations is responsible for running and supporting a solution once it has been put into production.

During the initial phases of the Service Operations, the PM includes a project review as a mechanism to review and record the Project learnings: what the business can learn from the Project and also to recognize what the Project Manager and the Project Team have learned and contributed during their experience and involvement with the project. This review can be valuable to the SLC by providing feedback of how CSV activities can be improved for similar projects.

During the Service Operations, the SLC delivers procedures related with the Operational Life, resulting in the ITIL standard process definitions. As depicted in Table 11.1, Alignment – New Technology/Service Life Cycle, on the Operational Life Period the SLC aligns in three stages: early operational life, maturity, and aging. Service support ends when the service is retired from production.

Alignment – Service Deployment

Service Deployment is the process by which a solution is realized to address a specific set of customer needs. It begins when there is both an approved project/work request requiring a solution, and that solution has been designed, developed and ready for implementation. Service Deployment ends once the solution has been implemented, the user has accepted it, and it has shown itself to be stable.

Service Deployment sits between Service Design and Development, which is responsible for designing a solution to a business need, and service operations. On complex base business implementations, robust controls are required to successfully implement the solution.

If this is the case, PM can be applied exclusively to the Service Deployment phase. Table 11.2, Alignment – Base Business Services, depicts the alignment of PM and SLC during the service delivery.

Table 11.1 Alignment – New Technology/Service Life Cycle

<table>
<tr><td colspan="12">Alignment: SLC, PM and ITIL.</td></tr>
<tr><td>Processes</td><td colspan="5">Service Design & Development</td><td colspan="3">Service Deployment</td><td colspan="2">Service Operations</td><td></td></tr>
<tr><td>SLC</td><td colspan="3">Conceptualization</td><td colspan="5">Development</td><td>EOL*</td><td>Operational Life</td><td>Retirement</td></tr>
<tr><td rowspan="2">PM</td><td colspan="3">Start-up</td><td colspan="2">Development</td><td colspan="4">Implementation and Review Project</td><td colspan="2"></td></tr>
<tr><td>Identify Project Leaders</td><td>Define Project</td><td>People in the Project</td><td>Prepare and Plan</td><td>Execute and Monitor</td><td>Prepare and Plan</td><td colspan="2">Execute Change and Monitor</td><td>Review</td><td colspan="2"></td></tr>
<tr><td>ITIL</td><td colspan="7"></td><td colspan="3">Service Delivery and Service Support Process</td><td></td></tr>
</table>

* Early Operational Life.

Table 11.2 Alignment – Base Business Services

<table>
<tr><td colspan="7">Alignment: SLC, PM and ITIL.</td></tr>
<tr><td>Processes</td><td colspan="3">Service Deployment</td><td colspan="2">Service Operations</td><td></td></tr>
<tr><td>SLC</td><td>Conceptualization</td><td colspan="2">Development</td><td>EOL*</td><td>Operational Life</td><td>Retirement</td></tr>
<tr><td>PM</td><td>Start-up</td><td>Development</td><td colspan="2">Implement and Review Project</td><td colspan="2"></td></tr>
<tr><td>ITIL</td><td colspan="2"></td><td colspan="3">Service Delivery and Service Support Process</td><td></td></tr>
</table>

* Early Operational Life.

For the PM context the majority of the service deployment effort is dedicated to the implementation of the service/technology. The PM "Start-up" and "development" may be of short duration. During the "Start-up" the implementation team is organized and there is further definition of the project, including the specific customer requirements. During the "Development" the technology/service is tailored to the specific customer requirements. Similar activities are performed during the SLC "Conceptualization" period.

As in the PM, during the SDLC the deployment implementation takes the main stage.

After the technology/service is put into production the Operational Life takes into effect supported by ITIL.

Additional Readings

Grigonis, G. J., Subak, E.J., and Wyrick M. L. "Validation Key Practices for Computer Systems Used in Regulated Operations." *Pharmaceutical Technology*, June 1997; 74–98.

Office of Government Commerce. *ITIL Service Design*. United Kingdom: The Stationery Office, 2011.

Office of Government Commerce. *ITIL Service Support*. United Kingdom: The Stationery Office, 2003.

Herr, R. R., and Wyrick., M. L. "A Globally Harmonized Glossary of Terms for Communicating Computer Validation Key Practices." *PDA Journal of Pharmaceutical Science and Technology*, 53(2) 1999; 97–103.

Chapter 12

Computer Systems Operational Life*

Introduction

In the life science industries, plenty of attention is placed in the validation of computer systems throughout the Conceptualization and Development periods of new systems and associated infrastructure (refer to Chapter 6).

After deploying the computer systems to operations, the Operational Life of these systems initiates. This is the period of time that relevant processes are in place to run the computer system in its operational environment, monitored for satisfactory performance, and modified as part of corrective, adaptive, perfective, and preventive maintenance (refer to Chapter 6).

> **CORE PRINCIPLE**
>
> "There should be written procedures for performance monitoring, change control, programme and data security, calibration and maintenance, personnel training, emergency recovery and periodic re-evaluation."
>
> *WHO Technical Report Series, No. 937, 2006. Annex 4. Appendix 5, Section 1.6*

The Operational Life creates a set of threats to all baselines of validated computer systems. These threats take into account meeting the changing environment and/or changing needs of users.

* López, O. "Maintaining the Validated State of Computer Systems." *Journal of GxP Compliance* 17(2) 2013.

Over 67% of the relative cost of the system will be accounted to the computer systems maintenance.* This cost includes the correction of latent defects in the computer software and changes that occur in its operational environment. A percentage of this maintenance budget will be assigned to the re-validation effort.

It is very common in the life science industry to observe that a few years after deploying a computer system, deficient operational supporting processes and/or the incorrect implementation of such processes nullify the validated state of the computer system causing remediation activities. This situation is typical across multiple computer systems thereby provoking a remediation project across the company and adding cost to the Operational Life of many computer systems.

This chapter provides a brief description of the typical Operational Life activities and processes in support to preserve the validated state of computer systems performing regulated operations.

Operational Life

After the system has been released for operation, the computer system Operational Life activities take over.

The Operational Life is governed by two key processes: operation and maintenance.

The operation process defines the activities of the organization that provides the service of operating a computer system in its live environment for its users.

The maintenance process defines the activities of the organization that provides the service of managing modifications to the software product to keep it current and in operational fitness. This process includes, as applicable, the migration and retirement of the computer system.

To maintain uniformity during the maintenance period, the maintenance activities must be governed by the same procedural controls followed during the development period.

Written procedural controls must be available for the operation and maintenance of computer systems.†

* Zelkowitz et al., 1979.

† ICH. *Good Manufacturing Practice Guide for Active Pharmaceutical Ingredients*, Q7, Section 5.44, November 2000.

Operation Activities

Routine use of computer systems during the Operational Life requires procedural controls that describe how to perform operational activities. These operational procedural controls must be in place and approved by the appropriate individuals. The execution of these procedural controls should be monitored by the regulated user to verify the accurate implementation and adherence.

The execution of these procedural controls should be reviewed on a periodic basis as according with the local retention policy.

In addition, it is vital that management should ensure that all users are trained accordingly.

Key operational procedural controls are:

- *Archiving*. In the context of the regulated user, archives consist of records that have been selected for permanent or long-term preservation on grounds of their evidentiary value.

  All computer system baselines should be archived in an environmentally controlled facility, as applicable, that is suitable for the material being archived and which is both secure and, where possible, protected from environmental hazards. Archived records should include, as applicable, associated metadata and electronic signatures. A record of all archived materials should be maintained.

  Archived e-records should be periodically verified for accessibility, readability and integrity. If applicable changes are to be made to the system (e.g. computer hardware or software), then the capability to retrieve the e-records should be guaranteed and confirmed (EU Annex 17).
- *Backups*. A backup process must be implemented to allow for recovery of the system following any failure that compromises its integrity.* Integrity and accuracy of backup data, and the ability to restore e-records should be checked during validation and monitored periodically (EU Annex 11.7.2).

  Backup copies should be made of such data that are required to reconstruct all CGMP-relevant documentation. This also applies to the system programs required to store and restore the e-records.

---

* OMCL Network/EDQM of the Council of Europe. *Validation of Computerised Systems – Core Document*, July 2009.

The frequency of backups depends on data criticality, amount of stored data, and frequency of data generation.

The procedural controls establishing the backup process must be in place to ensure the integrity of backups (secure storage location, adequately separated from the primary storage location, and so on). This may be part of a more general disaster recovery plan.

As part of the backup strategy, users can configure extra automatic backups. This process is far more robust than the traditional backup system that relies on transporting manually labeled rotational tapes by truck.

If relevant changes are to be made to the system, change control should ensure the availability and integrity of the e-records on the backup copies by restoring the e-records on a trial basis.

- *Business Continuity.* Business continuity procedural controls, including disaster recovery procedural controls, ensure minimal disruption in the case of loss of data or any part of the system. It is necessary to ensure that the integrity of the data is not compromised during the return to normal operation. At the lowest level, this may mean the accidental deletion of a single file in which case procedural controls should be in place for restoring the most recently backed-up copy. At the other extreme, a disaster such as a fire could result in loss of the entire system.

  The procedural control employed should be tested regularly and all relevant personnel should be made aware of its existence and trained to use it. A copy of the procedural controls should be maintained offsite.
- *Infrastructure Maintenance.* The procedural controls applicable for the preventative maintenance and repair of the infrastructure provide a mechanism for anticipating problems and, as a consequence, possible loss of data.

  In addition to the typical infrastructure elements such as system-level software, servers, wide area network, local area manager, and the associated components, the infrastructure includes UPSs and other emergency power generators.

  Modern infrastructure hardware usually requires minimum maintenance because electronic circuit boards, for example, are usually easily replaced and cleaning may be limited to dust removal. Diagnostic software is usually available from the supplier to check the performance of the computer system and isolate defective integrated circuits. Maintenance procedural controls should be included in the organization's procedural control. The availability of spare parts and access to qualified service personnel are important for the smooth operation of the maintenance program.

- *Problem Reporting*. The malfunction or failure of computer system components, incorrect documentation, or improper operation that makes the proper use of the system impossible for an undetermined period characterizes some of the incidents that can affect the correct operation of a computer system. These system incidents may become non-conformances.

  In order to remedy problems quickly, a procedural control must be established to record any computer system failures from the users of the system. These enable the reporting and registration of any problem encountered by the users of the system.
- *Problem Management*. Reported problems can be filtered according to whether their cause lies with the user or with the system itself and then fed back into the appropriate part of the supplier's organization. In order to remedy problems quickly, a procedural control must be established if the system fails or breaks down. Any failures, the results of the analysis of the failure, and, as applicable, any remedial actions taken must be documented.

  Those problems that require a remedial action involving changes to any baseline are then managed through a change control process.
- *Retirement*. The retirement of computer systems performing regulated operations is a critical process. The purpose of the "Retirement Period" is to replace or eliminate the current computer system and, if applicable, ensure the availability of the data that it has generated for conversion, migration, or retirement.
- *Restore*. A procedural control for regular testing of restoring backup data to verify the proper integrity and accuracy of data must also be in place.
- *Security*. Computer systems security includes the authentication of users and access controls. Security is a key component for maintaining the trustworthiness of a computer system and associated records. Security is an ongoing element to consider and is subject to improvement.

  In particular, after a system has been released for use, it should be constantly monitored to uncover any security violations. Any security violation must be followed up and analyzed and proper action taken to avoid a recurrence.
- *Training*. All staff maintaining, operating, and using computer systems that perform regulated operations must have documented evidence of

training in the area of expertise. For users, the training will concentrate on the correct use of the computer system, security, and how to report any failure or deviation from the normal operating condition.

Maintenance Activities

The validated status of computer systems performing regulated operations is subject to threat from changes in its operating environment, which may be either known or unknown.

The January 2011 revision of the Eudralex, Volume 4, Annex 11, "Computerised Systems" establishes in Item 10 that "any changes to a computerised system including system configurations should only be made in a controlled manner in accordance with a defined procedure."

The above statement is consistent with other regulations and guidelines such as: FDA *Code of Federal Regulations* Title 21 Part 211.68, 820.30(i), 820.70(i), 820.40, 11.10(d), 11.10(e); *World Health Organization (WHO) Technical Report Series*, No. 937, 2006. Annex 4. Section 12, and PIC/S PI 011-3 (Refer to Part Three – SYSTEM OPERATION/INSPECTION/REFERENCES).

Explicitly in Section 3.3 of the WHO* guidance stipulates three events to cover during the maintenance of computer systems:

- *Verification and revalidation*. After a suitable period of running a new system, it should be independently reviewed and compared with the system specification and functional specification. The periodic verification must include data checks, including any audit trail.

  Computer systems used to control, monitor, or record functions that may be critical to the safety of a product should be checked for accuracy at intervals of sufficient frequency to provide assurance that the system is under control. If part of a computerized system that controls a function critical to the safety of the product is found not to be accurate, then the safety of the product back to the last known date that the equipment was accurate must be determined.
- *Change control*. Modifications and adjustments to computer systems shall only be made in accordance with a defined procedural control that includes provision for checking, approving, and implementing the modification and/or adjustment.

* WHO. "Validation of Computerized Systems." *WHO Technical Report Series*, No. 937, Annex 4, Appendix 5, 2006.

- *Checks*. Data should be checked periodically to confirm that they have been accurately and reliably recorded and/or transferred. These checks include the following EU Annex 11 items: Data (11.5), Accuracy Checks (11.6), and Data Storage (11.7).

Summary

The regulated applications and infrastructure must be well-maintained during the Operational Life assuring that the systems remain in a validated state and providing cost savings to the maintenance of the computer systems.

The Operational Life comprises of:

- Ensuring that system changes are performed according to the approved change control procedure.
- Maintaining training records for users and technical support personnel;
- Controlling user access.
- Conducting periodic reviews based on established criteria.
- Ensuring that data is backed up and archived in accordance within established schedules.
- Identifying and tracking system problems and related corrective actions.
- Maintaining configuration items.

The above activities must be outlined in written and approved procedural controls.

Core Principle

Once the system has been accepted, the user should follow adequate system management and operational procedural controls.

Chapter 13

Suppliers and Service Providers*

Introduction

> "When third parties (e.g. suppliers, service providers) are used e.g. to provide, install, configure, integrate, validate, maintain (e.g. via remote access), modify or retain a computerised system or related service or for data processing, formal agreements must exist between the manufacturer and any third parties, and these agreements should include clear statements of the responsibilities of the third party."
>
> *EU Annex 11-3.1*

Service providers are all parties who provide any services irrespective of whether they belong to an independent (external) enterprise, to the same company group/structure, or to an internal service unit.

The role of the service providers and suppliers has been put in the spotlight due to the trend by the regulated users† of purchasing computer systems, software products or software services.

The choice of a contractor/supplier management by a regulated user must be documented. The contractor's/supplier's suitability demonstrated by means of compliance with the prerequisites in the vendor

* López, O. "Suppliers and Service Providers" in *EU Annex 11 Guide to Computer Validation Compliance for Worldwide Health Agency GMP*. Boca Raton, FL: CRC Press, 2015; 33–38.

† In this chapter the regulated user is also the "acquirer" or the organization that acquires or procures a system, software product or software service from a supplier.

requirements document and/or performance measurement contained in the service level agreement (SLA).

Even where tasks are partly contracted out to external companies, the regulated user is ultimately responsible to ensure the suitability and operability of the computer systems. The regulated user must have processes in place to ensure the supplier's suitability for the service and/or task to which the supplier is to be entrusted and the quality of contracted tasks. The regulated user must have the control of outsourced activities (contractor/supplier management) and have the ability to measure the quality of contracted tasks.

The responsibilities and specific requirements, including communication processes, should be clearly defined in the agreement between the contract giver and contract acceptor, Service Agreements and/or Quality Agreements.

These processes and controls must incorporate quality risk management to determine whether a supplier should be audited* and include:†

- The quality controls and quality assurance procedures, documentation and records related to the development and production of the system, software product, or software service from a supplier are of critical importance. Compliance with a recognized Quality Management System (QMS) provides the regulated user and regulatory agencies or competent authority with the desired confidence in the structural integrity, operational reliability and ongoing support for system, software product, or software service utilized in the system.‡
- Evaluating§ prior to outsourcing operations the suitability and competence of the provider to carry out the critical systems/activity using a defined supply chain. For application software used specifically for CGMP regulated activities, at least for GAMP type of software Configured Products (GAMP5 software category 4) and Custom Applications (GAMP5 software category 5), the validity of potential suppliers should be evaluated appropriately (EU Annex 11-4.5) and the evaluation documented.

---

* Audit: Conducted by an authorized person for the purpose of providing an independent assessment of software products and processes in order to assess compliance with requirements (ISO 12207:1995). (Note: The 1995 revision is not the most recent version.)

† ICH Q10. "Section 2.7 Management of Outsourced Activities and Purchased Materials," June 2008.

‡ Pharmaceutical Inspection Cooperation Scheme (PIC/S). *Good Practices for Computerized Systems in "GxP" Regulated Environments*, PI 011-3, September 2007.

§ Evaluation: A systematic determination of the extent to which an entity meets its specified criteria. (ISO 12207:1995). (Note: The 1995 revision is not the most recent version.)

This evaluation should consider:

- The potential impact of the system being supplied based on patient safety and data integrity.
- Vendor's QMS.
- Operational reliability.
- The novelty or complexity of the system.
- Software engineering practices.
- The history and experience in supplying these systems.
- Ongoing support for software and hardware products.

The regulated user may wish to consider additional means of evaluation fitness for purpose against predetermined requirements, specifications and anticipated risks. Techniques such as supplier questionnaires, (shared) supplier audits (Annex 11-3.2) and interaction with user and sector focus groups can be helpful.*

- Documented justification should be provided for not evaluating suppliers of CGMP regulated systems, software products, or software services.
- A report of the documented supplier selection should exist for review by inspectors (EU Annex 11-3.4). Any deviation from the requirements observed during this evaluation and/or audit should be addressed. This report is an element of the validation lifecycle and provides an insight into the evaluation processes. Confidentiality agreements should be adjusted accordingly.
- The evaluation and/or audit may:
  - Determine the level of governance by the regulated company.
  - Identify potential risks to the project due to gaps in the vendor QMS.
  - Use vendor's documentation results in support of the verification of the manufacturing critical aspects.
  - Build a common quality understanding/partnership between the supplier and the vendor.
- If the supplier proves the correct implementation to the established quality system for the application's intended use, except for the review of the performance of the supplier, no additional controls are required to the suppliers by the regulated user.

---

* Pharmaceutical Inspection Cooperation Scheme (PIC/S). *Good Practices for Computerized Systems in "GxP" Regulated Environments*, PI 011-3, September 2007.

The decision and justification to use vendor's documentation results in support the verification of the manufacturing critical aspects should be based on the correct implementation to the established quality system, intended use of the computer system, and should be documented and approved by subject matter experts including the quality unit (ASTM E 2500-07). These work and tests should be not repeated again by the customer.

- Monitoring and review of the performance of the supplier or the quality of the services from the provider, and the identification and implementation of any needed improvements. The regulated user should check regularly that the external company is developing, maintaining, or operating the computer system properly and in accordance with the approved SLA.
- Monitoring outsourced activities to ensure they are from approved sources using the agreed supply chain.

  It is the belief of particular regulated users that a mere certification of suitability from the vendor, for example if the off-the-shelf application is Annex 11 compliant, will be adequate. When validation information is produced by an outside firm, e.g. computer vendor, the records maintained by the company need not include all of the voluminous test data. However, such records should be sufficiently complete (including general results and protocols) to allow the company to evaluate the adequacy of the validation.

Following the ISO/IEC International Standard,* the primary SLC processes can be used to guide the reader on how to put together the elements discussed in this chapter.

In the context of the regulated user, the Acquisition Process is the main process to acquire a system, software product, or service.

In the context of the service provider, the Supply Process is the main process to provide the system, software product, or software service to the regulated user.

The referenced Annex 11 item, as applicable, can be found on each equivalent sub-process.

* ISO 12207:1995. *Information Technology – Software Life Cycle Processes.* (Note: The 1995 revision is not the most recent version. The primary SLC processes are only discussed in the 1995 revision.)

Acquisition Process

The activities of the Acquisition Process include:

- Acquisition Planning (EU Annex 11-1)
- Requirements gathering, including technical constraints (EU Annex 11-4.4)
- Requirements gathering and specification (EU Annex 11-4.4)
- Contract preparation an update (EU Annex 11-3.1)
- Supplier monitoring
  - In-process audits (EU Annex 11-4.5)
  - Code reviews, inspections, audits (EU Annex 11-3-2)
- Acceptance and completion (EU Annex 11-4.7)
  - FAT
  - SAT

Supply Process

The activities of the Supply Process include:

- Initiation; preparation of response; contract (EU Annex 11-3.1)
- Planning (EU Annex 11-1)
- Execution and control
  - Develop product based on Development Process (Project Phase, Relevant EU Annex 11-4.1 and EU Annex 4.5)
  - Maintain product based on Maintenance Process (Operational Phase).
- Review and evaluation
  - In-process audits (EU Annex 11-4.5)
  - Code reviews, inspections, audits (EU Annex 11-3-2)
  - FAT (EU Annex 11-4.7)
  - SAT (EU Annex 11-4.7)
- Delivery and completion
  - Formal release for use

Additional Readings

ASTM E 2500-13. *Standard Guide for Specification, Design, and Verification of Pharmaceutical and Biopharmaceutical Manufacturing Systems and Equipment*, 2013.

ISPE. *GAMP 5: A Risk Approach to Compliant GxP Computerized Systems*, 5th Edition. Management Appendices M2 and M6. International Society for Pharmaceutical Engineering (ISPE), February 2008.

ICH Harmonized Tripartite Guideline. *Good Manufacturing Practice Guidance for Active Pharmaceutical Ingredients*, Q7, November 2000.

ICH Harmonized Tripartite Guideline. *Pharmaceutical Quality Systems*, Q10, Section 2.7 Management of Outsourced Activities and Purchased Materials, June 2008.

ISO 12207. *Information Technology – Software Life Cycle Processes*, 1995. (The 1995 revision is not the most recent version.)

ISO 13485. *Medical Devices – Quality Management Systems*, Sections 5.5; 5.5.1; 5.5.3; 6.2; 6.2.1; 6.2.2; 7.4; 7.4.1, July 2012.

López, O. "Hardware/Software Suppliers Qualification" in *21 CFR Part 11: Complete Guide to International Computer Validation Compliance for the Pharmaceutical Industry*. Boca Raton, FL: CRC, 2004; 107–109.

PDA. "Auditing of Supplier Providing Computer Products and Services for Regulated Pharmaceutical Operations. Technical Report No. 32." *PDA Journal of Pharmaceutical Science and Technology*, Release 2.0, 58(5) 2004.

WHO. "Validation of Computerized Systems." *Technical Report Series*, No. 937, Annex 4, Appendix 5, Section 6.2, 2006.

Chapter 14

Trustworthy Computer Systems*

In previous written articles[†,‡] I have discussed the issues of the CGMP controls to preserve the integrity of critical e-records and how to assess the effectiveness of these controls. However, to ensure the integrity of e-records it is essential that the system handling these e-records must be, at the same time, trustworthy.

This chapter describes the concept of trustworthy computer systems in a CGMP regulated activity[§] and, the regulatory requirements and key guidelines associated with the trustworthiness of computer systems within the scope of the referenced competent authority. Examples of such computer systems performing CGMP regulated activity are those to:

- Make decisions on market release of drugs and, to create and retain market distribution records.
- Create and retain manufacturing orders and manufacturing records.
- Control/manage manufacturing processes and to retain relevant data.

---

* López, O. "Trustworthy Computer Systems." *Journal of GxP Compliance,* 19(2) 2015.

† López, O. "EU Annex 11 and the Integrity of Erecs." *Journal of GxP Compliance,* 18(2) 2014.

‡ López, O. "A Computer Data Integrity Compliance Model." *Pharmaceutical Engineering,* March/April 2015.

§ In this chapter "CGMP regulated activities" is defined as the manufacturing-related activities established in the basic legislation compiled in Volume 1 and Volume 5 of the publication *The Rules Governing Medicinal Products in the European Union* http://ec.europa.eu/health/documents/eudralex/index_en.htm, US FDA 21 CFR Part 211, *Current Good Manufacturing Practice in Manufacturing, Processing, Packing or Holding of Drugs; General and Current Good Manufacturing Practice For Finished Pharmaceuticals*, or any predicate rule applicable to medicinal products for the referenced country.

- manage storage and inventory, and so on, of raw materials and products (including intermediates);
- control/manage laboratory instruments used for quality control (QC) tests and systems to retain QC test results and relevant data;
- control/manage equipment and facilities, including HVAC and water supply systems, and so on, which may have a significant impact on quality of products, and systems to retain relevant data;
- create, approve and retain documents (SOPs, quality standard code, product standard code, and so on).

This chapter covers trustworthy computer systems key requirements and guidelines of worldwide competent authorities, and related organizations (e.g. Pharmaceutical Inspection Convention (PIC) and the Pharmaceutical Inspection Cooperation Scheme (PIC/S)).

For the purpose of this chapter, the terms and definitions given in 9000-3 and ISO 12207 are applicable. In the event of a conflict in terms and definitions, the terms and definitions specified in ISO 9000-3 apply.

Introduction to Trustworthy Computer Systems

Latest e-records integrity issues from the regulated users* uncovered by regulatory authorities have revived the dialog among the industry on the CGMP controls around e-records. There is a better understanding of the topic by the regulatory authorities and the regulated user after US Food and Drug Administration (FDA) 21 CFR Part 11, "Electronic Records: Electronic Signatures"† became effective in 1997.

Nevertheless, to ensure integrity to the e-records it is essential to assure trustworthy computer systems. Trustworthy computer systems are the first line of defense to protect the critical e-records managed by these systems.

Trustworthy computer systems consist of computer infrastructure, applications, and procedures that:

- Are reasonably suited to performing their intended functions
- Provide a reasonably reliable level of availability, reliability, and correct operation

* E-records integrity deviations, https://drive.google.com/drive/folders/0B0GT88vUt4U4S3pCODUtZlVNSE0?usp=sharing.

† 62 FR 13464, Mar 20, 1997.

- Are reasonably secure from intrusion and misuse
- Adhere to generally accepted security principles

The driver of the computer systems validation process is to ensure an acceptable degree of evidence (documented, raw data), confidence (dependability and thorough, rigorous achievement of predetermined specifications), intended use, accuracy, consistency, and reliability,* or that the computer system is a trustworthy system.

In the context of e-records integrity, the objectives of a trustworthy computer system are to ensure:

- Consistency of data; in particular, preventing unauthorized creation, alteration, or destruction of data (integrity)
- That legitimate users are not improperly denied access to information and resources (availability)
- That resources are used only by authorized persons in authorized ways (legitimate use)

Computer Systems Suited to Performing Their Intended Functions

This is one condition that links the intended use† of a computer system and the functionality of the computer system required by the regulated user.

"Intended use" is the effectiveness of the computer system to perform the prescribed operation and can be linked with what Joseph M. Juran called quality parameters. These parameters are: capability, installability, usability, performance, reliability, maintainability, documentation/information, and service.

Related with CGMP controls, computer systems executing CGMP regulated activities should‡ follow the quality management system requirements of the International Organization for Standardization (ISO) 9001 (e.g. ISO 9000-3),

* WHO. "*Validation of Computerised Systems*," *Technical Report Series*, No. 937, Annex 4. Appendix 5, 2006.

† Intended use: Use of a product, process or service in accordance with the specifications, instructions and information provided by the regulated user.

‡ Should: Used to express a non-mandatory provision. Statements that use "should" are best practices, recommended activities, or options to perform activities to be considered in order to achieve quality projects results. Other methods may be used if it can be demonstrated that they are equivalent.

or equivalent acceptable development methodology* (e.g. ISO 12207, ISO 12119). As an example, the origins of the Good Automated Manufacturing Practices (GAMP) embraced ISO 9000-3.

The intended use of a computer system is established during the Conceptualization Period, formalized as part of the requirements analysis and settles in the requirements specification.

The requirements specification describes the required functions of the computer system and, it is based on a documented risk and a CGMP impact assessment. This specification must be managed† (Chapter 8) and the requirements contained traceable throughout the computer system life cycle (SLC) (EU Annex 11, 4.4). The requirements specification is based on the inputs from many sources, including: computer system users, quality assurance, applicable regulations, information technology, infrastructure architecture, potential data migration, engineering, safety, and many more. Based on this specification, the system is developed or configured following the applicable best compliance practices transcribed as procedural controls.

The precise execution of an approved comprehensive quality management system enables both the regulated user and competent authority, to have a high level of confidence in the integrity of both the processes executed within the controlling computer system(s) and in those processes controlled by and/or linked to the computer system(s), within the prescribed operating environment(s).

The evidence to demonstrate the conformance of the computer systems with the established process requirements and applicable regulatory requirements of computer systems performing CGMP regulated activities is accomplished via the computer validation‡ process.

> "Software quality is the fitness for use of the software product."
>
> *Schulmeyer and McManus*

The definition of computer systems validation by PIC/S make reference to the "formal assessment and reporting of a computer systems validation." This reference can be interpreted as requiring a controlled documented

* Software life cycle process that contains the activities of requirements analysis, design, coding, integration, testing, installation, and support for acceptance of software products. (ISO 9000-3).

† López, O. "Requirements Management." *Journal of Validation Technology*, 17(2) 2011.

‡ Computer Validation: Formal assessment and reporting of quality and performance measures for all the life cycle stages of software and system development, its implementation, qualification and acceptance, operation, modification, requalification, maintenance, and retirement. (Pharmaceutical Inspection Cooperation Scheme (PIC/S). *Good Practices for Computerized Systems in "GxP" Regulated Environments*, PI 011-3, September 2007.)

methodology and records based on best compliance practices. The controlled documented methodology and records ensure that the regulated user has generated documented evidence (electronic and/or paper based), that gives a high level of assurance that both the computer system and the computerized system, will consistently perform as intended, designed, implemented, verified, tested, and maintained.*, †

The relevant requirements and/or guidelines about this topic are:

ISO 9000-3

Section 7.3.6.1 states that validation of software is aimed at providing reasonable confidence that it will meet its operational requirements.

US FDA

The FDA considers software validation to be the confirmation by examination and provision of objective evidence that software specifications conform to user needs and intended use, and that the particular requirements implemented through software can be consistently fulfilled.

The computer validation process takes place within the environment of an established SLC. The SLC contains software engineering tasks and documentation necessary to support the software validation effort. In addition, the SLC contains specific verification and testing tasks that are commensurate to the risk associated to the computer system.

European Medicines Agency (EU) Annex 11, Therapeutic Goods Administration (TGA)‡ and China SFDA.§

According to the interpretation of the GAMP Community of Practice (CoP) Task Team,¶ the second principle in the EU Annex 11: "The application should

---

* Pharmaceutical Inspection Cooperation Scheme (PIC/S). *Good Practices for Computerized Systems in "GxP" Regulated Environments*, PI 011-3, September 2007.

† Cappucci, W. et al. "ISPE GAMP CoP Annex 11 Interpretation." *Pharmaceutical Engineering*, July/August 2011.

‡ On 29 July 2009, the Therapeutic Goods Administration (Manufacturing Principles) Determination No. 1 of 2009 adopted the PIC/S Guide to Good Manufacturing Practice – 15 January 2009, PE 009-8, to be the Code of CGMP, except for its Annexes 4, 5 and 14 which are not adopted by Australia. Annex 11, Computerized Systems, was one of the PIC/S Guide to Good Manufacturing Practice annexes adopted. TGA is Australia's regulatory authority for therapeutic goods.

§ The China State Food and Drug Administration (SFDA) released in December 2015 GMP Annex 2 Computerized System. Actually, this document is based on the 1992 EMA GMP Annex 11.

¶ Cappucci, W. et al. "ISPE GAMP CoP Annex 11 Interpretation." *Pharmaceutical Engineering*, July/August 2011.

be validated; IT infrastructure should be qualified", reflects the GAMP 5 definition of computer system validation as achieving and maintaining compliance with applicable GxP* regulations and fitness for intended use.

PIC/S PI-011-3, Association of Southeast Asian Nations (ASEAN)† and Canadian HPFBI.‡

Some of the specifics PIC/S PI-011-3, intended for inspectors, may need some modification to account for the updated EU Annex 11, but overall it remains a good resource.

Consistent with the US FDA expectations on software validations, PIC/S considers that computer validation is the formal assessment and reporting of quality and performance measures for all the SLC stages of software and system development, its implementation, qualification and acceptance, operation, modification, requalification, maintenance, and retirement.

International Conference on Harmonization of Technical Requirements for Registration of Pharmaceuticals for Human Use (ICH)

The ICH Q7A CGMP Guidance for API (Chapter 5) calls for the suitability of the computer system is demonstrated during an "appropriate installation and operational qualifications".

World Health Organization (WHO)

The *Technical Report Series* (No. 937, Annex 4. Appendix 5, "Validation of Computerised Systems") establishes that the purpose of validation of a computer system is to ensure an acceptable degree of evidence (documented, raw data), confidence (dependability and thoroughness, rigorous achievement of predetermined specifications), intended use, accuracy, consistency, and reliability.

Japanese MHLW

The Japanese Ministry of Health, Labor and Welfare (MHLW) published on October 2011, the "Guideline on Management of Computerized Systems for

---

* GxP: The underlying international life science requirements such as those set forth in the US FD&C Act, US PHS Act, FDA regulations, EU Directives, Japanese MHLW regulations, Australia TGA, or other applicable national legislation or regulations under which a company operates. (GAMP Good Practice Guide, IT Infrastructure Control and Compliance, ISPE 2005)

† Based on the ASEAN Mutual Recognition Agreement recognition of CGMP inspections, it will follow PIC/S GMPs.

‡ In the Health Products and Food Branch Inspectorate (HPFBI) GMP Guidelines (2009 Edition, Rev 2), Health Canada establishes that guidance to validate computer systems performing GMP regulated activities is provided in PIC/S PI-011-3.

Marketing Authorization Holders and Manufacturers of Drugs and Quasi-Drugs". The purpose of this guideline is to specify the activities during development of computerized systems, validation items to verify such systems, and the activities to be observed during the operations of such systems, with the purpose of ensuring that such systems perform as intended.

Brazil ANVISA

Article 572 of the Brazilian Agência Nacional de Vigilância Sanitária (ANVISA) rules on good manufacturing practice of medicinal products establishes that the extent of validation depends on a number of factors, including the intended use of the system, the type of validation to perform (prospective, concurrent and retrospective), and inserting new elements.

Provide a Reasonably Reliable* Level of Availability, Reliability and Correct Operation

The best application will not meet user's need if it is unavailable. In the technical sense, availability is the measure of the percentage of time that an application is available for use. The typical end-user expects an application to be available 24/7/365. Anything else is deemed unacceptable. But up-time is not the only indicator of availability. Offutt[†] suggests that "using features available on only one platform" makes the application unavailable to those with a different platform. The user will go invariably elsewhere.

Maturity, fault tolerance, and recoverability are related with reliability or the amount of time that the computer system is available for use.

In the event of a system failure there should be a general procedure to remedy and restore the hardware or software from any situation to a correctly functioning and basic condition and to reconstruct the relevant data reliably[‡] (EU Annex 11-16).

The procedure to remedy and restore system errors should consider the following:

- Conduct error analysis
- Commission and carry out repairs

---

* Reliable: Consistently good performance.

† Offutt, J. "Quality Attributes of Web Software Applications." *IEEE Software*, March/April 2002; 25–32.

‡ APV. The APV Guideline "Computerized Systems" based on Annex 11 of the EU-GMP Guideline, April 1996.

- Implement additional organizational measures (work around)
- Test software components
- Check stored data
- Reconstruct data
- System release for re-use
- Documentation instructions

All performance requirements, including reliability and recovery, that the software must meet are to be specified in the requirements specification.

Testing of the recovery related requirements include challenging the ability of the system to recover from programming errors, data errors, and hardware failures. If the recovery is automatic, re-initialization, checkpoints mechanism data recovery, and restart should be evaluated.

Incidents related to computer systems that could affect the reliability of records should be recorded and investigated.

GAMP5 Appendix M4 (Section 3.1.14) provides guidance on reliability and error recovery.

The correct operation consists of those attributes of the computer system that provide full implementation of the required functions. The application dependent algorithms consisting of manufacturing procedures, control, instructions, specifications, and precautions to be followed within such automated systems are embodied in the computer program(s) which drive the computer. It includes those instructions to enforce process sequencing with significant impact on drug product quality.

The lack of operational checks to enforce event sequencing is significant if an operator's ability to deviate from the prescribed order of computer system operation steps results in an adulterated or misbranded product, and/or data integrity.*

The relevant requirements and/or guidelines about this topic are:

ISO 9000-3

The operational environment requirements (Section 7.2.1.1) may include, but not be limited to, the following characteristics: functionality, reliability, usability, efficiency, maintainability, and portability.

---

* López, O. Operational Checks in *21 CFR Part 11: Complete Guide to International Computer Validation Compliance for the Pharmaceutical Industry*. Boca Raton, FL: CRC, 2004.

US FDA

The General Principles of Software Validation* establishes reliability as a quality factor to be addressed during the quality planning and clearly established in the requirements specification.

21 CFR 11.10(a) requires computer systems reliable and performing the correct operation.

EU and TGA

Annex 11 p. 11 stipulates that during the periodic reviews the reliability of a computer system must be evaluated.

PIC/S PI-011-3, ASEAN and Canadian HPFBI

Understanding that the majority of the software used in the healthcare industry is developed by suppliers, PIC/S guideline stresses the quality of the software engineering processes followed during the development of the software product by the supplier.

To have confidence in the reliability of the products, the regulated user should evaluate the quality methodology of the supplier for the design, construction, supply, and maintenance of the software. Refer to GAMP 5 Appendix M2, "Supplier Assessment".

After acquiring a system, software product or service, the regulated user needs to execute the activities, defined in the applicable procedural controls, to demonstrate the correct operation of the computer system associated components and the integration of the components.

ICH

There is no explicit statement related with the availability and reliability of the computer systems.

Implicit requirements linked with the correct operation of the computer systems can be found in the requirements associated with validation of computer systems.

---

* US FDA. *General Principles of Software Validation; Final Guidance for Industry and FDA Staff*, January 2002, www.fda.gov/cdrh/comp/guidance/938.html.

WHO

Refer to the previous note related with the WHO in which reliability and correct operation are referenced.

China SFDA

As in the ICH, there is no explicit statement related with the availability and reliability of the computer systems.

Implicit requirements associated with the correct operation of the computer systems can be found in Article 6:

> Computerized system validation, including application validation and infrastructure qualification, the scope and extent should depend on scientific based risk assessment. Risk assessment should adequately consider the scope and purpose of use a computerized system. Verification should be run throughout the life cycle of a computerized system.

Brazil ANVISA

As in the ICH and China SFDA, there is no explicit statement related with the availability and reliability of the computer systems in the ANVISA's "Rules on Good Manufacturing Practice of Medicinal Products in the Resolution of the Executive Board No. 17 (Title VII-Computerized Information)".

Implicit requirements associated with the correct operation of the computer systems can be found in Articles 577 and 578:

> The system should include, where applicable, verification of data entry and processing.

> Before starting to use a computerized system, one must test and verify the ability of the system to store the desired data, ensuring the technological infrastructure necessary to its full operation.

Secure from Intrusion and Misuse

To avoid the intrusion into computer systems, physical and/or logical controls must be established enabling access to authorized persons only.* For those

* Section C.02.005 Item 15 in the Computer Systems GMP Guidelines for API in Canada's GUI-0104, December 2013.

users allowed to access a computer system, the precise access level to the applications and resources must be assigned based on an authorization level. In all moments, it must be documented the creation, change, and cancellation of access authorizations and the level of authorization.*

In order to minimize intrusion risks to computer systems, computers inputs and outputs (I/Os) must be monitored for the correct and secure entry and processing of data. One illustration of an I/Os monitoring is an intrusion detection system. This is a device or software application that monitors network or system activities for malicious activities or policy violations. These systems produce reports that can be used to strength the security controls.

The misuse of computer systems by the users can be remediated by the system owner implementing a training program of the intended use of the related applications and all computer resources must be established.

All intrusion and misuse incidents should be reported and assessed. The root cause of an intrusion and misuse should be identified and should be the basis of corrective and preventive actions.

The relevant requirements and/or guidelines about this topic are:

ISO 9000-3

During the review of the requirements, risk associated with security issues are to be assessed (Section 7.2.2.2). The management of the security controls is performed during the system development lifecycle. ISO 9000-3 recommends writing a plan specifically to manage the implementation of the security controls. During the operational phase, the security controls are maintained and the effectiveness evaluated as applicable.

US FDA

Overall, 21 CFR Part 211.68 symbolizes the US FDA security-related requirements. Computer systems must have adequate controls to prevent unauthorized access or changes to data, inadvertent erasures, or loss.

According to the 2003 applicability to 211 CFR Part 11, 11.10(d) requires to the in scope e-records the computer system access to authorized individuals only.

* Article 579 Item 2 in the Resolution of the Executive Board No. 17, Brazilian GMPs, April 2010.

EU, TGA and China SFDA

According to EU Annex 11 p.12, physical and/or logical controls to restrict the access to the computer systems and data storage areas should be in place and based on a risk assessment. The user's authorization levels and the changes to such levels must be controlled and documented.

Similar to the 2003 US FDA 21 CFR Part 11 Guideline, high risk computer systems handling critical e-records should implement audit trail functionality.

PIC/S PI-011-3, ASEAN and Canadian HPFBI

The PI-011-3 provides a complete section, Section 19, covering the security of computer systems.

Summarizing this section, the security of the system and security of the data is very important and, the procedures and records pertaining to these aspects should be based on policies of the regulated user and in conformance with the relevant regulatory requirements. It is very important for the regulated user to maintain the procedures and records related to the access to the system(s). There should be clearly defined responsibilities for system security management, suitable for both small and complex systems, including:

- The implementation of the security strategy and delegation
- The management and assignment of privileges
- Levels of access for users
- Levels of access for infrastructure

ICH

Section 5.43 calls for sufficient controls by the computer system to prevent unauthorized access or changes to data. There should be controls to prevent omissions in data (e.g. system turned off and data not captured). There should be a record of any data change made, the previous entry, who made the change, and when the change was made.

ICH Q7 requires in Section 6.6 a complete record of all raw data generated during each test using laboratory equipment. The information to be collected by test includes graphs, charts, and spectra from laboratory instrumentation. A second person must verify this information for accuracy, completeness, and compliance with established standards.

WHO

The *Technical Report Series* (No. 937, Annex 4. Appendix 5) establishes that the security procedures should be in writing. Security should also extend to devices used to store programs, such as tapes, disks and magnetic strip cards. Access to these devices should be controlled.

Brazil ANVISA

Article 579 establishes that the entries and data modifications can only be performed by authorized persons.

- Measures should be taken that do not allow unauthorized persons to include, exclude or alter data in the system and can be used for security measures, such as the use of passwords, personal code, access profiles, keys, or restricted access to the system.
- A procedure should be established for Access Management, defining how to issue, amend, and cancel the passwords of persons who are no longer authorized to enter or change data in the system.
- Should be given preference to systems that allow registering attempting unauthorized access.

Adhere to Generally Accepted Security Principles

Each predicate rule (e.g. 21 Code of Federal Regulations [CFR] Part 211.68(b)) or guideline (e.g. Guidance for Industry Computerized Systems Used in Clinical Investigations), requires/outlines appropriate security-related controls over applications, infrastructure, and infrastructure components, to ensure that only authorized personnel have a hierarchy of permitted access to enter, amend, read, or print out e-records and information stored within. These controls must be adequately addressed during the development, validation, operation, and maintenance of any computer system.

The following are essential practices relevant to the security of applications.* The applications can be networked or stand-alone. If the application is networked, supplementary practices are contained in the next section.

* López, O. *Computer Technologies Security Part 1 Key Points in the Contained Domain*. West Sussex, United Kingdom: Sue Horwood Publishing Limited, 2002.

1. All applications must have a qualified authentication mechanism to control access (EU Annex 11-Principle 2).
2. Software "virus checking" must take place periodically to protect of the applications and data.
3. Procedural controls must be established to specify the manner in which application security is administered (ICH Q7 Section 5.44).
4. The process for setting up access to applications must be defined and executed by the appropriate application-specific security administration personnel. The technical preparation, education, and training for personnel performing administration tasks, and associated documented evidence, are a key regulatory requirement (EU Annex 11-2).
5. The management of the user application accounts is a key procedural control. This procedural control includes requesting the addition, modification, and removal of application access privileges (EU Annex 11-12.3). The request is approved by the appropriate manager, is carefully documented, and submitted to the application security administration for execution of the request.
6. There must be a procedure to grant temporary application-specific access for personnel (21 CFR Part 11.10(d)).
7. In the event that a user leaves the company, there must be a process to notify the appropriate security administration *as soon as* the employee departs (EU Annex 11-12.3).
8. A procedure must exist which defines the escalation process and actions to be taken upon discovery of unauthorized access (EU Annex 11-13).
9. A documented record of security administration activities must be retained.
10. Procedures must exist to control remote modem access to applications via the applicable infrastructure.*
11. In cases where data or instructions are only available from specific input devices (e.g. instruments, terminals), the system should be checked for, and the operator should verify, the use of the correct device (EU Annex 11-5).
12. When an individual has been authorized to use the system, time stamped audit trails (EU Annex 11-9) must record write-to-file operations and changes, and independently record the date and time of the application-specific operator's actions or entries.

* Pharmaceutical Inspection Cooperation Scheme (PIC/S). *Good Practices for Computerized Systems in "GxP" Regulated Environments*, PI 011-3, September 2007.

13. Time stamped audit trails (EU Annex 11-9) must be used to keep track of modifications by the database administrator to the application related e-records.
14. The use of operational checks is recommended to enforce sequencing (21 CFR Part 11.10(f)).
15. Authority checks (21 CFR Part 11.10[g]) must be used, when applicable, to determine if the operator can use the system, operate a device, or perform the operation at hand.
16. The e-records must not be altered, browsed, queried, or reported via external software applications that do not enter to the data repository area through the protective technological controls (US FDA,* EU Annex 11 p.7.1, and Annex 11 p.17, and TGA).†
17. Unauthorized modification to the system clock must be prevented (21 CFR Part 11.10(d)). One possible technological control around this item is the use of a digital time-stamping service or an infrastructure that supports time stamping from a trusted time service (e.g. coordinated universal time).

    As an example of the above item #17 is a recent Statement of Non-Compliance with CGMPs issued on December 2014‡ following an inspection by the Italian Medicines Agency in accordance with Article 111(7) of Directive 2001/83/EC as amended. One of the concerns was that the "analysts routinely use the terminal administrator privileges to set the controlling time and date settings back to overwrite previously collected failing and/or undesirable sample results. This practice is performed until passing and/or desirable results are achieved."

The relevant requirements and/or guidelines discussed in this chapter under "Secure from Intrusion and Misuse" are also applicable in this section.

Trustworthy Computer Systems Infrastructure

The following items are the key practices which are applicable for the security of the networked environments (Local Area Networks or Wide Area Network).

---

* US FDA. *Guidance for Industry Computerized Systems Used in Clinical Investigations*, May 2010.

† TGA. *CGMP Human Blood Tissues*, Section 1011, April 2013.

‡ http://eudragmdp.ema.europa.eu/inspections/gmpc/searchGMPNonCompliance.do?ctrl=searchGMPNCResultControlList&action=Drilldown&param=26750.

Table 14.1 Authentication

Requirement	*Implementation*
The following features must be implemented: • Automatic logoff, • Unique user identification. • In addition, at least one of the other listed implementation features must be a procedure to corroborate that an entity is who it claims to be.	• Automatic logoff • Biometrics • Password • PIN • Telephone callback • Token • Unique user identification

1. Network resources have a qualified authentication mechanism for controlling access (EU Annex 11-12.1). Table 14.1 shows the authentication requirements and the methods of implementation. These authentication requirements and methods of implementation are relevant to applications security as well.

   Access control decision function are defined using access right lists, such as Access Control Lists (ACLs), and these allow the allocation of use, read, write, execute, delete, or create privileges. Access controls enable a system to be designed in such way that a supervisor, for example, will be able to access information on a group of employees, without everyone else on the network having access to this information.

   The access controls are an element of the authority check requirements.
2. The process for setting up user access to a network is the responsibility of the appropriate network security administration personnel. The technical preparation, education, and training for personnel performing administration tasks are fundamental (EU Annex 11-2). The determination of what is required and the provision of documented evidence of the technical preparation, and the education and of personnel training is a key regulatory requirement (21 CFR Part 11.10(i)).
3. Procedural controls, which specify the manner in which network security is administered, must be established and documented. Network users must be trained in the policies, practices, and procedures concerning network security.
4. The management of network user accounts is a key procedural control. This process includes the request for the addition, modification, and removal of access privileges (EU Annex 11-12.3). The request must be approved by the appropriate manager, documented, and submitted to the network security administration for implementation.

5. There must be a procedure for granting controlled temporary network access for personnel (21 CFR Part 11.10(d)).
6. In the event that a user leaves the company, there must be a process for notifying the appropriate security administration as soon as the employee departs (EU Annex 11-12.3).
7. Provisions must be made for the regular monitoring of access to the network. There must be an escalation procedure for defining the actions to be taken if unauthorized access to the network is discovered (EU Annex 11-13).
8. A documented record of security administration activities must be retained.
9. Procedures must be established to control remote access to the network. Systems that have connections to telephone communications through modems should have strict access controls and restrictions. Access restrictions on these systems should be designed to prevent unauthorized access or change. One possible method for controlling remote access is telephone call back.
10. Access to applications remotely must be performed through the protective technological controls.
11. The use of time-stamped audit trails (21 CFR Part 11.10(c) and (e) and EU Annex 11-9) to record changes, to record all write-to-file operations, and to independently record the date and time of any network system # actions or data entries/changes.
12. Unauthorized modification of the system clock must be prevented (21 CFR Part 11.10(d)).

Computer System Procedures

Refer to Chapter 12 related to operational and maintenance procedures.

Summary

To ensure the integrity of e-records it is essential that the system handling these e-records must be, at the same time, trustworthy.

Trustworthy computer systems consist of computer infrastructure, applications, and procedures that:

- Are reasonably suited to performing their intended functions
- Provide a reasonably reliable level of availability, reliability and correct operation

- Are reasonably secure from intrusion and misuse
- Adhere to generally accepted security principles

No matter the selected storage model (traditional or cloud), the requirements for trustworthy and compliant computer systems performing regulated activities are the same.

Finally, consistent with the globalization of the healthcare industry, the above principles are contained in all key regulations and guidelines.

Additional Readings

López, O. "A Computer Data Integrity Compliance Model." *Pharmaceutical Engineering*, 35(2), 2015; 79–87.

López, O. *Computer Technologies Security Part I – Key Points in the Contained Domain.* West Sussex, United Kingdom: Sue Horwood Publishing Limited, 2002.

López, O. "Computer Systems Validation in *Encyclopedia of Pharmaceutical Science and Technology*, 4th ed. New York: Taylor & Francis, 2013; 615–619.

López, O. "EU Annex 11 and the Integrity of Erecs." *Journal of GxP Compliance*, 18(2), 2014.

López, O. *EU Annex 11 Guide to Computer Validation Compliance for the Worldwide Health Agency GMP.* Boca Raton, FL: CRC Press, 2015.

Chapter 15

Control of Data and Records

Introduction

ISO/IEC* 17025, General requirements for the competence of testing and calibration laboratories, is an International Organization for Standardization (ISO) standard used by testing and calibration laboratories. It is the standard for which most laboratories must hold accreditation in order to be deemed technically competent.†

ISO/IEC 17025 covers the control of records‡ in Section 4.13 and the control of data§ in Section 5.4.7. These controls can be extrapolated to the CGMP record.

This chapter covers the controls to e-records and associated data. The controls discussed in this chapter can be implemented on manual processes with paper records to the use of computer systems.

> "Records shall be established and maintained to provide evidence of conformity to requirements and of the effective operation of the quality management system. Records shall remain legible, readily identifiable and retrievable. A documented procedure shall be established to define the controls needed for the identification, storage, protection, retrieval, retention time, and disposition of records."
>
> *ISO 9001:2000, Quality Management Systems – Requirements, 4.2.4 Control of Records*

---

* IEC: International Electrotechnical Commission.

† https://en.wikipedia.org/wiki/ISO/IEC_17025.

‡ Record: Document stating results achieved or providing evidence of activities performed (ISO-9000).

§ Data: The contents of the record, is the basic unit of information that has a unique meaning and can be transmitted.

Even the data and record controls in ISO/IEC 17025 are applicable to the laboratory environments, these controls and associated regulations are analyzed and correlated in this chapter using manufacturing-related regulations/guidance.

Control of Data

The controls of data contained in ISO/IEC 17025 are:

- Calculations and data transfers shall be subject to appropriate checks in a systematic manner. (Section 5.4.7.1)

  If e-records are exchanged electronically, there should be verification for the correct computer inputs and outputs (I/Os) (EU Annex 11-5). The correct I/Os ensures the secure exchange of data between systems and, furthermore, correct inputs on the processing of data. These built-in checks mitigate any interface error.

  The built-in check is the mechanism that can ensure the authenticity, integrity, and confidentiality of transmissions, and the mutual trust between communicating parties

- When computers or automated equipment are used for the acquisition, processing, recording, reporting, storage, or retrieval of test or calibration data, the laboratory shall ensure that:
  a. computer software developed by the user is documented in sufficient detail and is suitably validated as being adequate for use;

     Any software used to automate any part of the healthcare production process or any part of the quality system must be validated. The extent of validation depends on a number of factors, including the risk analysis and intended use of the system (e.g. 21 CFR 211.68, 21 CFR 820.70(i); EU Annex 11-4; PI 011-3 (14); WHO Appendix 5 in Section 1.1 in Annex 4 – Computer Systems; Brazilian GMP Resolution of the Executive Board No. 17 – Title VII-Computerized Information Systems).

  b. procedures are established and implemented for protecting the data; such procedures shall include, but not be limited to, integrity and confidentiality of data entry or collection, data storage, data transmission and data processing;

In the context of the technological and procedural controls associated with e-records controls, the following are key controls that must be adopted for records retained by computer storage:*

- e-records must be regularly and progressively backed up, and the backup retained at a location remote from the active file;
- data collected directly from equipment and control signals between computers and equipment must be checked by verification circuits/software to confirm accuracy and reliability;
- interfaces between computers and equipment must be checked to ensure accuracy and reliability;
- there must be documented contingency plans and recovery procedures in the event of a breakdown. The recovery procedures should be periodically checked for the return of the system to its previous state;
- the system must be able to provide accurate printed copies of relevant data and information stored within. Printed matter produced by computer peripherals must be clearly legible and, in the case of printing onto forms, should be properly registered onto the forms;
- a hierarchy of permitted access to enter, amend, read, or print out data must be established according to the nature of the change and the operator involved;
- suitable methods of preventing unauthorized access entry should be in place;
- the system in place must ensure that any critical data being entered into the computer manually are accurate and acceptable.

c. computers and automated equipment are maintained to ensure proper functioning and are provided with the environmental and operating conditions necessary to maintain the integrity of test and calibration data (Section 5.4.7.2). NOTE: Commercial off-the-shelf software (e.g. word processing, database, and statistical programs) in general use

* TGA, *Australian Code of Good Manufacturing Practice for Human Blood and Tissues*, 2000.

> within their designed application range may be considered to be sufficiently validated. However, laboratory software configuration/modifications should be validated as in 5.4.7.2.

Refer to Chapter 12.

Control of Records

The controls of records contained in ISO/IEC 17025 are:

- The laboratory shall establish and maintain procedures for identification, collection, indexing, access, filing, storage, maintenance, and disposal of quality and technical records. Quality records shall include reports from internal audits and management reviews as well as records of corrective and preventive actions. (Section 4.13.1.1)

  Critical e-records*, as informational objects, have a lifecycle that begins "from initial data generation and recording, through processing (including transformation or migration), use, retention, archiving and retrieval."†

  Based on the manufactured product, the critical e-records are identified. The workflows associated with these critical e-records are validated.

  As applicable, the e-records workflows that may be validated are:
  - generation of the data;
  - recording of the data;
  - completeness of the data;
  - processing of the data;
  - data error checking;
  - integration of data;
  - security of data and associated warehouses;
  - data mappings to warehouses;
  - correctness and completeness of printouts;
  - generation of audit trails, as applicable;
  - management of the metadata;

---

* Critical e-records: E-records with high risk to product quality or patient safety. (ISPE GAMP COP Annex 11 – Interpretation, July/August 2011).

† MHRA, *MHRA GMP Data Integrity Definitions and Guidance for Industry*, March 2015.

  - disposal of data during the retirement of the associated system(s) and during the end of the retention period.

    After the deployment of the system, the following procedures are activated: archiving, backup, business continuity, e-records quality control, e-records storage, infrastructure maintenance, problem reporting, retirement, restore, risk management, security, and training.

- All records shall be legible and shall be stored and retained in such a way that they are readily retrievable in facilities that provide a suitable environment to prevent damage or deterioration and to prevent loss. Retention times of records shall be established. (Section 4.13.1.2)

  Computer equipment should be located in appropriate conditions where environmental factors cannot interfere with the system.

  The system should be able to provide accurate copies of relevant data and information stored within (EU Annex 11-8). The information stored within includes the units and the respective context.* Units and the respective context are considered metadata.

  Each predicate rule establishes the records retention requirements. As an example, the retention records requirements of Finished Pharmaceuticals can be found at 211.180(c).

- All records shall be held secure and in confidence. (Section 4.13.1.3)

  Computerized systems should have sufficient controls to prevent unauthorized access or changes to data. (ICH Q7† Section 5.43)

  Physical and/or logical controls should be in place to restrict access to computerised system to authorised persons. (EU Annex 12.1)

  The extent of security controls depends on the criticality of the computerised system. (EU Annex 12.2)

---

* Mangel, A., "Q&As on Annex 11." *Journal for GMP and Regulatory Affairs*, Issue 8, April/May 2012.

† The ICH Q7 Guideline is a quality standard that governs the manufacturing of active ingredients. The ICH Q7 Guideline was established by an international organization known as the International Conference on Harmonization, which includes several countries, including the United States, Japan, and the countries of the European Union.

Creation, change, and cancellation of access authorisations should be recorded. (EU Annex 12.3)

Management systems for data and for documents should be designed to record the identity of operators entering, changing, confirming, or deleting data including date and time. (EU Annex 12.4)

- The laboratory shall have procedures to protect and back-up records stored electronically and to prevent unauthorized access to or amendment of these records. (Section 4.13.1.4)

Regular backups of all relevant data should be done. Integrity and accuracy of backup data and the ability to restore the data should be checked during validation and monitored periodically. (EU Annex 7.2)

Data should only be entered or amended by persons authorised to do so. Suitable methods of deterring unauthorised entry of data include the use of keys, pass cards, personal codes with passwords, biometrics, restricted access to computer equipment and data storage areas. (EU Annex 12.1)

There should be a defined procedure for the issue, cancellation and alteration of authorisation to enter and amend data, including the changing of personal passwords. Consideration should be given to systems allowing for recording of attempts to access by unauthorised persons. (TGA CGMP Human Blood Tissues, Section 1011)

Core Principle

Data integrity arrangements must ensure that the accuracy, completeness, content, and meaning of data is retained throughout the data life cycle.

Additional Reading

ISO/IEC 17025. "General Requirements for the Competence of Testing and Calibration Laboratories." 2005.

Chapter 16

Technologies Supporting Integrity of E-Records*

Introduction

An expectation pertinent to the computer systems performing production-related regulated functions is the integrity† of the electronic records‡ (e-records) managed by these systems. This expectation takes the highest priority and foundation in any Regulatory Authorities CGMPs. The electronic information properly recorded and managed is the basis for manufacturers to assure the competent authority about the product identity, strengths, purity, and safety.§ The e-records also demonstrate that the regulated entity production computer systems adhere to the GMPs, including instructions.

All operations with e-records should be performed in a secure environment. This requirement applies to e-records at rest, in transit, and during processing.¶

Any unintended changes to the e-records as the result of a storage, retrieval or processing operation, including malicious intent, unexpected

* López, O. "Technologies Supporting Electronic Records Integrity." *Journal of GxP Compliance,* 21(3) May 2017 (Part I) and 21(5) September 2017 (Part II).

† Integrity: The degree to which a system or component prevents unauthorized access to, or modification of, computer programs or data. (IEEE)

‡ Electronic record: Information recorded in electronic form that requires a computer system to access or process. (SAG. "A Guide to Archiving of Electronic Records." February 2014).

§ Wechsler, J. "Data Integrity Key to GMP Compliance," *Pharmaceutical Technology,* September 2014.

¶ NIST SP 800-33. *Underlying Technical Models for Information Technology Security,* December 2001.

hardware failure, and human error, is considered a failure of e-records integrity.

To assure the integrity of e-records, the computer systems managing such e-records must be essentially trustworthy (refer to Chapter 14). The computer system must execute the intended function free from unauthorized e-record manipulations.

E-records integrity is a critical aspect to be well thought out during the design, implementation, and usage of any system which stores, processes, or retrieves e-records. A quality-by-design approach should be adopted. The system design must make provisions such that original e-records cannot be deleted and for the retention of audit trails reflecting changes to original e-records. Security must be built into the infrastructure and the applications* managing the creation, storage, archiving, modifying, and/or transmission of e-records. Another example is the communication security through an open link can be reinforced by using controls such as encryption processes.

The quality-by-design approach supports the e-records integrity. The idea of "data integrity/quality by design" (DIQbD) is something that aligns with the computer-related quality processes such as the EMA Annex 11, ICH Q7, US FDA 21 CFR 211.68, and many more. In order to apply the applicable regulations appropriately, the regulated user must understand the:

- Required e-records
- Criticality of the e-records to the patient
- Collection method and processing
- Risk of the e-record integrity
- Technical and procedural controls required

Based on the intended use of the system, each of the requirements establishing e-records integrity must be documented and the associated risks assessed before implementing the e-records integrity technical and procedural controls. The validation process provides an ideal framework for documenting the e-records integrity life cycle.†

* Vibbert, J.M. The Internet of Things: Data Protection and Data Security. *Global Environment Information Law Journal,* 7(3) 2016.

† Davis, L. "MHRA: Data Integrity Defined?" PharmOut, https://www.pharmout.net/mhra-data-integrity-defined/.

Centered on information security,* this chapter provides a broad overview of the cryptographic† technologies that can keep e-records integrity for any GMP regulated activity.‡

It describes each individual technology, such as: e-records encryption, digital signatures,§ and services family (e.g. Virtual Private Network¶). These are the set of tools and techniques ensuring the integrity and validity of the information throughout the e-records life cycle.**

In addition, this chapter describes how the combination of these tools can mitigate threats to and vulnerabilities related with e-records integrity.

Implementing the applicable cryptographic tools, access control, and authority checks to computer resources; audit trails controls; authentication; security of the electronic signatures; signature-e-records linkage; time controls; uniqueness of the electronic signatures; and integrity and privacy of e-records in transit are some of the technical controls in which the e-records can be protected. The applicable level of control may be as the result of the criticality of the e-records and associated risks. Only within the control of business needs and risks can management define security.†† Risks to be considered are, for example, the degree to which e-records or the system generating or using the e-records can be configured, and therefore potentially manipulated.‡‡

---

* Information security: Is a set of strategies for managing the processes, tools and policies necessary to prevent, detect, document, and counter threats to digital and non-digital information. Infosec responsibilities include establishing a set of business processes that will protect information assets regardless of how the information is formatted or whether it is in transit, is being processed, or is at rest in storage. http://searchsecurity.techtarget.com/definition/information-security-infosec.

† Cryptographic: It is the practice and study of techniques for secure communication in the presence of third parties. http://searchsoftwarequality.techtarget.com/definition/cryptography.

‡ In this chapter "GMP regulated activities" is defined as the manufacturing-related activities established in the basic legislation compiled in Volume 1 and Volume 5 of the publication, *The Rules Governing Medicinal Products in the European Union* http://ec.europa.eu/health/documents/eudralex/index_en.htm; US FDA 21 CFR Part 211, *Current Good Manufacturing Practice In Manufacturing, Processing, Packing or Holding of Drugs; General and Current Good Manufacturing Practice For Finished Pharmaceuticals*, or any predicate rule applicable to medicinal products for the referenced country.

§ Digital signature: Digital signature means an electronic signature based upon cryptographic methods of originator authentication, computed by using a set of rules and a set of parameters such that the identity of the signer and the integrity of the data can be verified. (US FDA 21 CFR Part 11.3[5]).

¶ Virtual Private Network: Describes the use of encryption to provide a secure telecommunications route between parties over an insecure or public network, such as the Internet.

** López, O. "Electronic Records Lifecycle." *Journal of GxP Compliance,* 19(4) 2015.

†† ITIL. *The Official Introduction to the ITIL Service Lifecycle*, 2007.

‡‡ MHRA. *MHRA GxP Data Integrity Definitions and Guidance for Industry*, March 2018.

Encryption is one of the most well-understood mechanisms for data reliability. There are well-established, mature standards for encryption and the related key management technologies.

Cryptographic Technologies

The following paragraphs contain a simplified depiction of cryptographic technologies* supporting e-records integrity.

Hashing refers to the process of computing a condensed message or record of any length to a string of a fixed length with the use of a one-way mathematical function so that one cannot retrieve the message from the hash. The output of a hashing or hash value is called a message digest. The probability that two-different e-records will generate the same message digest is 1 in 10^{87}. Consequently, a message digest is unique and has a low probability of collisions providing a digital identifier for each e-record. A minor change in a message will result in a change to the message digest (Figure 16.1).

Because hashing is a one-way function and the output of the function has a low probability of collisions, hashing can be used with a cryptographic product or services family for authentication, nonrepudiation, and

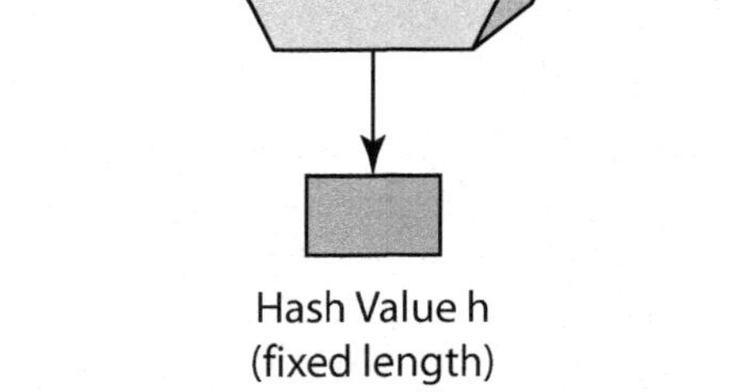

Figure 16.1 Hashing.

* López, O. "Technologies Supporting Part 11" in *21 CFR Part 11: Complete Guide to International Computer Validation Compliance for the Pharmaceutical Industry*. Boca Raton, FL: CRC Press, 2004; 141–146.

e-records integrity. Hashing also is a key element in the digital signature algorithm (DSA).

Encryption refers to the process of scrambling input clear text or records, called the plaintext, with a user-specified password (password-based encryption algorithm) or key (secret-key algorithm) to generate an encrypted text or output called a cipher text. No one can recover the original plaintext from a cipher text in a reasonable amount of time without the user-specified password or key. The algorithms that combine the user-specified password or key and plaintext are called *ciphers*. Encryption most often is used to protect the privacy of messages or e-records (Figure 16.2).

The Data Encryption Standard (DES) was once a predominant symmetric-key algorithm* for the encryption of e-records. It was highly influential in the advancement of modern cryptography in the academic world.

DES is now considered to be uncertain for many applications primarily due to the 56-bit key size being too small. In January 1999, the DES key was broken in 22 hours. There are also results which demonstrate speculative weaknesses in the cipher text, although they are undetectable to mount in practice. The algorithm is believed to be practically secure in the form of Triple DES, although there are theoretical attacks. In recent years, the cipher text has been superseded by the Advanced Encryption Standard (AES).

AES is used by the United States government to protect classified information and is implemented in software and hardware throughout the world to

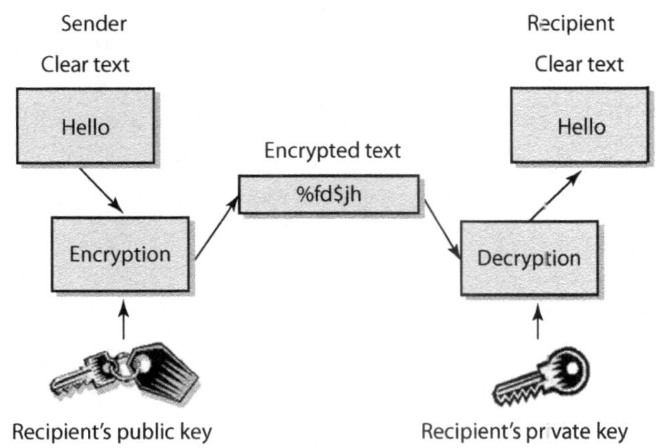

Figure 16.2 Encryption.

* Symmetric-key algorithm: It is a cryptographic algorithm that uses the same key to encrypt and decrypt data.

Table 16.1 Encryption Strength Comparison

Factor	*AES*	*Triple DES*	*DES*
Key length	128, 192, or 256 bits	(k1, k2 and k3) 168 bits (k1 and k2 is same) 112 bits	56 bits
Time required checking all possible keys at 50 billion keys per second.	For a 128-bite key: 5×10^{21} years.	For a 112-bit key: 800 days.	22 hours

encrypt sensitive e-records. It was published by NIST as the US FIPS PUB 197. The AES became effective as a federal government standard in 2002. It is also part of the ISO/IEC 18033-3 standard which specifies block ciphers for the purpose of e-records confidentiality.

The following table compares the encryption strength as determined by key length in bits* of the above referenced encryption algorithms (Table 16.1).

Public-key infrastructure (PKI) is the combination of software, encryption technologies, server platforms, workstations, policies, and services used to administer public-key certificates† – credentials issued by a trusted authority – and public- or private-key sets.

PKI enables regulated entities to protect the security of their communications and business transactions on networks. PKI is used to secure emails, web browsers, virtual private networks (VPNs), and end applications.

In a traditional PKI design, a certification authority (CA) is a trusted party that guarantees for the authenticity of the entity in question by confirming the integrity of the public-key value in a certificate. The CA issues and manages, from a certificate server, security credentials and public-keys for message encryption and decryption. The CA notarizes public-keys by digitally signing public-key certificates using the CA's private key and links to entities. An entity, which is a person, server, organization, account, or site, can present a public-key certificate to prove its identity or its right to access information. It links a public-key value to a set of information that identifies the entity associated with the use of the corresponding private key. This entity is known as

* Alanazi, H., et al. "New Comparative Study Between DES, 3DES and AES within Nine Factors." *Journal of Computing*, 2(3) 2010; 152–157.

† A public-key certificate (also known as a digital certificate or identity certificate) is an electronic representation of an identification or passport, issued by a certification authority (CA) to a PKI user, stating identification information, validity period, the holder's public-key, the identity and digital signature of the issuer, and the purpose for which it is issued.

the *subject* of the certificate. Certificates are authenticated, issued, managed, and digitally signed by a trusted third party, the CA.

A certificate server is the repository for public-key certificates. End applications that are PKI-enabled verify the validity and access privileges of a certificate by checking the certificate's profile status is protected in the repository. The certificate server provides services for managing users, security policies, and trust relationships in a PKI-enabled environment.

Certificate servers must possess controls that provide tamper evidence such as logging, alerting, and tamper resistance such as deleting keys upon tamper detection. Each server may contain one or more secure cryptoprocessor chips to prevent tampering and bus probing. Bus probing is an action to get information from the communication bus. These may come in the form of a plug-in card or an external device that attaches directly to a computer or networked server.

The next critical concept in a PKI is the root certificate. It is an unsigned or a self-signed public-key certificate that identifies the root CA. A root certificate contains the private key of which is used to "sign" other certificates. The most common commercial variety is based on the X.509 standard which normally includes a digital signature from a CA. The ISO/IEC 9594-8 defines frameworks for public-key certificates.

An X.509 certificate* binds a name to a public-key value. The role of the certificate is to associate a public-key with the identity contained in the X.509 certificate.

Authentication of a secure application depends on the integrity of the public-key value in the application's certificate. If an impostor replaces the public-key with its own public-key, it can impersonate the true application and gain access to secure e-records. To prevent this type of attack, all certificates must be signed by a CA.

A CA signs a certificate by adding its digital signature to the certificate. A digital signature is a message encoded with the CA's private key. The CA's public-key is made available to applications by distributing a certificate for the CA. Applications verify that certificates are validly signed by decoding the CA's digital signature with the CA's public-key.

An X.509 certificate contains information about the certificate subject and the certificate issuer (the CA that issued the certificate). A certificate is encoded

* https://access.redhat.com/documentation/en-US/Fuse_ESB_Enterprise/7.1/html/ActiveMQ_Security_Guide/files/X509CertsWhat.html.

in Abstract Syntax Notation One (ASN.1), a standard syntax for describing messages that can be sent or received on a network.

The role of a certificate is to associate an identity with a public-key value. In more detail, a certificate includes:

- A subject distinguished name (DN) that identifies the certificate owner.
- The public-key associated with the subject.
- X.509 version information.
- A serial number that uniquely identifies the certificate.
- An issuer DN that identifies the CA that issued the certificate.
- The digital signature of the issuer.
- Information about the algorithm used to sign the certificate.
- Some optional X.509 v.3 extensions. For example, an extension exists that distinguishes between CA certificates and end-entity certificates.

Digital signature is an advanced form of electronic signature that encrypts documents with digital codes that is particularly difficult to duplicate. The use of digital signatures provides the mechanism to verify the integrity of a signature or e-record linkage and the identity of the signatory. Digital signatures can be implemented in software, firmware, hardware, or any combination (Figure 16.3).

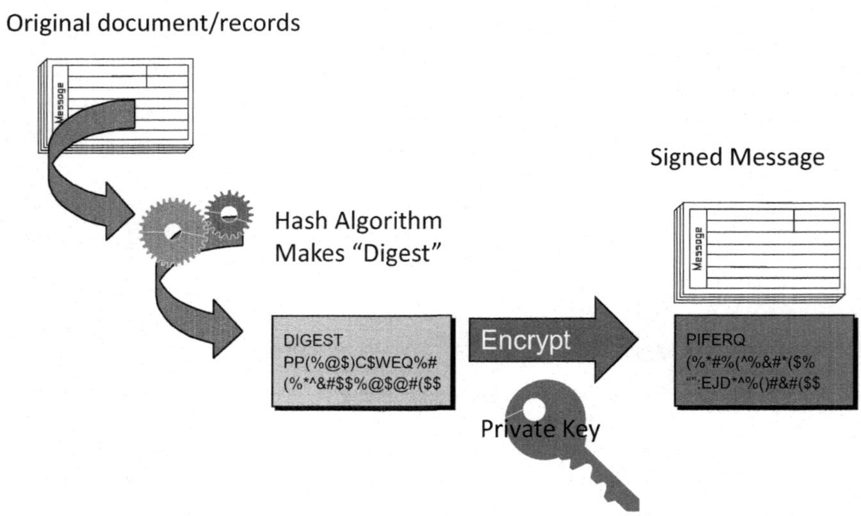

Figure 16.3 Digital signature.

At the time writing this book, in the US, Turkey, India, Brazil, Indonesia, Mexico, Saudi Arabia, Uruguay, Switzerland, and the EU, electronic signatures have a legal significance.

The Public-Key Cryptography Standards (PKCS) describes how to sign a message or e-record in such way that the recipient can verify who signed it and that the message or e-record hasn't been modified since it was signed. Figure 16.4 shows a typical digital signature verification process.

Summary:

- The sender's digital signature is associated with a pair of keys: private key and public-key.
- To sign an e-record, the e-record and the private key are the inputs to a hashing process.
- The output of the hashing process is a bit of strings (message digests) appended to the e-record. The plaintext, the digital signature, and the sender's digital signing certificates are sent to the recipient. A signing certificate contains the public signing key assigned to an individual (Figure 16.4).
- At the recipient site, after the sender's certificate is received, the CA digital signature is checked to ensure that someone the recipient trusts issued it.

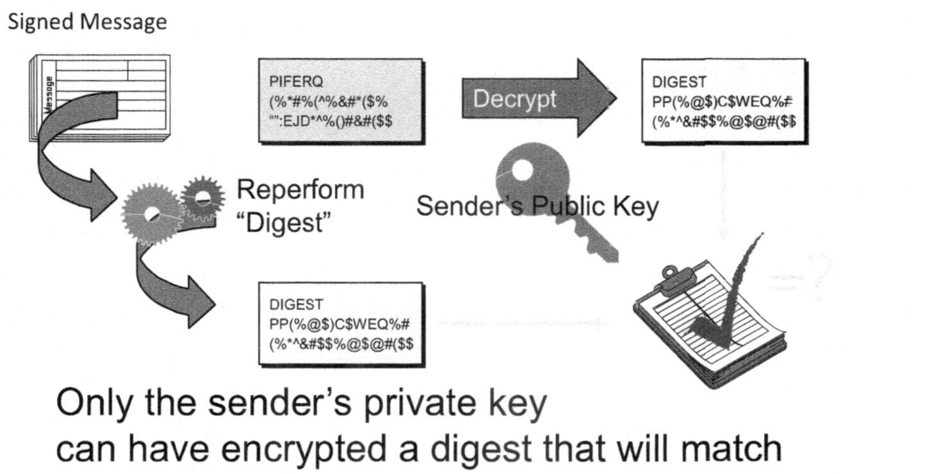

Figure 16.4 Verification digital signature.

- The recipient of the transmitted e-record decrypts the message digest with the originator's public-key, applies the same message hash function to the e-record, and then compares the resulting message digest with the transmitted version. Any modification to the e-record after it was signed will cause the signature verification to fail (integrity).
- If the signature was computed with a private key other than the one corresponding to the public-key used for verification, then the verification will fail (authentication).

In digital signatures, the private key signs and the public-key verifies the authenticity of signatures. For confidentiality, the public-key encrypts messages, and the private key decrypts messages.

The DSA, in which hashing is a key element, is a Federal Information Processing Standard (FIPS) for digital signatures. It was proposed by the National Institute of Standards and Technology (NIST) in August 1991 for use in their Digital Signature Standard (DSS). The most recent DSA revision is the FIPS 186-4 in 2013.

Digital signature is a technology that fully supports the trustworthiness of signed e-records.

The following sections in this chapter depicts a combination of the tools based on the above technologies to mitigate threats and vulnerabilities related with e-records integrity

Cryptographic Technologies Applicable to E-Records Integrity

The electronic environments, such as computer systems, pose particular challenges establishing the integrity of the e-records. This is due to the ease with which e-records may be altered and copied, which can result in the possibility of a multiplicity of versions of particular e-records and the associated document.

Trustworthy computer systems (Chapter 14) provide the confidence to the regulated users that the e-records are the same as those expected, based on a prior reference or understanding of what they purport to be. This expectation includes that the e-records have not been altered in an unauthorized manner (NIST SP 800-33 and IEEE Glossary).

Methods used in storing, transmitting or representing e-records may result in misrepresentations, must be investigated and the investigation results documented.

A range of strategies for affirming the integrity of e-records have been developed, and the choice of a particular method will depend upon the criticality for which e-record integrity verification is required through a risk analysis process. Hashing and digital time stamping (Chapter 21) are 'public' methods confirming the integrity of e-records which in the case of the latter method, involve a specific time.

Another class of methods to establish the authenticity of an e-record includes encapsulation techniques and encryption strategies. A digital watermark can only be detected by appropriate software and is primarily used for protection against unauthorized copying. Digital signatures are used to e-record authorship and identify the people who have played a role in a document.

The types of security services that are needed to support e-records integrity vary depending upon the requirements of the application managing the e-records and the e-records by themselves. As a rule of thumb, it is needed to deal with identity and Access Management (Chapter 22), encryption of e-records retained at rest, and encryption of the e-records in transit (e-records moving from storage to storage).

The required security services must be designed in a way to encourage compliance with the principles of e-records integrity.*

E-records integrity is an essential element of any successful enterprise information technology (IT) program. It is required to have a strong plan behind it, and a strategy embracing all of the major issues.

E-Records at Rest

E-records at rest are retained by computer storage. Computer storage is a device that records (stores) or retrieves (reads) e-records from any medium, including the medium itself.

E-records should be secured by both physical and electronic means against damage.† This guideline is found in several worldwide regulatory and guidance documents and it is applicable to short and long-term storage of e-records.

---

* MHRA. *MHRA GxP Data Integrity Definitions and Guidance for Industry*, March 2018.

† EudraLex. "EU Guidelines to Good Manufacturing Practice, Medicinal Products for Human and Veterinary Use Part 1, Annex 11 – Computerized Systems." *The Rules Governing Medicinal Products in the European Union*, Volume 4. June 2011.

Critical e-records retained by computer storage can be protected via encryption or a comprehensive service such as PKI.

Access Controls and Authority Checks to Computer Resources

User access controls to computer resources are a basic security function for the reason that trustworthiness of the computer system may be compromised even if the e-records themselves are not directly accessed.

User access controls shall be configured and enforced to prohibit unauthorized access to, changes to, and deletion of e-records (EMA Annex 11-12.1 and US FDA 21 CFR 211.68(b)).

Access controls and authority checks "ensure that people have access only to functionality that is appropriate for their job role, and that actions are attributable to a specific individual."*

Access controls are applicable to the system administration functions as well. These functions can be in the applications or infrastructure levels. "System administrator rights (permitting activities such as e-records deletion, database amendment or system configuration changes) should not be assigned to individuals with a direct interest in the e-record (generation, review, or approval)."†

Public-key certificates can be used to authenticate the identity of a user, and this can be used as an input to access-control decision functions. Access-control decision functions are defined through access rights lists – for example, access control lists (ACLs) with functions such as use, read, write, execute, delete, or create privileges.

In Windows, as an example, an ACL is a list of security protections that apply to an entire object, a set of the object's properties, or an individual property of an object. Each active directory object has two associated ACLs: the discretionary access control list (DACL) and the system access control list (SACL).

A DACL is a list of user accounts, groups, and computers that are allowed (or denied) access to the object. A DACL is a list of access-control entries (ACEs) in which each ACE lists the permissions granted or denied to the authentication (EMA Annex 11-12.3). This feature is a challenge–response exchange with a new key that is used at each log-in.

---

* MHRA. *MHRA GxP Data Integrity Definitions and Guidance for Industry*, March 2018.

† MHRA. *MHRA GxP Data Integrity Definitions and Guidance for Industry*, March 2018.

A SACL enables administrators to log attempts to access a secured object. Each ACE specifies the types of access attempts by a specified trustee* that cause the system to generate a record in the security event log. An ACE in a SACL can generate audit records when an access attempt fails, when it succeeds, or both.

As an example of access controls in a typical manufacturing room, an operator logs into the system to perform an operation in a process area. After the operator types the user ID and password, a digital ticket is created that asks the training system to verify the operator's training record and confirm whether the area and equipment were cleaned and released for production. The system returns the appropriate authorization to perform the operation. In this example, authentication, public-key certificate certificates, and ACL are combined to provide the necessary control to operations.

ACLs must be current and reviewed on a regular basis.

Audit Trails Controls

As part of the integrity of e-records, audit trails refer to a journal that records modifications to the e-records. The person or automated processes operating on the user's behalf may perform these modifications. An audit-trail mechanism provides the capability to reconstruct the modified e-records and therefore does not obscure previously recorded e-records. The tracking mechanism includes a computer-generated time stamp that indicates the time of the entry.

Audit trails are computer generated and can be part of the e-record or an e-record by itself. The controls associated with e-records are applicable to electronic audit trails.

Controls to the audit trails include: restrict user access rights to audit trial file to prevent e-record amendments; switch off the audit trails; time stamp must be reliable (refer to "Time Controls"); the system administrator rights should not be assigned to audit trails review or approval; record-audit linkage; audit trails cannot be modified; access to the audit trials is limited to print–read only.

The combination of authentication, public-key certificates, encryption, and ACLs provides the mechanisms to control the access to audit trail-related files.

---

* A trustee is the user account, group account, or *logon session* to which an access control entry (ACE) applies. Each ACE in an access (ACL) has one security identifier (SID) that identifies a trustee.

Authentication

Authentication is a process in which the credentials provided are compared to those on file in a database of authorized users' information on a local operating system or within an authentication server. If the credentials match, the process is completed, and the user is granted authorization for access to the applicable computer resources (Figure 16.5).

There are various ways for authenticating a person: user IDs and static passwords; user IDs and dynamic passwords; biometric devices. Certificate-based authentication is a user ID and dynamic password process that uses public-key certificates.

Figure 16.5 refers to the typical authentication via user ID and static/dynamic password.

The gathering of the identification documentation (EMA Annex 11-2) of a regulated user is typically performed by the regulated entity Human Resources. Similar regulatory requirement is summarized in US FDA 21 CFR Part 11.100(b).

The authentication of an entity in a PKI-enabled environment is performed by using a CA. The CA issues and manages security credentials and public-keys for message encryption and decryption. The objective of a security credential is to associate an identity with a public-key value.

The identity is not of the user, but of the cryptographic key of the user placed on file in a database of authorized users' information on a local

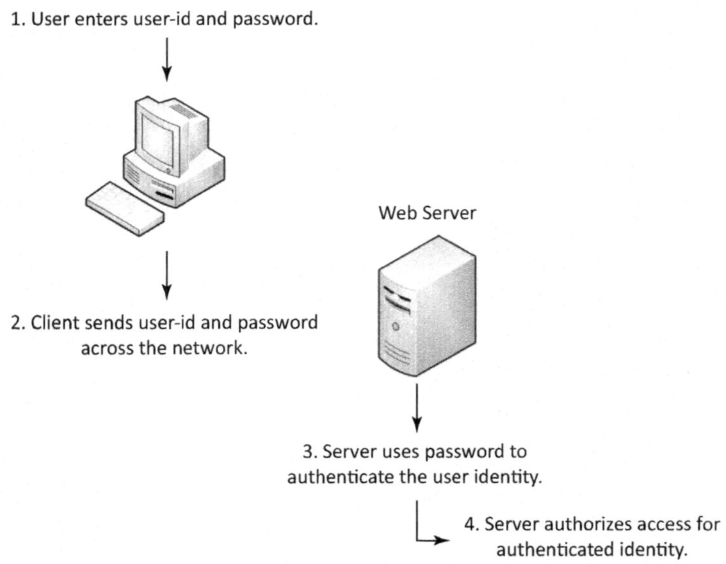

Figure 16.5 Authentication.

operating system or within a certificate server. Having a less secure key lowers the trust we can place on the identity.

The certificate-based authentication is a technique for strong authentication. A party wishing to be authenticated presents a public-key certificate. If the certified party is still trusted in the organization, then the certificate server trusts that the party is who it claims to be. One benefit of certificate-based authentication is that the entity does not have to have an established relationship with, for example, a server before being authenticated.

The digital signature is another method to authenticate a person. This method prevents the sender to deny sending a message. When the verifier validates the digital signature using the public-key of a sender, the verifier is assured that the signature has been created only by the sender who possesses the corresponding secret private key and no one else.

The authentication of a server, as an example, can be performed using a computer networking protocol. Such protocols include mechanisms for servers to identify and make connections with each other.

Secure Sockets Layer (SSL) is an example of a computer networking protocol using cryptographic technologies that authenticates regulated users and performs encrypted communication between servers and regulated users. Using a cryptographic system, it can establish the identity of a remote user (or system). A typical example is the SSL certificate of a web server providing proof to the user that he/she is connected to the correct server.

The SSL protocol establishes an encrypted link between a server and a regulated user, typically a web server (website) and a browser; or a mail server and a mail client (e.g. Outlook). By authenticating a server, the person is assured communication with the correct site. SSL also signs the transmitted e-records so the person is assured that the e-records have not been changed in transit. Server certificates follow the X.509 certificate format.

Security of the Electronic Signatures

The output of a digital signature, hashed data, is considered an e-record. All technical controls applicable to e-records are applicable as well to the hashed data.

In digital signature implementations, the integrity and security of the signatures private key must be considered. The degree of confidence in the linkage between a public-key and its owner depends on the confidence in the CA that issues the public-key certificate.

Within the cryptographic module, the part of a system or application providing cryptographic services such as encryption, authentication, or digital signature generation and verification, public-keys shall be protected against unauthorized modification and substitution. Private keys must be securely managed. These are implemented in various other services, including unauthorized disclosure, modification, and substitution.

Provisions in X.509 compliant public-key certificates enable the identification of policies that indicate the strength of the mechanisms used as well as the criteria for certificate handling. The rules expressed by certificate policies are reflected in security policies that detail the operational rules and system features of CAs and other PKI components. Logical security and proper configuration to the CA, certificate server, and security server help ensure security during the creation and management of public-key certificates.

The private key may be stored in a user's local disk in an encrypted format or as part of a token that interfaces with the computer. Personal cryptographic tokens have been considered to be the obvious secure repository for private keys, and the options for on-board cryptographic processing ensure that a private key is never clear outside of the token.

Signature E-Records Linkage

An electronic signature solution must secure electronic signatures through encrypted copy protection and make it impossible to copy, cut, or paste signatures and audit trails from an approved e-record. This requirement is consistent with 21 CFR Part 11.70 and EMA Annex 11.14(b).

In addition, any changes to the e-record after an electronic signature has been assigned should invalidate the signature until the e-record has been reviewed again and re-signed.*

The above requirements support the integrity of digitally signed e-records. It is vital to consider the integrity and security of the main components of the digital signatures: the PKI components. The level the user is confident about the linkage between a public-key and its owner depends significantly on how confident the user is about the system that issued the certificate that links them.

* Pharmaceutical Inspection Cooperation Scheme (PIC/S). *Good Practices for Data Management and Integrity in Regulated GMP/GDP Environments*, (Draft 2), PI 041-1, August 2016.

In addition to the system issuing public-key certificates, access-control technologies, and procedures, the signature and e-record linkage must have supporting tools to verify the integrity of this link. PKI uses hashing algorithms and keys to demonstrate the integrity of signed e-records. A digital signature is linked to an e-record by incorporating an encrypted message digest of the e-record into the signature itself. This link is retained for as long as the e-record is kept and provides the trustworthiness of electronically signed e-records for that period of time.

Time Controls

The digital time-stamping service (DTS) issues a secure time stamp that can be used for digital signatures and audit trails. The DTS includes the time, a hash of the e-record being time stamped, and a time certification.

The DTS gives strong legal evidence that the contents of the time stamped work existed at a point-in-time and have not changed since that time. The hashing as part of the DTS maintains complete privacy of the e-records themselves.

The workflow of the digital time stamping practice consists of a message digest created from the e-record and sent to the DTS. The DTS sends back the time stamp, as well as the date and time the time stamp was received, with a secure signature. The signature proves that the e-record existed on the stated date. The e-record contents remain unknown to the DTS – only the digest is known. The DTS must use lengthy keys because the time stamp may be required for many years.

DTS and public-key certificates provide the mechanism to authenticate the source (device checks) of the time stamp in the audit trails and electronic signatures. Access-right lists and public-key certificates can be used to control access to the DTS.

In addition to DTS, other supporting time controls include an infrastructure that supports time stamping from a trusted time such as the coordinated universal time. This technology, which in some cases is compliant with X.509 is tied into a time-calibration service. Applications or computer logs may require time-stamping services on the server.

The access controls to the time server and all associated infrastructure must ensure proper security restrictions to protect the time/date settings.

The time controls using cryptographic technologies provide a secure time/date mechanism that cannot be altered by personnel. A minor change in the e-record will result in a change to the message digest.

Uniqueness of the Electronic Signatures

Electronic signatures replacing handwritten signatures must have appropriate controls to ensure their authenticity and traceability to the specific person who electronically signed the record(s).*

The main element for signing e-records and messages in the digital signature is the private key.† Users of PKI may generate key pairs (private and public). When generated by PKI, key pair is produced by prime numbers, which are created from large, random numbers (e.g. candidate prime numbers). ANSI X9.17 specifies a key generation technique. A private key is uniquely associated with an entity and is not made public.

No matter who generates the key pairs, the CA certifies the public-key. However, many organizations mandate that the CA generate the key pair to ensure the keys' quality.

In a certificate-based authentication scheme, a browser generates a session key that is encrypted with a server's public-key.

The uniqueness of the electronic signatures is one element of attributable e-records.

E-Records in Transit

Records must remain unaltered while in transit. The unauthorized manipulation of records, audit trail records, and replay of transmissions will be reliably identified as errors. Below are explained the typical cryptographic controls associated with e-records in transit (Figure 16.6).

Integrity of E-Records in Transit

The integrity of e-records in transit is required by the US FDA 21 CFR 211.68. Similar requirements can be found as guidelines in EMA Annex 11-4.8 and 5.

Hash and encryption functions can be used for assuring integrity of transmitted e-records and message verification.

---

* EudraLex. "EU Guidelines to Good Manufacturing Practice, Medicinal Products for Human and Veterinary Use Part 1, Annex 11 – Computerized Systems." *The Rules Governing Medicinal Products in the European Union*, Volume 4. June 2011.

† Private key: A cryptographic key that can be obtained and used by anyone to encrypt messages intended for a particular recipient, such that the encrypted messages can be deciphered only by using a second key that is known only to the recipient.

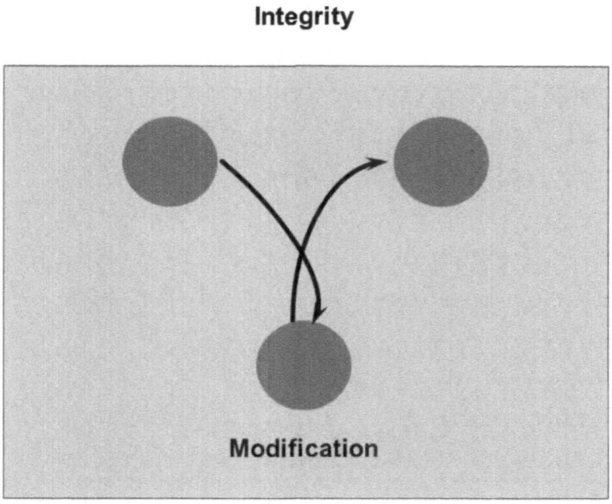

Figure 16.6 E-rec in transit.

Hash protects the integrity and privacy of e-records and prevents their loss. For example, e-records must be protected when confidential patient e-records are sent to other locations.

Records and messages authentication provides the means to evaluate the integrity of the e-records and message in transit. It involves technical controls to detect unauthorized modifications to e-records and messages. A recipient can use two approaches to authenticate e-records in transit and messages:

- *Encrypt records or messages using the recipient's public-key*

  A cryptographic hash function allows one to easily verify that some input e-records maps to a given hash value, but if the input e-records is unknown; it is deliberately difficult to reconstruct it (or equivalent alternatives) by knowing the stored hash value. This is used for assuring integrity of transmitted e-records and is the building block for the Hash Message Authentication Code (HMACs*), which provide message authentication. Consequently, a way that the recipient can make sure that it is the right file is if by the sender posting the hash value publicly. The recipient can then compute the hash value of the file received and check of it matches the hash value.

* A keyed-hash message authentication code (HMAC) is a specific type of message authentication code (MAC) involving a cryptographic hash function (hence the 'H') in combination with a secret cryptographic key.

Encryption protects the privacy of messages and e-records in transit between networks, including wireless LAN and Internet. Tools such as network diagnostics or protocol analyzers can read information easily as it is transmitted. To mitigate this difficulty, systems such as SSL transport layer security, or virtual private networks (VPNs) can provide the necessary protection of critical e-records across networks. These solutions use encryption, digital signatures, or public-key certificates to ensure data privacy, identification of the originator of messages, and verification of message integrity.

- *Sign the records or message*

  A digital signature can also confirm the integrity of a message. In case an attacker has access to the digitally signed records and modifies the e-records, the digital signature verification at receiver end fails. The hash of modified data and the output provided by the verification algorithm will not match. Hence, receiver can safely deny the message assuming that data integrity has been broken.

Device Checks

The device checks are justified where only certain devices have been selected as legitimate sources of e-records input or commands. As an example, in a network environment it may be necessary for security reasons to limit the issuance of critical commands to a particular authorized workstation. US FDA 21 CFR 11.10(h) is a regulatory requirement related with device checks.

Public-key certificates can be used to implement any of these verifications. In the above example it can determine the identity of the file server extracting e-records.

Summary

The cryptographic technologies support e-records integrity in the Regulatory Authorities GMP. Hashing, e-records encryption, digital signatures, and/or services family (e.g. Virtual Private Network) are a set of tools and techniques that can be implemented to properly control the integrity of e-records.

These technical controls have an important advantage over other controls. These cryptographic set of tools and techniques mitigate threats to, and vulnerabilities connected with, e-records integrity.

Table 16.2 Cryptographic Tools Supporting E-records Integrity

	Hashing	*Data Encryption*	*Digital Signatures*	*Services Family*
Access controls				Public-key certificate
Audit trail controls		√		Public-key certificate
Authentication	√		√	Public-key certificate SSL
Device checks				Public-key certificate
Integrity and privacy of e-records in storage.	√	√	√	
Integrity and privacy of e-records in transit.	√	√	√	HMAC VPN
Security of the electronic signature	√			
Signature-e-records linkage		√	√	DSA
Time controls	√			DTS
Uniqueness of the electronic signatures				Private key

The following table recaps the cryptographic tools supporting e-records integrity (Table 16.2).

The implementation of these technologies should be following a security-by-design approach. That is, design the security into devices and applications from the beginning, including the cost of doing so.

Core Principle

> Regulated users who use open systems* to create, modify, maintain, or transmit e-records shall employ procedures and controls designed

* Open system means an environment in which system access is not controlled by persons who are responsible for the content of e-records that are on the system. (21 CFR Par 11.3[9])

to ensure the authenticity, integrity, and, as appropriate, the confidentiality of electronic records from the point of their creation to the point of their receipt. Encryption and use of appropriate digital signature standards are additional controls that ensure record authenticity, integrity, and confidentiality.

Disclaimer

Any mention of products or references to organizations intended only to convey information; it does not imply recommendation or endorsement nor does it imply that the products mentioned are necessarily the best available for the purpose.

The opinions expressed in this chapter are strictly those of the author.

Additional Readings

American Bar Association. *Digital Signature Guidelines*, August 1996, www.americanbar.org/content/dam/aba/events/science_technology/2013/dsg_tutorial.authcheckdam.pdf.

American Bar Association. *PKI Assessment Guidelines*, May 2003, www.americanbar.org/content/dam/aba/events/science_technology/2013/pki_guidelines.authcheckdam.pdf.

Institute of Electrical and Electronics Engineers Working Groups. *IEEE Standard Specification for PKI*, http://grouper.ieee.org/groups/1363/.

NIST Computer Security Resource Center, http://csrc.nist.gov/.

López, O. *Data Integrity in Pharmaceutical and Medical Devices Regulation Operations: Best Practices Guide to Electronic Records Compliance*. Boca Raton, FL: CRC Press, 2016.

Pharmaceutical Inspection Cooperation Scheme (PIC/S), *Good Practices for Data Management and Integrity in Regulated GMP/GDP Environments*, (Draft 2), PI 041-1, August 2016.

Public-Key Cryptography Standards Website: www.rsasec.urity.com/rsalabs/pkcs/.

RFC 2527. "Internet X.509 Public-Key Infrastructure, Certificate Policy, and Certification Practices Framework." www.ietf.org/rfc/rfc3647.txt.

RSA. "Understanding Public-Key Infrastructure (PKI) Technology." ftp://ftp.rsa.com/pub/pdfs/understanding_pki.pdf.

Vibbert, J. M. "The Internet of Things: Data Protection and Data Security. *Global Environment Information Law Journal*, 7(3), 2016.

WHO. "Guidance on Good Data and Record Management Practices." *Technical Report Series*, No. 996, May 2016.

Chapter 17

Infrastructure Qualification Overview

What Is Infrastructure?

In this book, computer infrastructure is an element of a computer system such as hardware, system-level software, devices, integrated components, and networks that run the business other than the software applications. In the context of Figure 17.1,* the computer infrastructure comprises the computer hardware and system-level software. The application software is out of the scope.

This combination of system-level software and hardware is associated with the management and monitoring of the performance, security, accessibility, and integrity of the computer infrastructure. Examples of the computer infrastructure comprise the following:

- System-level software (e.g. operating systems, middleware)
- Application servers
- Service components (e.g. domain controllers, web, and remote access servers)
- Wide Area Network (WAN)/Local Area Network (LAN) components (e.g. networking equipment such as junction devices, bridges, gateways).
- WAN/LAN systems
- Miscellaneous equipment (e.g. network cabling, patch panels, and cable drops)

* Herr, R. R. and Wyrick, M. L. "A Globally Harmonized Glossary of Terms for Communicating Computer Validation Key Practices." *PDA Journal of Pharmaceutical Science and Technology,* 53(2) 1999; 97–103.

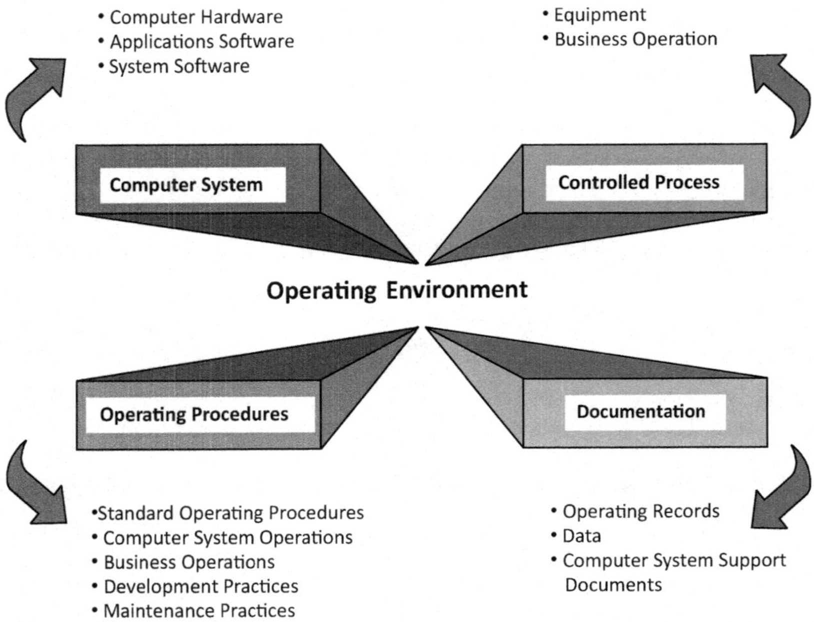

Figure 17.1 A computer system and the operating environment.

- Desktop computers
- Data/network centers

The above items run the business other than the application software. Examples of e-sourcing or services delivered over a computer network are:

- Virtual privates networks (VPNs)
- Security management
- Secure sockets layer (SSL)
- Digital signatures
- Remote access services (B to E)
- Business partner data connectivity (B to B)
- Network-based applications (e.g. secure file transfer, web enabled mail and network scanners)
- Wireless services

Excluded from this book are the following:

- Stand-alone and networked software applications
- Private branch exchange (PBX)

- Videoconferencing infrastructure
- Personal computing devices (e.g. PDAs)
- Infrastructure owned by other parties that are out of the scope of the company

In the regulatory context, computer and network infrastructure components, and associated services are integrated into the computer system domain related with the operating environment (Figure 17.1). The operating environment may include the process or operation being controlled or monitored by the computer system, the procedural controls, process-related documentation, and the people. Computer systems performing activities covered by the medicines' manufacturing practices regulation may control the quality of a product during its development, testing, manufacturing, and handling processes; manage information business operations; manage data used to prove the safety; efficacy and quality of the product and formulation; and provide data for drug submissions.

What Is Infrastructure Qualification?

The infrastructure qualification is a process that provides documentary evidence of the design, development, integration, implementation, operational life cycle, and retirement of all infrastructure hardware components,* products, and/or services. The objective of this process is to ensure that the integrated infrastructure hardware and associated devices are appropriate for the intended use. "Intended use" can be linked with what Joseph M. Juran called quality parameters. These parameters are: capability, installability, usability, performance, reliability, maintainability, documentation/information, and service.

By approaching the computer infrastructure hardware as equipment, the CGMP regulations applicable to equipment are applicable to the infrastructure hardware. (Refer to Chapter 3, CGMP Applicability to Hardware and Software). Equipment needs to be qualified once and, when applicable, as part of any modification.

Once the computer infrastructure is qualified, the various applications that operate over the computer infrastructure can be validated without repeating the computer infrastructure qualification effort, unless the new application

* Hardware component: Hardware module of a hardware unit. Hardware components may contain other hardware components and hardware modules.

requires new computer infrastructure or system-level software not previously included as part of the computer infrastructure qualification effort.

When a new application will operate over the computer infrastructure it is always practical to perform an impact analysis of the new application over the computer infrastructure.

The "documentary evidence" is established after a number of formal and informal activities, many of which must be completed in a pre-defined order. These activities comprise the SLC (refer to Chapter 7). The work products of each phase in the SLC provide the "documentary evidence" that is required to demonstrate that the infrastructure conforms to the needs and intended uses of the user, and that all requirements were consistently fulfilled.

Why Do We Qualify Computer Infrastructure?

The infrastructure is basically a transport means that is used to move information from one location to another.

As required by the FDA, after the process equipment is designed or selected, it should be evaluated and tested to verify that it is capable of operating satisfactorily within the operating limits required by the process.*

The computer infrastructure, including the network infrastructure components, enable sharing of data that may be part of electronic records that are required or submitted to the regulated entity. As such, the trustworthiness of the computer (Chapter 14) and network infrastructure components for the in-transit e-records must be established.

Similar requirements can be found at other government agencies such as:

- Sarbanes-Oxley Act 2002
- US Public Law 104-191, the Health Insurance Portability and Accountability Act of 1996 (HIPAA)
- European Data Protection Acts
- Generally Accepted Accounting Principles (US GAAP)

In addition to the regulatory requirement, it is a good business practice to incorporate assurance of the trustworthiness of the data and information, including an effective business continuity program.

* US FDA. *Process Validation: General Principles and Practices*, January 2011.

When crucial servers and networks crashed, businesses pay dearly in terms of productivity, damaged reputation and financial performance. According to *USA Today*, US companies lost an estimated $100 billion due to network outages in 1999 alone. Even for average companies, the Avaya* warns that the cost of a single minute of downtime for a mission-critical application is an average of $140,000. For large companies, the price can reach millions of dollars per minute.

Other reasons to satisfy good business practices include:

- Demonstrating the suitability of computer hardware and software to perform the assigned task.
- Facilitating the relationships between the company and its suppliers.
- Improving the level of control and maintainability.

Introduction to the Infrastructure Qualification Process

The SLC is the "period of time that begins when a product is conceived and ends when the product is no longer available for use".† Refer to Chapter 6.

The development model associated with the SLC contains the engineering tasks and associated work products necessary to support the infrastructure qualification effort. It breaks the infrastructure development and implementation process down into sub-periods during which discrete work products are developed. This approach leads to well-documented products and services that are easier to test and maintain, and for which an organization can have confidence that the infrastructure-related products and services functions will be fulfilled with a minimum of unforeseen problems.

The development model contains specific inspection and testing tasks that are appropriate for the intended use of the computer system.

Figure 6.1‡ depicts an SLC adapted to different system acquisition strategies, and products and services development models. It is focused on engineering key practices. It does not specify or discourage the use of any particular development method. The acquirer determines which of the activities outlined by

* www.avaya.com/en/about-avaya/newsroom/news-releases/2014/pr-140305/.

† ANSI/IEEE Std 610.12-1990. *Standard Glossary of Software Engineering Terminology, Institute of Electrical and Electronic Engineers*, New York, 1990.

‡ Herr, R. R. and Wyrick, M. L. "A Globally Harmonized Glossary of Terms for Communicating Computer Validation Key Practices." *PDA Journal of Pharmaceutical Science and Technology*, 53(2) 1999; 97–103.

the standard will be conducted, and the developer is responsible for selecting methods that support the achievement of contract requirements. A modifiable framework must be tailored to the unique characteristics of each project. It includes the following periods:

- Conceptualization
- Design
- Development
- Implementation
- Early operational life
- Maturity
- Aging

Project Recommendation, Project Initiation, Release for Use, and Retirement Are Events. These events are considered phase gates or major decision points, which include formal approvals before the development can proceed to the next period.

Certain discrete work products are expected when evidencing the development and maintenance work of infrastructure compliance to regulatory requirements.

To demonstrate the suitability of a given infrastructure component, product, and/or service to the intended use and, consequently, the qualification state of the infrastructure, the main work products that the FDA expects includes:

- Written design specification* that describes what the software is intended to do and how it is intended to do it.
- A written test plan and procedures† based and procedure on the design specification.
- Test results and an evaluation‡ of how these results demonstrate that the predetermined design specification has been met.

---

* In the context of this book, a design specification may include a set of documents containing the technical requirements, technical configuration, functional requirements, and/or technical design. Refer to US FDA, *Guidance for the Industry: Computerized Systems Used in Clinical Trials*, April 1999.

† Written test plan and procedures are equivalent to qualification protocols.

‡ Test results and an evaluation are equivalent to executed qualification protocols and the associated summary reports.

The information obtained from the executed test plan and procedure is used to establish written procedures covering equipment calibration, maintenance, monitoring, and control.

In assessing the suitability of a given piece of equipment, it is usually insufficient to rely solely upon the representations of the equipment supplier, or upon experience in producing some other product. Sound theoretical and practical engineering principles and considerations are a first step in the assessment.

It is important that equipment qualification simulate actual production conditions, including those which are "worst case" situations. The selected SLC should specify the overall periods and the associated events, and dictates the minimum requirements regardless of the chosen development method. These development methods and deliverables are also known as the development methodology. The development methodology establishes the detailed discrete work products by phases and events and by associated activities. The computer infrastructure development approach must be consistent with the selected SLC.

Development and maintenance teams shall receive adequate training in the use of the chosen methodology.

To evaluate adherence to the selected methodology, quality checkpoints (e.g. audits) are conducted during the project. Considering Figure 6.1 as an example, each event associated with the SLC is a checkpoint when quality checks can be conducted.

All Together

Figure 17.2 depicts the application and computer infrastructure development and installation correlation.

Application developers should define the required infrastructure technology/services in their requirements definition document and verify the delivery of these services during the installation qualification and the integration of these services to be tested during the installation, qualification, and the integration of these services during the operational and/or performance qualification.

Based on the system requirements, during the design period the application and infrastructure teams decide how the computer system is to be built, including the detailed information about the interfaces between the computer system and its operating environment.

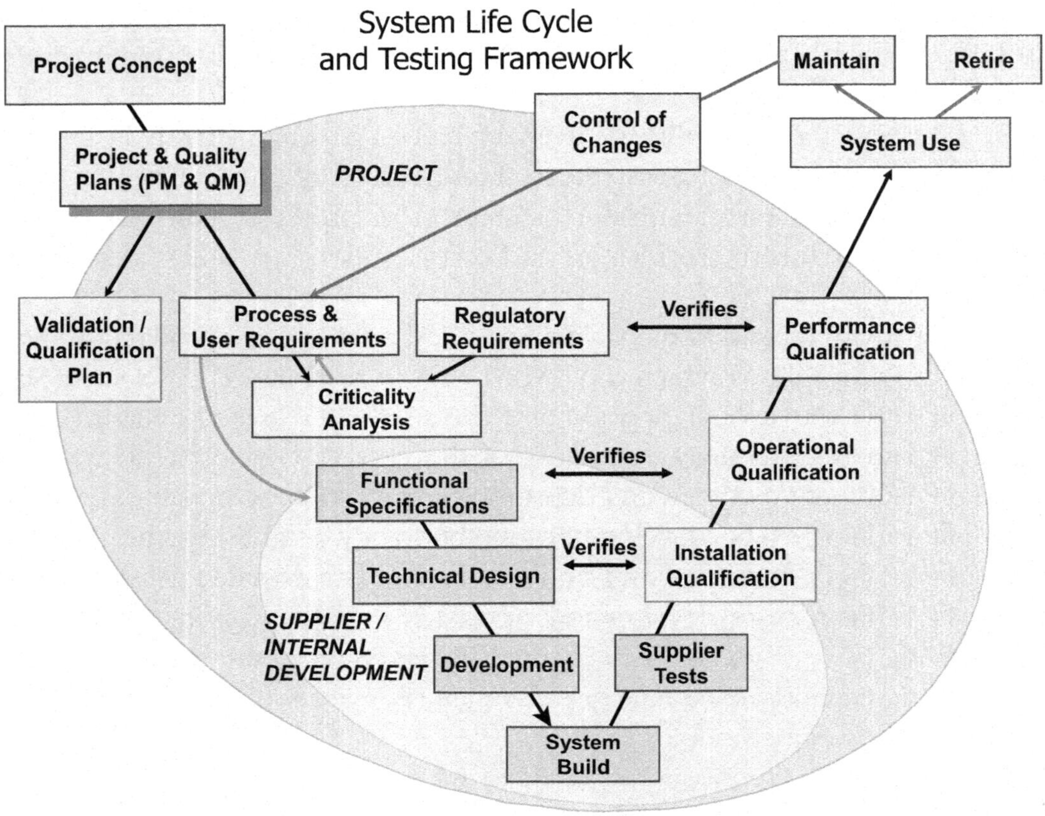

Figure 17.2 Application/Infrastructure development and installation correlation.

Another area to be evaluated during the designing team meetings is the risk analysis results and the distribution of the implementation of some requirements and/or risk mitigation between the application, system-level software, and/or the infrastructure hardware.

At the same time the application team develops the application software, the computer infrastructure deployment team is installing and qualifying the computer infrastructure that will support the application.

The computer system is to be integrated and tested in their operational environment during the OQ and/or PQ.

Chapter 18

Remediation Projects

Introduction*

Legacy computer systems are computer systems that are operating using old computer hardware, based on older software applications, and/or the applicable regulation is new (e.g. 21 CFR Part 11 in 1997) or was updated (e.g. EU Annex 11 in 2011). In some cases, a vendor may no longer support the hardware or software. For a variety of reasons, some of these computer systems may be generally characterized by lack of adequate GMP compliance-related documentation and records pertaining to the development and operational life periods of the SLC. Additionally, because of their age there may be no records of a formal approach to the validation of the system.

The remediation activities should be based on the requirements document. If the requirements document is not available or it is outdated, then one of the foremost corrective actions is to reverse engineer the requirements document. "Experience reports" supported by additional testing have reportedly been used to retrospectively derive a requirements document.

The validation strategy should be consistent with the principles established for classic retrospective evaluation where the assurances are established, based on compilation and formal reviews of the historical operation including historical data, maintenance, error report and change control system records, and risk assessment of the system and its functions. An experience report on the historical operation of the computer system is developed.

* Pharmaceutical Inspection Cooperation Scheme (PIC/S). *Good Practices for Computerised Systems in Regulated "GxP" Environments*, PI 011-3, September 2007.

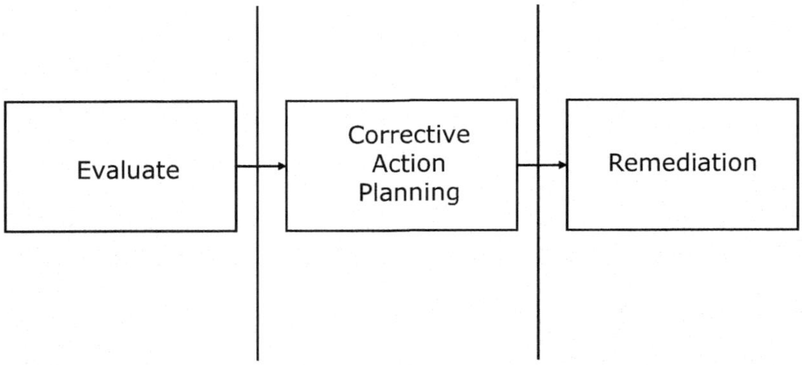

Figure 18.1 Complete remediation project.

If historical data do not encompass the current range of operating parameters, or if there have been significant changes between past and current practices, then retrospective data would not of itself support the evaluation of the current computer system.

The retrospective evaluation on computer systems should not be based only on historical data. The historical data reflects the system's performance only under the conditions of past use, and makes no assumption regarding system operation involving different parameters in the future.

For existing legacy systems, a gap analysis must be undertaken against the identified problems. The issues found during the gap analysis are remediated and documented following a formal qualification plan/report.

Figure 18.1 illustrates a complete remediation project. Like any project, the schedule is based on priorities, time, and the availability of resources.

This chapter identifies the key principles for remediating a non-compliant computer system, but it is not intended to cover everything that an organization's management needs to do in order to achieve and to maintain a computer system in compliance.

Evaluate Systems

The evaluation of legacy computer systems performing regulated operations is the first step to achieving an organized, prioritized, and balanced remediation project approach. The objective of the assessment of a computer system is to evaluate the completeness of the documentation including as applicable: current functionality testing and performance, reliability, system (e.g. design documents) and system life cycle documentation, implementation of the risk mitigations, configuration management (e.g. modifications history), SOPs, trainings, environmental control, preventative maintenance, hardware calibration, system operation history and support, infrastructure management, security, deviation records, incidents/faults, risk assessment, and the e-records management.

The results of the assessment will determine whether the operational, maintenance and security procedures specific to the system provided a controlled environment which ensures the confidence (dependability and thoroughness, rigorous achievement of predetermined specifications), intended use, accuracy, consistency and reliability.*

An assessment plan should be developed in order to define the nature, extent, schedule, and responsibilities of the evaluation and process.

Each system performing a regulated operation must be identified and the operation it performs must be well understood in order to totally evaluate the computer system and estimate the work needed. Data and process flow diagrams may be used as tools for reviewing the operation.

After determining the gaps associated with each system, and based on the effect on product quality and data integrity, a risk assessment is performed on the gaps found. For example, a risk ranking and filtering method can be used to break down a basic risk question into as many components as needed to capture factors involved in the risk. These factors are then combined into a single relative risk score that can then be compared, prioritized, and ranked.

By performing a risk assessment to each system the specific priority rating is obtained. Other factors to take into account during the prioritization process are the components and functions which have regulatory implications.

An assessment report must be generated for each computer system, which summarizes the current operation of the computer system, allocates its priority relative to other computer systems, provides a reference to any supporting documentation, and identifies the compliance gaps in the system. Based on the information in the evaluation reports, a Corrective Action Plan can be generated.

Corrective Action Planning

The purpose of the Corrective Action Plan is to define the overall activities, schedule, costs, and responsibilities necessary to guide the development and

* WHO. "Validation of computerized systems." *WHO Technical Report*, No. 937, Annex 4. Appendix 5, 2006.

implementation of technological and/or procedural controls to bring the systems into compliance. The plan should identify any existing technological/procedural controls that may be modified or new technological/procedural controls which need to be implemented in order to ensure that the gaps are corrected in a consistent and uniform manner. The remedial action items identified in the assessment should be documented in a detailed implementation plan.

Using the evaluation reports, the remediation activities, available resources, and project schedule, the business cost of the remediation approach can be estimated. This will enable a business decision to be made regarding the remediation or replacement of the current system based on the cost-effectiveness of the system and its operational feasibility.

The plan must contain the activities that place emphasis on achieving consistent, high quality, sustainable compliance solutions.

Once the Corrective Action Plan has been approved, it can then be executed.

Remediation

During the remediation phase, the computer systems are brought into compliance by implementing the procedural and technological controls documented in the Corrective Action Plan. In addition, the processes needed to sustain the compliance solutions are implemented.

The remediation process consists of six major activities. These activities are:

- Interpretation
- Training
- Remediation execution
- New applications assessments
- Application upgrade assessments
- Supplier qualification program

Interpretation

In case of a new/updated regulation, the ability to evaluate the risks of a particular system in relation to the new/updated applicable regulation requires a thorough understanding of the regulation and a consistent interpretation. The objective of the interpretation phase of this plan is to provide current, consistent, regulatory interpretation of the regulation to all stakeholders.

Training

In the context of new technologies, upgrades to technologies and/or new/updated regulation, awareness and understanding of these items is fundamental to the success of the remediation plan. The objective of the training is to ensure that all system owner and technical subject matter experts have an appropriate level of knowledge of the remediation work.

As applicable, the implementation user's training is necessary in preparation to the user acceptance testing and the correct operation of the system.

Other forms of training need to be developed in order to support the maintenance of regulatory compliance of computer systems.

Remediation Execution

Once the Corrective Action Plan is approved, the computer technology suppliers and developers are requested to identify how the deficiencies can be overcome. When appropriate, procedural controls need to be developed in order to address the deficiencies which cannot be solved by technological controls.

It is probable that the implementation of technological controls will require a comprehensive SLC including the recommendation, conceptualization, and implementation of the new technology, the release and early operation of the new technology, and the decommissioning and disposal of the old technology. If the technological implementation fails, the failure should be documented along with details of the corrective action taken. Once this action has been taken, the system must be re-evaluated in the same way as any other system which had been subject to an upgrade or correction.

When all of the action items applicable to a computer system have been implemented, it can be formally released for operation, and for support under a maintenance agreement.

The Corrective Action Plan should be periodically reviewed for the reason that the evolving technology requirements will need to be considered and the plan revised accordingly.

New Applications and Application Upgrade Assessments

The objective of regulatory assessments for new applications, and for application upgrades, is to identify the regulatory requirements gaps before releasing the system into production. All gaps must be managed using procedural and/or technological controls.

New systems and upgrades to systems, which are released into production must have a high level of compliance. However, due to limitations on the technology used by suppliers, it is not always possible to implement systems that are fully compliant.

These systems must be assessed, the gaps recorded, and a formal plan established to remediate the gaps.

The project team is responsible for completing this assessment.

Suppliers Qualification Program

A key business strategy has been the outsourcing of work to computer technology suppliers and developers. The objective of qualifying computer technology suppliers and developers is to evaluate and monitor these "strategic" partners for regulatory compliance and to provide an input to the partner selection and partner relationship management processes.

For each qualification performed, a report must be prepared which describes the results of the qualification (refer to Chapter 13).

Remediation Project Report

The Remediation Project Report provides evidence of successful project completion. It must describe the technological and procedural controls and associated activities that were performed to make the computer technologies compliant. This report and all supporting documentation are archived according to the applicable retention schedules.

Once a legacy system has achieved a satisfactory, documented compliant state, any subsequent changes can be prospectively addressed through a change control process.

After the approval of the remediation project report, the computer system is deployed to operations.

Special Case – Retrospective Evaluation

When computer systems are characterized by lack of adequate GMP compliance-related documentation and records pertaining to the development and operational life, a retrospective evaluation is performed in order to properly document and validate changes made to previously unvalidated software.

It is extremely difficult to "retrospectively" evaluate a computer system and generally is more costly and time consuming that prospective validation. Retrospective evaluation might be justified, for example, if a non-GxP system is newly classified as a GxP system.

If it must be attempted, significant information can be obtained through observation, documentation, and performance history. Generally, retrospective evaluation should be used only as a corrective measure in response to deficiencies noted concerning prior validation efforts and/or lack of GMP documentation.

For retrospective evaluation, the User's Manual, Operators Manual, Program Maintenance Manual, and the Training Manual provided by the vendor(s) will help to provide the general structure of the systems. The operational SOP should identify the tasks (including all steps) that are performed with the aid of the computer. The personnel responsible for designing test cases can avoid making assumptions about the system functions if this documentation is complete. Missing or incomplete information may be reconstructed by researching:

- Assembly specifications
- System history: maintenance logs, change logs, error logs, failure reports, and records
- Project files
- Evaluation of user manuals and SOPs
- Source code
- Software structure and data flow diagrams
- Computerized system test results
- Previous versions of software

It is interesting to note that on June 16, 1998 the FDA Philadelphia District Office issued a Warning Letter (WL) to a regulated company containing a view about legacy equipment. The Philadelphia district does not expect the recipient of the WL to run "comprehensive installation, operational, and performance qualification studies on those pieces of equipment whose initial qualification work may not reflect current GMP standards." According to the WL, the Philadelphia district office anticipates GMP controls to the related legacy equipment.

The medical device guideline* establishes an alternative when necessary documentation (source code and design specifications) is not available from the vendor or the developer. The device manufacturer will need to perform sufficient system-level "black box" testing† to establish that the software meets their user needs and intended uses.

To be able to develop the test cases to perform a significant system-level "black box" testing the requirements document is needed. This document establishes the actual allocation of system functions to the hardware/software, operating conditions, user characteristics, potential hazards, non-functional requirements, intended use, and other requirements.

As in a typical remediation project, Figure 18.1 illustrates complete retrospective evaluation and associated remediation activities.

Essentials Retrospective Evaluation Management‡

Based on the current EU Annex 11-4.1 and 4.5, the following retrospective evaluation procedure should be adopted.

- Prepare an experience report on the past operation of the computer system.
- Assess the completeness of the documentation against the life cycle and evaluate the quality of the documentation (a manufacturer's audit may be required for this purpose).
- Conduct a risk analysis to the GMP-relevant components and functions.
- Create a Corrective Action Plan defining activities and responsibilities.
- Create/revise the documentation necessary for testing the computer system.
- Test the GMP-relevant component of the computer system in the risk analysis using this documentation.
- Release for operations the computer system, if necessary implementing additional organizational QA measures.

* Comment #136 Preamble of 21 CFR Parts 808, 812, and 820 Medical Devices; Current Good Manufacturing Practice (CGMP); Final Rule, Federal Register/Vol. 61, No. 195/Monday, October 7, 1996.

† Black-Box Test: The test cases are derived solely from the description of the test object, the inner structure of the object is thus not considered when creating the test plan.

‡ APV. The APV Guideline "Computerized Systems" based on Annex 11 of the EU-GMP Guideline, April 1996.

- Introduce all cross-phase activities/evaluations applicable to the existing system, as in the life-cycle model (see Section 2.2 of the APV Guideline).
- Freeze system status or develop it further according to the life cycle.

Ultimately, regulated users have to be able to demonstrate*:

- Defined requirements.
- System description, or equivalent.
- Verification evidence that the system has been qualified and accepted and that GxP requirements are met.

The above guidance is consistent with the US FDA CDRH guidance.

In the absence of adequate retrospective evaluation evidence this could be a reason to suspend, discontinue, or turn-off any legacy system(s).

Core Principles

> The regulated user should have a reasonable timetable for promptly modifying any systems not in compliance to make them compliant with the applicable regulation, and should be able to demonstrate progress in implementing their timetable.

Regulatory Requirements/Guidance

- A significant number of legacy systems may operate satisfactorily and reliably, however, this does not preclude them from a requirement for validation. (PIC/S PI 011-3)
- If an existing system was not validated at time of installation, a retrospective validation could be conducted if appropriate documentation is available. (ICH Q7A, Section 5.4 – Computerized Systems)
- Firms will be required to justify the continued use of existing computerized systems that have been inadequately documented for validation purposes. Some of this may be based on historical evidence but much will be concerned with re-defining, documenting, re-qualifying, prospectively validating applications and introducing GxP related life cycle controls. (PIC/S PI 011-3)

---

* (PIC/S). *Good Practices for Computerised Systems in Regulated "GXP" Environments*, PI 011-3, September 2007.

SIPOC (Figure 18.2)

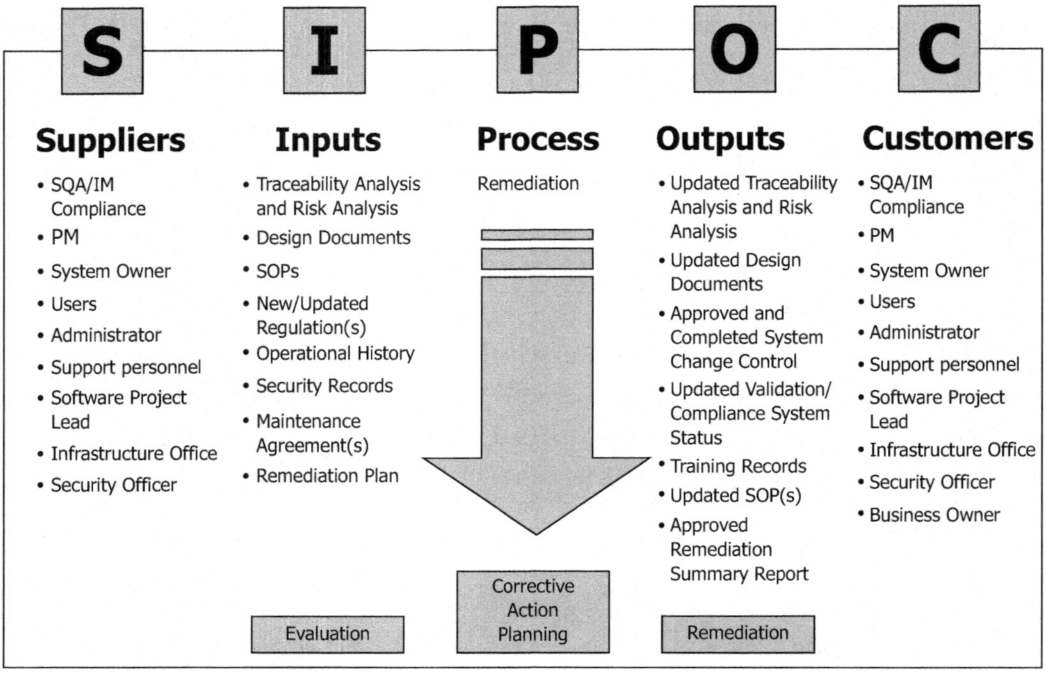

Figure 18.2 Remediation project.

Chapter 19

Production CSV Program Organization

Many groups, both within and outside of an organization, support the validation of computer systems. It is the responsibility of executive management to provide adequate resources to attain compliance in the production area.

Responsibilities are often similar across multiple functional groups such as information technology, engineering, laboratories (QC), manufacturing/operations, contract developers, and SaaS suppliers.

In order to manage the execution and supervision of computer systems validation activities there needs to be an organizational structure established. This chapter suggests an organizational structure for supporting a computer validation program in a production environment.

Organizational Model

This model, Figure 19.1, is an example of how computer systems validation and its related activities can be organized and how responsibilities can be allocated. Each organization should prepare a document that identifies the roles and responsibilities appropriate for its business environment.

CSV Executive Committee

The Computer Systems Validation Executive Committee is composed of validation, compliance, regulatory affairs, quality control laboratory, engineering,

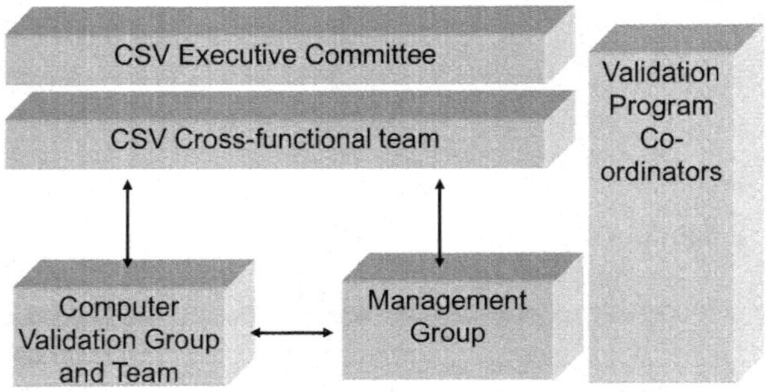

Figure 19.1 Organizational model.

and information technology senior management. Another possible member of this committee is a "process innovation".

In the context of production-related systems, the Computer Systems Validation Executive Committee is responsible for:

- Establishing and supporting the awareness of the production-related CSV strategy through resourcing training, and procedure and guideline development.
- Reviewing and approving computer systems validation guidelines.
- Reviewing and approving the computer systems validation master plans.
- Providing direction and guidance concerning the validation program.
- Arbitrating on organizational issues and validation program issues.

CSV Cross-Functional Team

The Cross-Functional Computer Systems Validation Team is a multidisciplinary team (Figure 19.2) which represents the overall needs of the production-related operation. This team comprises representatives from production, engineering, quality control, quality assurance, and other groups as needed.

The members and their deputies are assigned by the CSV Executive Committee. For ad hoc activities, the team can be complemented with representatives from departments that perform activities which support production-related computer validations. Examples of such departments are IT, QA validation, QA compliance, operations, engineering, and representatives from each manufacturing facility concerned.

In the context of production CSV, the Cross-Functional Computer Systems Validation Team is responsible for:

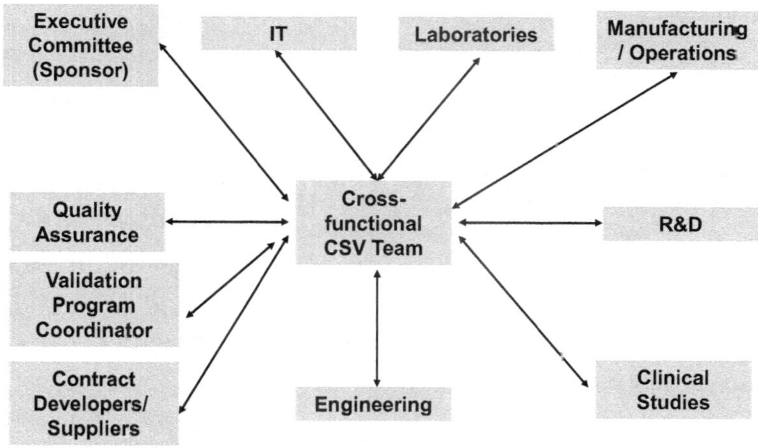

Figure 19.2 Cross-functional teams.

- Implementation of the production-related CSV strategy; including the implementation of the validation policy, validation guidelines, and computer system validations procedural controls.
- Support computer-related company and/or executive committee strategies.
- Developing and maintaining the computer system validation approach to be followed by the manufacturing computer validation team.
- Reviewing validation plans and protocols as needed.
- Assisting the validation program coordinator in compiling the validation master plans.
- Developing and maintaining a QA framework for computer system validations.
- Assisting QA compliance during audit of a computer system.

The importance of the QA unit in validation is evident in the context of regulatory compliance. The QA unit has the responsibility and authority for:

- Reviewing and approving the validation policy and requirements documents, to verify the correct execution of the validation plans and summary reports
- Assessing the compliance of computer systems to the validation policy, validation guidelines, validation procedural controls, and to related predicate regulations
- Auditing the readiness of computer systems for regulatory inspections
- Supporting Management Group during regulatory inspections

- Documenting the results of audits via QA audit reports
- Ensuring that any audit report issues are resolved
- Organizing capability assessments on external and internal suppliers

Computer Systems Validation Groups and Teams

The Computer Systems Validation Groups and Teams mainly focus on the execution of manufacturing computer systems validation projects.

The Computer Systems Validation Group is responsible for the delivery of a production validated system. This includes:

- Developing, approving and executing the CSV Plan and associated summary report for GMP production computer systems
- Developing the required documentation
- Ensuring that the production computer system is maintained in a validated state by ongoing qualification of the platform and validation of the application

The members of the Computer System Validation Group include the:

- System Validation Team designated by the Management Group
- Supplier of the standard/configurable software packages used, the system integrator (software system and platform), and/or cloud service provider
- Platform owner, system owner, system users, Validation Project Coordinator, e-records owners, and specialists in various fields related to computer systems validation

One of the most important members of the Computer Systems Validation Team is the Validation Project Coordinator. The Validation Project Coordinator is responsible for planning, coordinating, and reporting the validation activities during a project. The Validation Project Coordinator may act as the liaison between the Validation Program Coordinators and other teams and groups in the organization, and approves consultancy.

The Validation Project Coordinator must be familiar with the contents of the validation practices and procedures; and must have participated in appropriate training activities in the area of e-compliance.

When embarking on the implementation of a regulatory computer system, it is recommended that the project managers appoint an individual to act as the Validation Project Coordinator.

The involvement of the Validation Project Coordinator on a project will vary depending on the size of project. For a small project, the coordinator role may require only a part-time assignment. For a large project, the role may require the assignment of a full-time person.

Management Group

The Management Group consists of:

- System Owner
- System User(s)
- E-Records owner

The Management Group is responsible for:

- Preparing, approving, and implementing procedural controls which are appropriate for the system
- Managing the system throughout its entire project life cycle
- Providing information needed by the Validation Groups and Teams to develop the computer validation master plan
- Setting up, managing, and resourcing the Computer Systems Validation Team
- Approving the validation reports for the computer systems
- Enforcing the quality records practices and records retention periods of e-records and SLC documentation
- Ensuring the validation status is maintained throughout the operational life of the systems
- Providing support during regulatory inspection

Validation Program Coordinators

This is a dedicated corporate consulting group. The principle task of this group is to provide consultation and to review/approve validation documentation. A benefit of this approach is that a consistent production computer validation program is implemented across all sites and units.

For any validation activity to be effective, an independent and qualified third party, someone that is neither a developer nor a user of the system, must review it. Although the developers and users of the system may generate most of the SLC products, a qualified third party should review the SLC related documentation and give objective assurance to management that the computer systems validation was carried out properly.

This third party review function can be performed by a dedicated Validation Group who has sufficient objectivity as well as sufficient expertise in computer systems validation methods. The members of a Computer Systems Validation Group should include system, software, and hardware engineers with experience in the regulations and project management.

A dedicated CSV Group should have experience and knowledge of:

- Computing infrastructures
- Security and controls
- Corporate, industry, and regulatory standards
- Solving computer systems problems
- The roles and responsibilities of the integrators and service providers

The Validation Programs Coordinators may be part of the QA unit, technical services unit, or the information technology unit.

The advantages of the dedicated Validation Program Coordinators are that the employees in such a group are totally dedicated to and responsible for the computer validation effort. Interaction with production and quality assurance scheduling is important and therefore must be taken into consideration.

The value added by a dedicated computer systems validation group to the validation process includes:

- Reducing the learning curve to the Management Group, System Validation Team and System Validation Group by providing validation consultation
- Producing a smoother path for reviewing the manufacturing systems validation documentation and reviewing protocols at the start of the development effort
- Reducing inefficiencies by ensuring the quality and consistency of the validation methodology
- Improving working inefficiencies by reusing validation experience between similar computer systems and in manufacturing facilities

To summarize, the Validation Program Coordinators are responsible for:

- Managing the computer systems validation program, consisting of the validation policy, validation guidelines, validation procedural controls development and implementation, computer validation training, and other activities which have been identified
- Coordinating the development of validation guidelines and validation procedures and organizing regular reviews, and the development and review of generic validation plans and protocols
- Reviewing the computer validation work and documentation and signing to verify the correct execution of the validation plan, protocols, and summary report for computer systems and to ensure the uniformity and quality of the approach
- Compiling the computer validation master plan
- Keeping an inventory of the validation status of the computer systems
- Providing support, consultancy, tools (e.g. templates), and expertise on computer systems validation matters to the CSV Teams
- Supporting QA during audits which assess the readiness of computer systems for regulatory inspections
- Supporting Management Groups during regulatory inspections
- Developing and providing validation training based on procedural controls

Chapter 20

Integration Between Computer System and E-Records Life Cycles

Introduction

Before the current emphasis by the worldwide regulatory agencies or competent authorities to e-records integrity, the focus was the computer systems life cycle.

After placing the emphasis on e-records integrity by the worldwide regulatory agencies or competent authorities, the regulated industry is now providing the same attention to the system life cycle and the e-records life cycle.

To avoid additional work and as part of the computer system workflows, it is relevant to incorporate integrity-related controls to the e-records and build in the correct management of e-records during processing.* This design-related work must be incorporated to the computer system as part of the Development Phase.

After the computer system is released to operations, the prominence in the e-records management turns out to be the management of the e-records in the computer storage† and the records in transit.‡ The importance to the computer

* López, O. "Electronic Record Controls: During Processing" in *Data Integrity in Pharmaceutical and Medical Devices Regulation Operations*. Boca Raton, FL: CRC Press, 2017; 179–184.

† López, O. "Electronic Record Controls: During Processing" in *Data Integrity in Pharmaceutical and Medical Devices Regulation Operations*. Boca Raton, FL: CRC Press, 2017; 169–177.

‡ López, O. "Electronic Record Controls: During Processing" in *Data Integrity in Pharmaceutical and Medical Devices Regulation Operations*. Boca Raton, FL: CRC Press, 2017; 185–188.

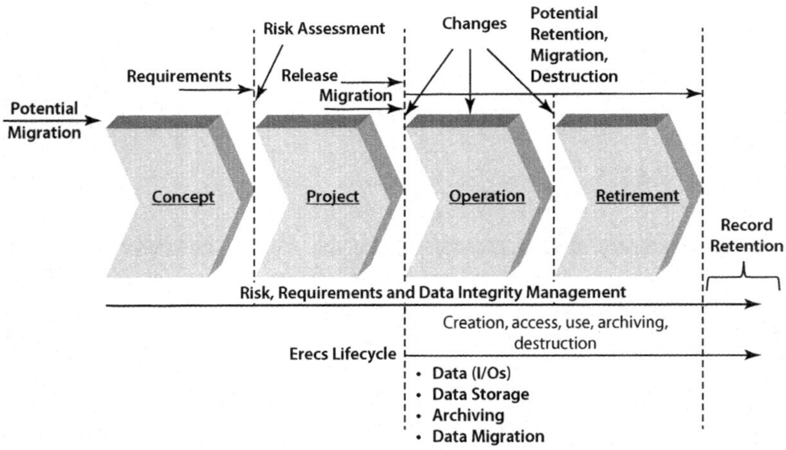

Figure 20.1 Data integrity management.

systems after release for operations is the typical GMP controls associated with the operational life of the computer system.

Figure 20.1 depicts an approach to integrating the e-records life cycle during the Development Period and Operational Life Period. The selected system life cycle is from the EU Annex 11.

The following sections explain this integration.

Development Period

Computer Systems Validation

An element in the e-records governance* is the computer validation process. This process provides the initial assurance of the successful implementation of the e-records integrity controls. These records controls are to be maintained through the operation, maintenance, and even after the retirement of the computer system.

Computer systems validation is the formal assessment and reporting of quality and performance measures for all the life cycle stages of software and system development, its implementation, qualification and acceptance, operation, modification, re-qualification, maintenance, and retirement. This should

* MHRA. *MHRA GMP Data Integrity Definitions and Guidance for Industry*, Section 5, (Draft) July 2016; Pharmaceutical Inspection Cooperation Scheme (PIC/S). *Good Practices for Data Management and Integrity in Regulated GMP/GDP Environments*, (Draft 2), PI 041-1, August 2016.

enable both the regulated user, and competent authority to have a high level of confidence in the integrity of both the processes executed within the controlling computer system(s) and in those processes controlled by and/or linked to the computer system(s), within the prescribed operating environment(s).*

In the context of Regulatory Authorities, the validation process applicable to computer systems incorporates the intended purpose of the systems.

As part of the Development Period, the application is built, tested, documented, and installed.

The following is addressed by the EU Annex 11 guideline:

- As part of the qualification of the application and associated controls, test the backup and restoration procedure(s), and verify the output of the backup (11-7.2). Each backup set should be checked to ensure that it is error-free, including the metadata and all configuration related files.
- The ability to retrieve the e-records and audit trails should be ensured and tested (11-7.1).
- Verify accuracy of reports and audit trail reports (11-8).
- As applicable, and based on the operational sequencing, test accuracy of the e-records (11-7.1).
- IT infrastructure must be qualified to ensure security and electronic records integrity (11-Principle b).

Requirements

Business requirements† are gathered as part of the feasibility at the beginning of the computer system project, including the e-records integrity-related requirements. These e-records integrity-related requirements are traced to the regulated company e-records governance (Annex 11-4.4 a.k.a 11-4.4).

The following e-records integrity requirements are critical:

- Identify the critical e-records.‡
- Based on a risk assessment, identify the e-records integrity-related controls. The identified risk must be managed through the SLC (11-1).

* Pharmaceutical Inspection Cooperation Scheme (PIC/S). *Good Practices for Computerized Systems in "GxP" Regulated Environments,* PI 011-3, September 2007.

† Business requirements are the critical activities of an enterprise that must be performed to meet the organizational objective(s) while remaining solution independent.

‡ Critical data: Data with high risk to product quality or patient safety. (ISPE GAMP COP Annex 11 – Interpretation, July/August 2011).

- If e-records are transferred to another data format, the new format must be established* (11-4.8 and 11-8.1).
- Identify interfaces (11-5) and the data to be entered manually (11-6).
- Based on risk assessment, assess the need of audit trails (11-12.4), and controls to prevent unauthorized access to the application and the operating systems (11-7.1, 11-12 and 21 CFR 11.10(g)) by restricting the access via passwords or other means.
- Recording of access attempts.
- A reliable time source must be used to update server's time. This reliable time must be used for the generation of time stamps.
- Design the applicable reports (11-8.1), operational system checks (21 CFR Part 11.10(f)), authority checks (21 CFR Part 11.10(g)) and device checks (21 CFR Part 11.10(h)).

The appropriate methods to prevent unauthorized manipulation of e-records include:

- Use of keys
- Passwords
- Personal codes
- Restricted access to computer terminals

Of special interest are the system administrator access and the access to the e-records retained by computer storage (11-7.1). According to the MHRA Data Integrity Definitions and Guidance document,† MHRA expects that each system administrator should have unique access to the computer system. Every employee with administrative privileges is logged into the computer system with his distinct password, to ensure that there is traceability of actions performed in the computer and the respective user, including an audit trail.

During the Development Period of a new system in which a legacy system is replaced, the requirements stage must consider the e-records migration from the legacy system to the new system. If this is the case, it will require:

- Considering storage and infrastructure requirements
- Mapping source and destination fields

* "Establish" is defined in this book as meaning to define, document, and implement.

† MHRA. *GxP Data Integrity Definitions and Guidance for Industry* (Draft), July 2016.

- Specification of the mandatory fields for e-records
- Extracting and loading requirements
- Specifications of the e-records inputs (e.g. format, decimal places, units, ranges, limits, defaults, and the conversion requirements)
- Defining what constitutes an error and how errors must be handled
- Verification requirements to ensure that source e-records are the same as the e-records in the destination

As the reader can evaluate of the above requirements, this is a project by itself.

The business requirements are transformed to user requirements or capabilities needed by a user to solve or achieve an objective. Finally, the user requirements are translated to functional requirements or requirements that specify behavior or functions of the computer system (11-4.4).

Risk Assessment

A mature e-records governance system adopts a "quality risk management" approach across all areas of the quality system* (11-4.5). The critical e-records integrity risk will vary depending upon the degree to which e-records generated by the computer system can be configured, and therefore potentially manipulated† (11-12.2).

Based on the above statements, an evaluation of risks is performed to uncover potential e-records manipulations in an unauthorized manner and, via a root analysis, finding the mitigation(s) to the potential unauthorized manipulation of the e-records. These analyses may lead to architecture and design tradeoffs during the system development.

The MHRA guidance suggests mitigations to address the risk of e-records manipulations in an unauthorized manner.

- Access controls to ensure that only authorized individuals can access and use the system based on the job role (11-12). The access controls are applicable to database servers or any server containing GMP-related e-records.

---

* Churchward, D. "Good Manufacturing Practice (GMP) Data Integrity: A New Look at an Old Topic, Part 2." July 2015.

† Churchward, D. "Good Manufacturing Practice (GMP) Data Integrity: A New Look at an Old Topic, Part 1." June 2015.

- The regulated entity must have documentation about users and access level (11-12.3).
- In cases that technological or design constrains don't allow unique access to the computer application and/or database server(s), a paper-based method must provide access traceability.
- The access to system administrators should be minimal, unique per administrator and traceable. The preferred traceability method for actions performed by a system administrator is audit trails (11-9). It is not specified if the audit trails must be electronically recorded.
- Separation of roles must be enforced on e-records maintenance.
- E-records maintenance must be controlled (11-12.4) and an approval method must be implemented (11-10).

The above are controls to prevent e-records manipulation.

Another area to consider is the risk associated with e-records migration from existing system(s) over to a new system. The risk of e-records migration may be mitigated by verifying "that data are not altered in value and/or meaning during this migration process" (11-4.8).

Annex 20* summarizes an approach to a quality risk management pertinent to computer systems and computer controlled equipment.

- Determine the GMP criticality of the system, impact on patient safety, product quality, or e-records integrity; identification of the critical performance parameters; determine the extent of validation.
- Develop requirement specification considering the basis of the criticality; perform a detailed risk assessment to determine critical functions.
- Select of the design of computer hardware and software (e.g. modular, structured, fault tolerance); implementation of appropriate controls via design as much as possible;
- Perform code review, as applicable.
- Determine the extent of testing and test methods of the controls implemented during the design.
- Evaluate reliability of electronic records and signatures, as applicable.
- The risks uncovered during this activity must be managed through the SLC (11-1).

* EudraLex. "EU Guidelines for Good Manufacturing Practices for Medicinal Products for Human and Veterinary Use. Annex 20 – Quality Risk Management" *The Rules Governing Medicinal Products in the European Union*, Volume 4. February 2008.

The risk management process supports the assessment against the computer requirements and within its operational environment. Decisions regarding risks identified must be made prior to start the design of the computer system.

According to the MHRA guidance "the effort and resource assigned to data governance should be commensurate with the risk to product quality."

In addition, the MHRA had communicated to the regulated user that must carry out a routine effectiveness review of their governance systems to ensure e-records integrity and traceability is maintained. The effectiveness review can be performed during the periodic review.

The requirements document must include requirement(s) related with the mitigation of the uncovered risks.

Manufacturers must develop and employ a system which allows an acceptable state of control based on the e-records integrity risk.

E-records Migration and Computer Systems Release to Operations

If e-records are transferred to a new environment changing the format of the e-records, the qualification must include test cases and the associated verifications that the electronic records' new format does not alter the content of the records and associated metadata during the migration process (11-4.8). The migrated records and the application(s) are integrated, and testing executed to demonstrate such integration.

As part of the implementation, one of many e-records integrity-related requirements addressed in the MHRA guideline is the recording of transactions contemporaneously by computer systems. These are typical transactions in which the user agrees, completes by performing certain pre-defined actions, or acknowledges a deviation. These actions must not be combined into a single computer system transaction with other operations.

The above guideline can be traced to Section 4.8 in the Volume 4, Chapter 4 (Documentation) from the EudraLex *Rules Governing Medicinal Products in the European Union.*

"Records should be made or completed at the time each action is taken and in such a way that all significant activities concerning the manufacture of medicinal products are traceable."

Recording e-records contemporaneously is a key factor related with e-records reliability.*

* Data reliability is a state when data is sufficiently complete and error free to be convincing for its purpose and context. In addition to being reliable, data must also meet other tests for evidence.

Operations

During this stage it's when e-records are generated, recorded, transformed, accessed, used, logically deleted, migrated, and retired. It is when the integrity of the e-records can be compromised. The objective of all e-records requirements, and the implementation of such requirements, are to preserve the e-records integrity.

During the Operational Stage the procedural controls associated with e-records integrity must be enforced:

- Only authorized people can modify the e-records stored on data servers or any other media.
- There are record of changes made.
- Entry of e-records considered critical are checked by a designated person other than the one who made the records or checked by the system itself.
- Availability of a procedural control for cancellation, changes to the level of approval and for entering or editing e-records, including changing of personal passwords.

To keep the focus on the e-records integrity technical controls during the operational stage, the e-records integrity controls can be categorized in three spaces: e-records storage; e-records during processing; and e-records while in transit.* Refer to Figure 20.2.

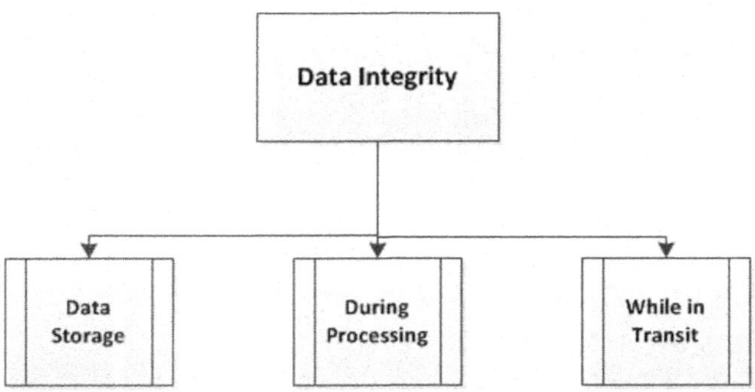

Figure 20.2 Data integrity.

* NIST SP 800-33. Underlying Technical Models for Information Technology Security, December 2001.

Computer System Retirement – E-Records Migration

The activities to migrate e-records as part of a computer system retirement are not different from the migration of e-records as part of the transfer of e-records to a new computer system, discussed previously.

E-records must be preserved as part of the planning to retire the computer system generating e-records.*

The e-records preservation plan must include one of the following options:

- Make sure that a new system will be able to retrieve e-records from previous systems.
- Preserve previous applications (not contemplated, the system is to be retired).
- Archive hard copies (when allowed).
- Completion of system documentation and validation dossier.

If archiving hard copies, computer records reproduced in paper copies, is the selected method to migrate the e-records, the paper copies must be certified as true copies of the original e-records, and the paper copies are to be signed and dated as verified true copies. All electronic metadata must be part also part of the fixed record. The verified hard copy must then be stored with other paper-based records.

After executing the e-records preservation plan, ensure that the quality assurance (QA) unit of the regulated user performs an audit on the preserved records. The audit will verify the traceability between planning and implementation, and will assess the successful execution of the preservation plan.

E-records migration must ensure the protection of e-records from deliberate or inadvertent alteration or loss. (Refer to Chapter 8)

E-Records Archiving†

In the context of e-records no longer active, these e-records are archived. This is considered a long retention environment.

E-records archiving is the process of moving e-records that are no longer actively used to a separate records storage device for long-term retention,

---

* CEFIC, API Committee. "Computer Validation Guide." December 2002.

† López, O. *Data Integrity in Pharmaceutical and Medical Devices Regulation Operations: Best Practices Guide to Electronic Records Compliance*, Chapter 13. Boca Ratón, Fl: CRC Press, 2016.

often disabling the e-records from any further changes. The retention period of these e-records has not been finalized.

The controls applicable to e-records in storage are also applicable to archived records.

The archiving process is an activity that may involve a modification of format, media, and/or physical storage. It must be performed in a controlled manner in accordance with a procedural control.

There are multiple types of archiving disposition:

- *Extract/Migrate* – The migration of digital information from one hardware/software configuration to another or from one generation of computer technology to a later one, offers one method of dealing with technological obsolescence. Data is extracted from the current system and moved to another location, or the entire instance is migrated elsewhere.
- *Host* – These are single-instance database systems that are not typically managed by the site and are hosted elsewhere.
- *Archive* – Will contain the following types:
    - Report – In this case, the official record is considered to be in hard copy currently or the most effective end state will become hard copy.
    - Physical to virtual (P2V) (Encapsulate) – In order to be able to access the e-record effectively, in some cases it is necessary to have both the application and the database in a virtual environment. Encapsulation is a technique for grouping together a digital object and anything else necessary to provide access to that object. In this case, software will be used to encapsulate the data and application and the product housed in a server designated for this purpose.
    - Technology emulation creates an environment that behaves in a hardware-like manner. It potentially offers substantial benefits in preserving the functionality and integrity of digital objects.
    - Keeping every version of software and hardware – the requirement for keeping every version of software and hardware, operating systems and manuals, as well as the retention of personnel with the relevant technology skills. This option makes the preservation of obsolete technologies to access the archived e-records unfeasible.

If the e-records in storage are transferred to another format, media or system, the archiving process must include verifications that the e-records are not altered in value and/or meaning during this migration process. The metadata must be also transferred and verified. Refer to "Data Migration" in this chapter.

The computer system holding the archived records must implement all security-related functions to restrict access to authorized person only. Periodically, archived records need to be verified for accessibility, readability, integrity, and the state of security control.

If changes are implemented to the computer infrastructure and/or application, then it is required to ensure and test the ability of the application to access the e-records.

E-records may be retained on archived media for a very long period of time. The procedure addressing the e-records in storage should also address the stability of the storage media itself.*

After completing the specified record retention requirements, the records can be physically deleted.

Each country has their particularity about each best practice discussed in this book. One example of such particularity is the clinical e-records archiving guidelines established in South Africa. In South Africa, e-records must be reproduced in hard copy, which are to be signed and dated as a verified accurate copy of the original data. The verified hard copy should then be stored with other paper-based records. This requirement in South Africa is established to overcome the possibility of loss or inability to read the information due to technological redundancy.†

The MHRA guidance document recommends that archive e-records should be locked such that they cannot be altered or deleted without detection and audit trail.

The archive arrangements must be designed to permit recovery and readability of the e-records and metadata throughout the required retention period.

E-Records Destruction

After meeting the approved retention time, the e-records are tagged to discard and removed according to an approved procedure. The record information that is purged typically includes content, metadata, audit trails, and any

---

* Brown, A. "Selecting Storage Media for Long-Term Preservation." The National Archives, DPGN-02, August 2008, www.nationalarchives.gov.uk/documents/selecting-storage-media.pdf.

† Department of Health, *Guidelines for Good Practice in the Conduct of Clinical Trials with Human Participants in South Africa*. Pretoria, South Africa, Section 6.7. Department of Health, 2006.

pointers to the record and connections to related records. The record must be eliminated as well in the retention environment.

Where a record is deleted prior to meeting its approved retention schedule, an audit trail of the deletion is good practice until the end of the approved retention period.

Current good practice also includes, as part of a company's records handling program, a periodic practice to revisit the approved retention of periods of specific records as business, regulatory or legal requirements change. It is important, from a legal perspective, to remember that record handling programs include defined provisions to temporarily suspend the execution of the purge process (including backup tapes) when records are part of a legal discovery process during a pending litigation.

Additional Readings

DOD 5015.2-STD. *Design Criteria Standard for Electronic Records Management Software Applications*, June 2002.

MHRA. *MHRA GMP Data Integrity Definitions and Guidance for Industry,* March 2018.

NIST SP 800-33. *Underlying Technical Models for Information Technology Security*, December 2001.

Pharmaceutical Inspection Cooperation Scheme (PIC/S). *Good Practices for Computerized Systems in "GxP" Regulated Environments*, PI 011-3, September 2007.

Chapter 21

Digital Date and Time Stamps

Introduction

In digital environments, a time stamp is an electronic record (e-record) enclosing the time of occurrence of an event. Time stamping* refers to the use of an electronic time stamp to provide an order among a set of events.

The US Food and Drug Administration (FDA) rely on that recording time as a critical component in documenting a sequence of events. Within a given manufacturing batch a number of events and operator actions may take place, and without recording time, documentation of those events would be incomplete.†

In addition, time stamps are used during the creation of audit trails. These time stamps allow for reconstruction of the course of events relating to the creation, modification, and deletion of e-records.

Consequently, for the better understanding of good data integrity practices (GDIP), the time stamping to e-records is a key service that supports, if properly controlled, nonrepudiation of transactions adding integrity to e-records.

System Clock

As part of the controls to e-records integrity, the system clock or networked master clock provides the date and time stamps required to e-records

* López, O. "Overview of Technologies Supporting Security Requirements in 21 CFR Part 11 – Part II." *Pharmaceutical Technology*, March 2002.

† US FDA. *21 CFR Part 11 – Electronic Records; Electronic Signatures; Final Rule – Preamble*, Comment 74, March 1997.

and e-signatures. Typically the networked master clock is placed in the time server.

An accurate system clock is a necessary condition for the reliability of manufacturing-related e-records, it is therefore necessary to guarantee its reliability for all the e-records at the basis of all decisions that impact the quality of manufacturing products.

E-records to be time-stamped are those loaded in database structures during the insertion or update of the e-records.

Date and time stamps (or "timestamps") create a notation that indicates, at least, the correct date and time of an action. It is recognized as a valuable service that supports nonrepudiation of transactions.

A precise system clock is a necessary condition for the consistency of the related information; it is therefore an element to assure the reliability for all the e-records.

Timestamps add integrity and trust to messages and records sent by means of a network. Therefore, as part of the e-records controls, unauthorized modifications to the system clock and time drift* between servers must be prevented.†

Refer to www.fda.gov/ICECI/EnforcementActions/WarningLetters/2017/ucm563067.htm. It accounts for a WL report containing an observation that includes unauthorized access and manipulation of the system clock.

When writing an application program, the programmer is usually provided with a time-stamping service that the operating system provides, if required, during the execution of the application.

Computer Clock Reliability

The reliability of the system's date and time can be achieved by synchronizing:

- The networked master clock with a reliable source
- All networked computer clocks using the master clock

In addition to the above synchronization practices, the reliability of the system clock is enhanced by maintaining programs to verify the correct functionality of the master and networked computer clocks.

* Time drift is when two or more servers do not have identical times. The discrepancy can vary from seconds to minutes and can become extensive if left unchecked.

† López, O. "Overview of Technologies Supporting Security Requirements in 21 CFR Part 11 – Part II." *Pharmaceutical Technology*, March 2002.

A time server accomplishes the above two functions by reading the actual time from a reference clock and distributes this information to its clients using a computer network.

Supplementary controls to create reliable computer clocks can be found at "Computer Clock Controls."

Digital Time-Stamping Service*

Supporting time controls include an infrastructure that supports time stamping from a trusted time such as the coordinated universal. This technology, which in some cases is compliant with X.509 (Public-Key Infrastructure Certificate and Certificate Revocation List (CRL) Profile), is linked with a time-calibration service. Applications or computer logs may require time-stamping services on the server.

One of many time-stamping services is the digital time-stamping service (DTS). DTS issues a secure time stamp, which includes the time, a hash of the digital information being time-stamped, and a time certification, that can be used for digital signatures. A message digest is produced from the record and sent to the DTS. The DTS sends back the time stamp, as well as the date and time the time stamp was received, with a secure signature. The signature proves that the document existed on the stated date. The document contents remain unknown to the DTS – only the digest is known. The DTS must use lengthy keys because the time stamp may be required for many years.

DTS and digital certificates provide the mechanism to authenticate the source (device checks) of the time stamp in the audit trails and electronic signatures. Access-right lists and digital certificates can be used to control access to the DTS.

The certificate server and client clocks must remain synchronized as closely as possible. Kerberos† recommended maximum tolerance settings for computer clock synchronization is five minutes. Kerberos uses time stamps to determine the validity of entities' authentication requests and to help prevent replay attacks.

It is expected the periodic coordination between the service with the local computer clock, and to limit the access of the computer date and time local

---

* López, O. "Overview of Technologies Supporting Security Requirements in 21 CFR Part 11 – Part II." *Pharmaceutical Technology*, March 2002.

† Kerberos (www.isi.edu/gost/info/Kerberos/) is an industry-standard authentication system suitable for distributed computing by means of a public network.

function. The local computer date and time function must not be accessed by users.

Time Zone

A time stamp should be expressed in a form that clearly indicates its frame of reference so that time stamps are universally comparable, apart from different time zones and seasonal adjustments. It allows for the discerning of the timing of one activity relative to another (e.g. time zone).

ISO 8601, *Data elements and interchange formats – Information interchange – Representation of dates and times*, can be implemented to avoid misinterpretation of the significance of date and time representation, resulting in confusion and other consequential errors or losses of the time across national boundaries.

Computer Systems Not Networked

In case of systems not networked, a process must be implemented for the manual update of the clock for equipment that performs time stamping of production e-records. This process must cover the preventive maintenance and updates in case of recovery of the system.

Computer Clock Controls

Controls should be established to ensure that the system's date and time are reliable in all computers connected to the local network.

Some of the critical controls are:

- Maintenance procedural controls are established to ensure the accurate synchronization of time and date to regulated activities
- Alteration of the time server used to synchronize all networked computer clocks to record timed events is controlled and limited for modifications to authorized personnel
- Recording of any changes to the time server
- Discerning of the timing of one activity relative to another (e.g. time zone controls)

- Unit of time must be meaningful in terms of documenting human actions. The unit of time must be specified in the requirements document
- Implementation of time stamps with a clear understanding of the time zone referenced used to systems that extent different time zone. The time zone references must be specified in the requirements document

Additional Readings

Information Security Committee American Bar Association. *Digital Signature Guidelines*, August 1996.

ISO 8601. *Data Elements and Interchange Formats – Information Interchange – Representation of Dates and Times*, 2004.

US FDA. *Guidance for Industry – Computerized Systems Used in Clinical Investigations*, May 2007.

US FDA. *Guidance for Industry – 21 CFR Part 11; Electronic Records; Electronic Signatures, Time Stamps*, February 2002 (obsoleted).

Chapter 22

New Technologies and Critical Processes

Access Management, Big Data, Cloud Environments, E-Records Integrity, Internet of Things (Iot), SLAs, and Wireless are areas in e-compliance that are under the scrutiny of the regulated user and regulatory agencies attention.

E-records integrity are primarily discussed in Chapters 14 through 16 and 20.

Access Management

Since maintaining data integrity is a primary objective of the CGMP principles, it is important that everyone associated with a computer system is aware of the necessity for the related security considerations. As a function related to security, e-records integrity service maintains information exactly as it was recorded and it is auditable to affirm its reliability.

The regulated entity must ensure that personnel are aware of the importance of data security, the procedures and system features that are available to provide appropriate security and the consequences of security gaps. Such system features could include routine surveillance of system access, the implementation of file verification routines, and exception and/or trend reporting.

Security controls must be established for all computer systems as a mean of ensuring e-records protection. Computer security is the principal enabler to create the integrity of e-records.

A number of unrelated regulated entities have had problems linked to the proper control over computer systems to prevent unauthorized changes in e-records. Usually, these regulated entity sites alter or delete critical e-records.

The system owner* is the person responsible for providing the records protection suitable controls over the application, infrastructure (e.g. network, database server) and database components. These record protection controls ensure that only authorized personnel can make changes to any component of the computer system and the security of the e-records residing on the system.

Security must be instituted at several levels. Procedural controls must govern the physical access to computer systems (physical security). As part of the physical security it must be considered security to devices used to store programs, such as tapes, disks, and magnetic strip cards. Refer to Chapter 14.

The access to individual computer system platforms is controlled by network specific security procedures (network security and database server). Access to these devices should be controlled (logical security).

Unnecessary networked services should be disabled and secured. Database software, like most operating systems and complex applications, provides a number of services that allow remote system management, distributed processing, and other network-related functions. In many cases, those services are enabled by default and are often "protected" by using either no password or a vendor-supplied default password.

As with applications and operating systems, database servers can also have vulnerabilities that lead to unauthorized e-records access, loss of e-records integrity, or total system compromise. To minimize the impact of vulnerabilities, eliminate known security vulnerabilities by keeping the database servers up-to-date with security patches released by vendors.

Without the ability to selectively grant access to a database and its data, arbitrary users can add and delete information at will. Even if access controls are enforced by web applications, e-records contained within the database are still at risk if a malicious user circumvents the web application and accesses the database directly. If possible, use database access controls that can restrict what users, groups of users, or applications can access or change the database.

* System Owner – The person responsible for the availability, and maintenance of a computerized system and for the security of the data residing on that system (EU Annex 11).

E-records security includes integrity, reliability, and availability of these records. During validation of a database or system, consideration should be given to:*

- Implementing procedures and mechanisms to ensure data security (e.g. user access to the e-records and user permissions to perform activities in the database) and keeping the meaning and logical arrangement of data
- Load-testing, taking into account future growth of the database and tools to monitor the saturation of the database
- Precautions for necessary migration of data (Annex 11-17) at the end of the life cycle of the system

Procedures and technical controls should be put in place to prevent the altering, browsing, querying, or reporting of e-records via external software applications that do not enter through the protective system software.

Finally, application level security and associated authority checks control the access to the computer system applications (applications security).

A defined procedure(s), at all levels, should be established for the issue, cancellation, and alteration of authorization to enter and amend, including changing of personal passwords.

Where a record is deleted prior to meeting its approved retention, an audit trail of the deletion is required until the end of the approved retention period.

It should be considered recording activities of unauthorized attempts to access the computer system and/or e-records storage devices.

In those cases that the use of an explicit terminal is critical as the source of data inputs or operational instructions entered by the user terminal verification may be implemented.

An example of a potential security issue is the elevated access level by the database administrator. The database administrator could alter e-records in the database table without any traceability of the modification(s) to these e-records.

The database system administrator can modify, without traceability, any field in signed records including the signature field, time stamp and reason for

* European Medicines Agency (EMA). "Questions and answers: Good manufacturing practice: Annex 11 Computerised Systems Question 4." GMP/GDP Compliance. www.ema.europa.eu/ema/index.jsp?curl=pages/regulation/q_and_a/q_and_a_detail_000027.jsp&mid=WC0b01ac05800296ca#section9.

the signature. It should be ensured that electronic signatures applied to electronic record are valid all over the storage period of the e-records and documents. The updated signature will make the complete e-record invalid and the signature will not be permanently linked to the signed record.

There are three possibilities to fix the above example:

- Implement procedural control to maintain the segregation of duties,* including not allowing record changes by the system administrator. In addition, all modification to the records, each record must be submitted for electronic re-approval.
- Implement database software that provides audit trail capabilities at all access levels, including the database administrator. Establish procedural controls to maintain the segregation of duties, including not allowing record changes by the system administrator.
- Incorporate digital technologies (e.g. hashing†) to the database software. A minor change in the e-record will result in a change in the output of the hashing. An automated service verifies the original hashing and the calculated hashing, reporting any change to the hashing and, invalidating the record and associated signature if applicable.

Use all of the capabilities provided in the database to restrict the database administrator's access to any features beyond account management (and possibly configuration controls), your procedures and training materials.

During the validation of a database system, considerations should be given to implementing procedures and mechanisms to ensure data security and segregation of duties. The implementation of these procedures and mechanisms must be verified and/or tested.

Upon placing the e-records in retention environments, the same level of e-records security of which is controlled throughout their earlier life cycle, still needs to be maintained.

The Federal Information Processing Standards Publication (FIPS PUB) 199, "Standards for Security Categorization of Federal Information and Information Systems", is a security categorization standard for information and information systems. It is another method to perform a risk assessment.

---

* Segregation of duties: A process that divides roles and responsibilities so that a single individual cannot subvert a critical process.

† López, O. "Overview of Technologies Supporting Security Requirements in 21 CFR Part 11 – Part I." *Pharmaceutical Technology*, February 2002.

Big Data*

Big Data is the process of collecting large amounts of data and immediate analysis to find hidden information, recurring patterns, new correlations, and so on.

- The data set is so large and complex that traditional means of processing are ineffective.
- Additional challenges: analyzing, capturing, collecting, searching, sharing, storing, transferring, visualizing, etc.,
- Protection of personal data.
- The size to accommodate the entire process has been steadily increasing in order to be able to collect and integrate all the information.

In the context of Figure 22.1, e-records are stored in Data Warehouses. These are central repositories (e.g. databases (DBs)) of integrated data from one or more disparate sources. These sources are depicted in the figure as "operational applications".

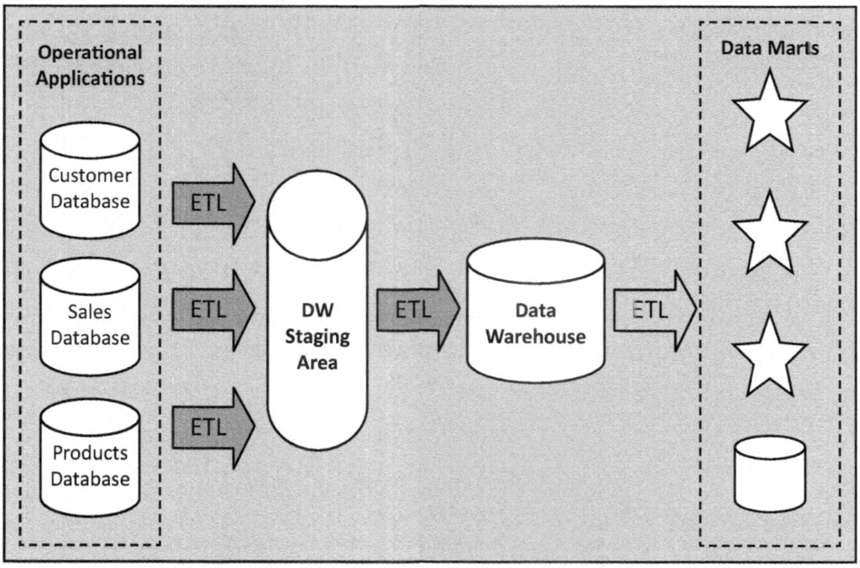

Figure 22.1 Sample Big Data environment.

* López, O. "Electronic Records Integrity in a Data Warehouse and Business Intelligence." *Journal of Validation Technology Compliance*, 22(2) 2016.

From the context of Big Data, the raw data* is extracted from its operational application or source repositories locations; may be processed/transformed by applying a series of rules or functions; the raw data is converted to data;† and then the data loaded into a final set of tables, "Data Marts," for the consumption of the users.

A data mart‡ is the access layer of the Data Warehouse environment that is used to get data out to the users. The data mart is a subset of the data warehouse that is usually oriented to a specific business line or team. Data marts are small slices of the data warehouse.

Similar to the figure in this section, the most common form of data integration is:

- Copy source data in DBs (warehouse) and keep it up-to-date. The usual method to copy the source data into the DBs is periodic reconstruction of the warehouse, usually overnight.
- Perform integration of data and store in the warehouse.
- For rapid access, a specific business line data is placed in the data mart usually oriented for consumption by a specific business line or team.

The e-records controls discussed in this book ensure that the data in the warehouse repositories, extracted raw data, transformed data, and loaded data are managed only by the relevant approved controls and/or validated software applications under a controlled infrastructure. These controls provide the trustworthy system§ environment required to manage e-records in support to GMPs related decisions.

The data acquisition process for Big Data storage uses standard technologies and procedures that replicate automatically each single byte of data in several locations. Some providers also guarantee the automatic reproduction in three different geographically separated data centers.

---

* Raw data: Original record (data) which can be described as the first-capture of information, whether recorded on paper or electronically (MHRA).

† Data: Facts, figures and statistics collected together for reference or analysis. All original records and true copies of original records, including source data and metadata and all subsequent transformations and reports of these data, that are generated or recorded at the time of the GxP activity and allow full and complete reconstruction and evaluation of the GxP activity. (MHRA).

‡ A data mart is the access layer of the data warehouse environment that is used to get data out to the users. The data mart is a subset of the data warehouse that is usually oriented to a specific business line or team. Data marts are small slices of the data warehouse.

§ López, O. "Trustworthy Computer Systems." *Journal of GxP Compliance,* 19(2) 2015.

The relevance of Big Data has motivated the European Medicines Agency (EMA) to establish on March 23, 2017, a taskforce to evaluate the use of Big Data to support pharmaceutical research, innovation, and development.*

Cloud Environments†

The cloud computing practice uses a network of remote servers hosted on the Internet to store, manage, and process e-records, rather than a local server or a personal computer.

Figure 22.2 provides a pictorial view of the typical models in cloud environments. In each model the dark colored portion relates the elements controlled by the cloud service provider.

A cloud service provider‡ is a company that offers some component of cloud computing, typically Infrastructure as a Service (IaaS), Software as a Service (SaaS) or Platform as a Service (PaaS), to other businesses or individuals.

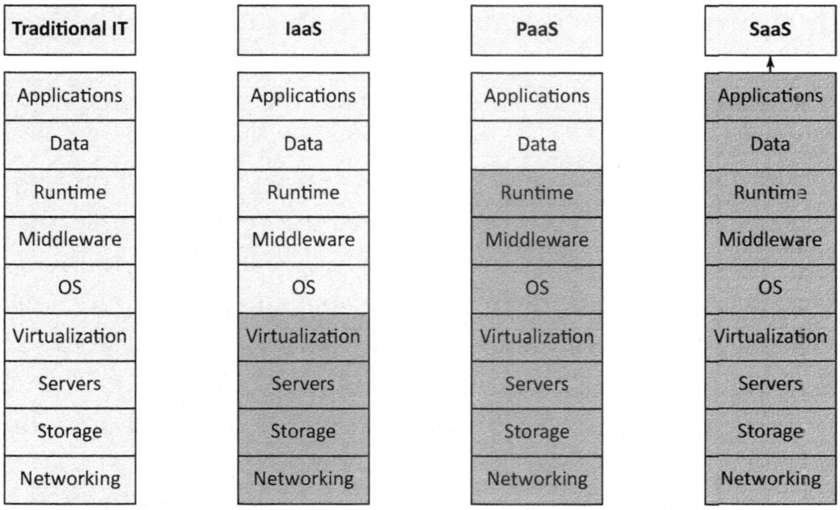

Figure 22.2 Cloud service models versus traditional IT (All).

* www.pharmtech.com/ema-creates-taskforce-big-data-0 and http://www.ema.europa.eu/ema/index.jsp?curl=pages/news_and_events/news/2017/03/news_detail_002718.jsp&mid=WC0b01ac058004d5c1.

† López, O. "Electronic Records and Cloud Computing" in *Best Practices Guide to Electronic Records Compliance*. Boca Raton, FL: CRC Press, 2017; 193–199.

‡ Service provider: An organization supplying services to one or more internal or external customers (ITIL Service Design, 2011 Edition).

IaaS: A virtual data center environment including servers, databases, network, storage, and so on, hosted at the cloud service provider's facility.

PaaS: A development environment for software application hosting by the cloud service provider who provide tools, programming codes, interface modules, and so on, that allows IT professionals to develop software applications and integrate them together in the cloud infrastructure environment either hosted by the service provider or contracted to another provider.

SaaS: Software application hosted by the cloud service provider in order to perform functions or processes. In this model a regulated user uses a vendor's software application from a web browser or program interface. The regulated user does not manage or control the underlying cloud infrastructure; including the network, servers, operating systems, storage, or application capabilities; with the possible exception of application configuration settings.

Business Process as a Service (BPaaS) is a new but popular model for cloud services where the cloud service provider takes full responsibility for not only the design, management, and control of its software application but also the operation of the business process on behalf of the client company.

From the perspective of the regulated user, the most complex scenario is the BPaaS model.

Where the regulated user chooses to outsource cloud computing, that can affect product conformity with requirements, the regulated user shall ensure control and hold responsibility for the suitability and operability over such computer-related service. Control of such outsourced computer-related service shall be identified within the quality management system* and clear statement of the responsibilities of the cloud service provider. The statement of responsibilities is defined in a formal contract/technical agreement (e.g. SLA).

The regulated user should ensure that GMP e-records ownership, governance and accessibility are included in the SLA (*MHRA Data Integrity Guideline and Definitions*, March 2018).

The way to achieve such regulated user controls over the cloud service provider is by defining clear regulated user requirements, all-inclusive vendor assurance program, comprehensive selection of the cloud service

* ISO 9001. *Quality Management Systems – Requirements*, Section 4.1, 2008.

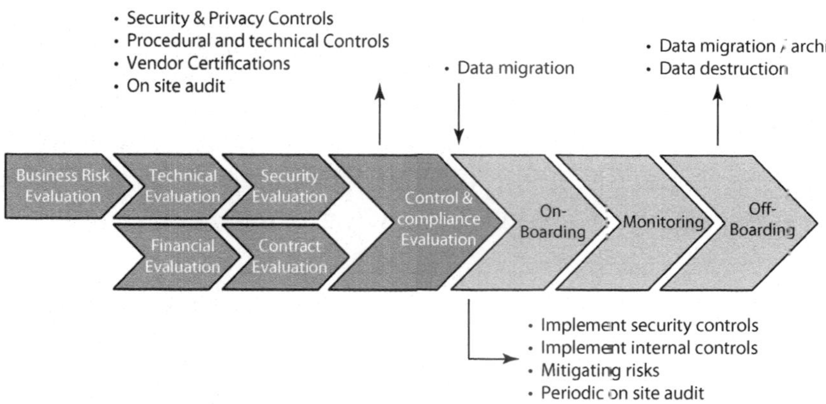

Figure 22.3 On boarding and monitoring cloud program.

provider, all-inclusive SLA between the regulated user and the cloud service provider, and periodic evaluation to the cloud service providers. Refer to Figure 22.3.

As part of the vendor assurance program, the regulated user should also perform a data governance review (*MHRA Data Integrity Guideline and Definitions*, March 2018).

In the context of EMA Annex 11, Figure 22.4 provides a pictorial view of the items that the regulated user and the cloud service supplier need to

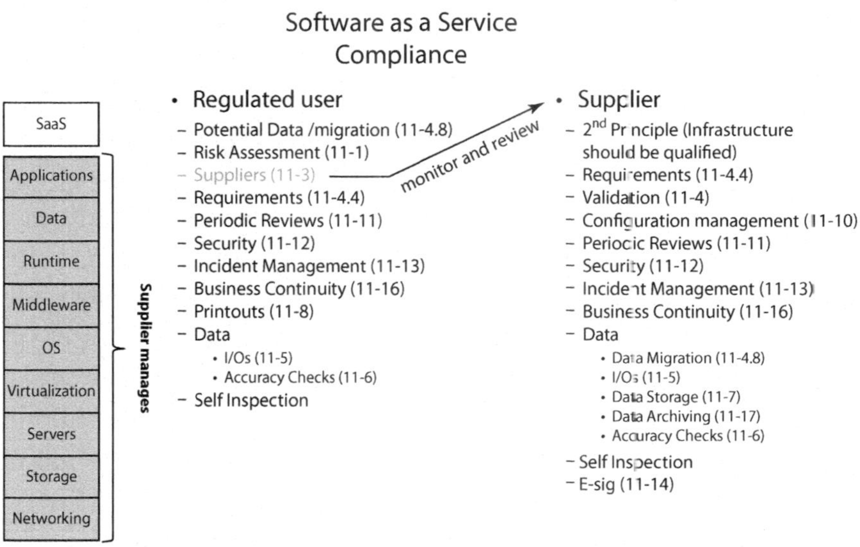

Figure 22.4 SaaS cloud compliance.

comply in a cloud environment. Note that during the operation of the system, the assurance contact points between the regulated user and the supplier are the periodic audits to the cloud computing supplier and the associated environment.

All the e-records integrity controls referenced somewhere else in this book are particularly applicable to the cloud environments.

Internet of Things

The IoT is changing manufacturing as we know it, together with improving manufacturing efficiency.

In the context of manufacturing, the IoT is the network of physical devices, automated guidance vehicles (AGVs), and other manufacturing items embedded with electronics, software, sensors, actuators, and network connectivity which enables these objects to connect and exchange data.

Through sensors and actuators linked through wired and wireless networks via the Internet Protocol, manufacturing plants are getting connected. This interconnectivity can provide processes that govern themselves, smart products can take corrective action to avoid damages, where individual parts are automatically replenished, and tracking products as they move through the supply chain.

In addition, this interconnection can provide data to evaluate the manufacturing plant workflows, including predicting maintenance needs before equipment breaks.

The validation of these systems comprises the qualification of the infrastructure and the associated interfaces to make the e-records flow in a reliable matter.

EU Annex 11-5 is key in IoT. If e-records are exchanged electronically, there should be a verification for the correct computer inputs and outputs (I/Os). The correct I/Os ensures the secure exchange of data between systems and, furthermore, correct inputs on the processing of data. These built-in checks mitigate any interface error.

The built-in check is the mechanism that can ensure the authenticity and integrity of data transmissions, and the mutual trust between communicating parties.

Networks using the Internet Protocol shall employ procedures and controls designed to ensure the integrity e-records in transit.

Service Level Agreements

Service providers are all parties who provide any services irrespective of whether they belong to an independent (external) enterprise, to the same company group/structure, or an internal service unit.

When service providers are providing any services (e.g. installing, configuring, integrating, validating, maintaining, modifying, or retaining a computer system or related service or for data processing), formal agreements must exist between the manufacturer and any third parties providing such services. (EU Annex 11-3.1)

These agreements outline a clear statement of the responsibilities and activities between the third parties and by the regulated entity.

The information technology (IT) department in the regulated entity should be considered a third party in the context of supporting activities provided to the regulated application and infrastructure (EU Annex 11-3.1).

As applicable, the information to be contained in the service level agreement may include:

- E-records ownership
- Transactional system data errors
- Business continuity
- Incidents/problems
- Change control
- Inspection readiness
- Interface monitoring
- Periodic reviews
- Security management
- System maintenance/outages
- System retirement
- Metadata management
- Documentation
- Training
- Records retention
- Other areas

Even the service level agreement provides the responsibility to execute the supporting activities to the service provider, the regulated entity continues to hold responsibility for the suitability and operability of the computer systems and the integrity of the e-records.

Reference

- US FDA. *Contract Manufacturing Arrangements for Drugs: Quality Agreements Guidance for Industry*, November 2016.

Wireless*

Bluetooth, Wi-Fi, radiofrequency, and so on, are typical wireless environments in which manufacturing-related data may be transported.

As an example in this section, I will use A Wireless LAN (WLAN).

WLAN is another type of media used to provide network connectivity to the local LAN and its resources. It serves the same purpose as the typical 'wired' LAN environment that most business locations use.

The major difference between the two network environments is that the wireless device accesses the network via a shared radio frequency band instead of using a physical cable and jack that is typically via a switched ethernet connection.

The implementation of wireless networking also has potential regulatory implications. Validated applications may use the wireless LAN data connectivity for the transmission of CGMP e-records. To protect the reliability of CGMP e-records, wireless security measures such as authentication and encryption must be implemented, and the proper implementation of these security measures shall require documented verification.

There is available various wireless networking standards: 802.11, Bluetooth, and HipeLAN/ 1 and 2.

802.11 and HiperLAN/2 are the most common standards for wireless LANs.

The wireless network still utilizes the existing network topology to accomplish its purpose of providing network connectivity. A wireless access point (AP) is physically cabled to a LAN switch and acts as a translator between the wired and wireless worlds. This access point links the wireless data devices to the physical hardwired network. A wireless data device is one that transmits and receives data between an AP and itself via a radio frequency.

Triple data encryption standard (DES) through a VPN tunnel is the method chosen for enterprise WLAN's, which is the same method used for remote

* López, O. "Qualification of Wireless Services" in *Computer Infrastructure Qualification for FDA Regulated Industries*. Bethesda, MD: PDA and DHI Publishing, LLC, 2006; 129–132.

access. The VPN tunnel is established between the wireless device and a local VPN Server to provide secure protection for all data transferred on VPN secured WLAN.

The intermediary devices (routers and/or switches) that are used to pass the tunnel traffic are typically unaware of the content, and pass the data along without performance impact.

The following illustration is a high-level drawing that depicts the key components involved with a basic wireless LAN connection for enterprise WLAN environments. The level of technological complexity can increase by varying amounts depending on the type of facility and the amount of wireless data networking coverage that is being provided.

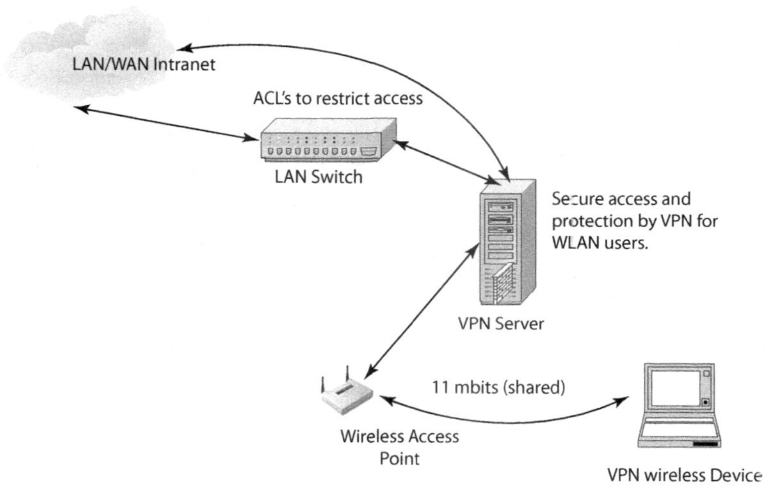

WLAN Devices

Access Point

An access point (AP) is a communication hub for users of a wireless device to connect to a wired LAN. The AP acts as a bridge for the clients and extends the physical range of service a wireless user has access to. There is an IP address for management configuration of the AP. The base stations typically have an SNMP* agent for remote management.

* SNMP: Short for Simple Network Management Protocol. It is a set of protocols for managing complex networks. SNMP works by sending messages, called protocol data units (PDUs), to different parts of a network. SNMP-compliant devices, called agents, store data about themselves in management information bases (MIBs) and return this data to the SNMP requesters.

The AP can be implemented as a hardware device or a computer's software.

At the wireless device a network interface adapter is installed with the purpose to work with the AP devices. The adapter shall be configured for data encryption to enable user-based authentication.

The qualification of hubs can be found in chapter 12, Qualification of LAN Devices.

VPN Server

A VPN Server provides the termination point with the client for the VPN session. This device encrypts and decrypts data and manages the session authentication process. It also verified that the wireless LAN components provide reliable and secure data communications based on the standard configuration.

A VPN Server qualification consist of:

- Verification of the installation and functionality of the system-level software associated with the VPN Server.
- Verification of the VPN Server, application servers and service components qualification.
- Testing of the services provided by the VPN Server.

LAN Switch

This switch interacts with the domain server and the access point device to authenticate the wireless user prior to granting access to the network.

A LAN switch qualification consist of confirming that the LAN switch provides a reliable authentication service based on the standard configuration.

WLAN System Qualification

A WLAN system qualification consists of:

- Verifying that the WLAN components were qualified.
- Verifying the availability of the WLAN diagrams.
- Verifying the training of WLAN supporting operators.
- Verifying that the data integrity and network security is not compromised.
- Verifying that the VPN remote access services (RAS). Refer to Chapter 17.

Data Integrity in Wireless Environments

If data integrity is defined as the "property that data have not been altered in an unauthorized manner" and it "covers data in storage, during processing, and while in transit." The "while in transit" provides the criteria that must be met for data to have remained unaltered while moving wirelessly from one point to another.

The following criteria to take into account are: qualification of infrastructure; built-in checks; and accuracy checks.*

- *Qualification of Infrastructure.*

  Refer to Chapter 17.
- *Built-in Checks.*

  The correct I/Os ensures the secure exchange of data between systems and, furthermore, correct inputs on the processing of data. These built-in checks maximize the mitigation associated with I/Os errors.

  Built-in checks as described in the Annex 11-5, includes the transmission integrity and transmission confidentiality. Transmission integrity guards against improper information modification or destruction while in transit. The implementation of the transmission integrity may be by encryption.

  The impact on network-based technologies is that insufficient error checking at the point of transaction entry can result in incorrect transaction processing and data integrity risks. Integrity can be lost when data is processed incorrectly, or when transactions are incorrectly handled due to errors or delayed processing.

  The built-in check is the mechanism that can ensure the authenticity, integrity, and confidentiality of transmissions, and the mutual trust between communicating parties.
- *Accuracy Checks.*

  Critical data transferred between computer systems or from a computer system to paper, the verification of accuracy can be performed by a second person or, if the system is properly validated, by the computer system itself.

  The impact on network-based technologies is that insufficient error checking at the point of transaction entry can result in incorrect transaction processing and data integrity risks. Integrity can be lost when data

* López, O. A computer data integrity compliance model. *Pharmaceutical Engineering*, March/April 2015.

is processed incorrectly, or when transactions are incorrectly handled due to errors or delayed processing.

In the context of the computer system check, verification is one that is programmed in to the background of the data entry and configured to ensure the accuracy of the data input. This could be specific checks on data format, ranges, or values.

Chapter 23

All Together

As indicated in Chapter 6, the typical SLC, Figure 23.1,* includes the following periods:

- Conceptualization
- Development
- Operational Life:
  - Early Operational Life
  - Maturity
  - Aging

Each period in the SLC must be controlled to maximize the likelihood that the finished computer system meets all requirements such as: quality, regulatory, safety, functional, non-functional, and so on. If an SLC approach is applied properly, no additional work will be required to complete the validation of the computer system. The SLC is a dynamic element of a broad CSV.

The SLC tasks to be executed depend of who initiates or performs the development, operation, or maintenance of a computer system. These primary

* Herr, R. R., and Wyrick, M. L. "A Globally Harmonized Glossary of Terms for Communicating Computer Validation Key Practices." *PDA Journal of Pharmaceutical Science and Technology,* 53(2) 1999; 97–103.

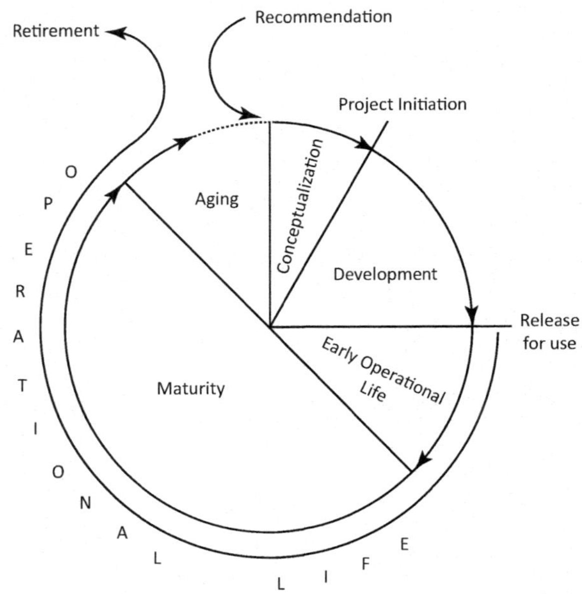

Figure 23.1 System life cycle.

parties are the acquirer,* the supplier,† the developer,‡ the operator,§, ¶ and the maintainer** of computer system products.

The following defines each primary SLC process and the activities associated with the process. These primary SLC processes are original from the ISO12207:1995, "Information Technology – Software Life Cycle Processes". Even though there is an updated version of the ISO12207, I selected these classifications to cluster the activities per primary process.

Acquisition Process

The Acquisition Process defines the activities of the acquirer, the organization that acquires a system, software product, or service.

The regulated user gives up SLC control, but still bears the responsibility for the continued safe and effective performance of the medical device. This

* Acquirer: An organization that acquires or procures a system, software product, or software service from a supplier (ISO 12207:1995).

† Supplier: An organization that enters into a contract with the acquirer for the supply of a system, software product, or software service under the terms of the contract (ISO 12207:1995).

‡ Developer: An organization that performs development activities (including requirements analysis, design, testing through acceptance) during the software life cycle process (ISO 12207:1995).

§ Operator: An organization that operates the system (ISO 12207:1995).

¶ Regulated user: The regulated Good Practice entity, that is responsible for the operation of a computer system and the applications, files and data held thereon (PIC/S PI 011-3).

** Maintainer: An organization that performs maintenance activities (ISO 12207:1995).

risk can be mitigated by supplier audit(s) recording the supplier SLC and by implementing accordingly.

This process consists of the following activities:

- Initiation.
  - Conceptualization Period.
  - Requirements gathering.
  - Document and execute an acquisition plan.
- Request-for-proposal preparation, distribution, analysis of response, selection of supplier.
- Contract preparation and update.
- Supplier monitoring:

  Project management and technical levels reviews are held throughout the life of the contract. In addition, audits are performed for determining compliance with the requirements, plans, and contract as appropriate.
- Acceptance and completion:

  An acceptance review and acceptance testing of the deliverable software product or service and will accept it from the supplier when all acceptance conditions are satisfied. After acceptance, the acquirer should take the responsibility for the configuration management of the delivered software product.

Supply Process

The Supply Process contains the activities and tasks of the supplier.

This process consists of the following activities:

- *Initiation:*

  The supplier conducts a review of requirements in the request for proposal taking into account organizational policies and other regulations. The supplier makes a decision to bid or accept the contract.
- *Preparation of response:*

  The supplier should define and prepare a proposal in response to the request for proposal, including its recommended tailoring.
- *Contract:*

  The supplier negotiates and enters into a contract with the acquirer organization to provide the software product or service. The supplier may request modification to the contract as part of the change control mechanism.

- *Planning:*

  The supplier conducts a review of the acquisition requirements to define the framework for managing and assuring the project and for assuring the quality of the deliverable software product or service. In addition, planning may establish requirements assuring the quality of the project and of the deliverable software product or service. Requirements for the plans should include resource needs and acquirer involvement.

  Once the planning requirements are established, the supplier considers the options for developing the software product or providing the software service, against an analysis of risks associated with each option.

  The supplier develops and documents project management plan(s) based upon the planning requirements and selected options.

- *Execution and control:*

  The supplier implements and executes the project management plan(s).

  The supplier shall monitor and control the progress and the quality of the software products or services of the project throughout the contracted life cycle. This shall be an ongoing, iterative task, which shall provide for:

  - Monitoring progress of technical performance, costs, and schedules and reporting of project status;
  - Problem identification, recording, analysis, and resolution.

    If applicable, the supplier manages and controls the subcontractors in accordance with the acquisition process.

    The supplier interface with the independent verification, validation, or test agent as specified in the contract and project plans. In addition, the supplier interface with other parties as specified in the contract and project plans.

- *Review and evaluation:*

  The supplier coordinates contract review activities, interfaces, and communication with the acquirer's organization.

  The supplier conducts or supports the informal meetings, acceptance review, acceptance testing, joint reviews, and audits with the acquirer as specified in the contract and project plans.

The supplier performs verification and validation to demonstrate that the software products or services and processes fully satisfy their respective requirements.

The supplier makes available to the acquirer the reports of evaluation, reviews, audits, testing, and problem resolutions as specified in the contract.

The supplier provides the acquirer access to the supplier's and, as applicable, subcontractor's facilities for review of software products or services as specified in the contract and project plans.

The supplier performs quality assurance activities.

- *Delivery and completion:*

  The supplier delivers the software product or service as specified in the contract. The supplier provides assistance to the acquirer in support of the delivered software product or service as specified in the contract.

Development Process

The Development Process contains the activities and tasks of the developer. The process contains the activities for requirements analysis, design, coding, integration, testing, and installation and acceptance related to the computer systems. It may contain system-related activities if stipulated in the contract. The developer performs or supports the activities in this process in accordance with the contract.

This process consists of the activities of a typical development methodology (refer to Chapter 6).

Operation Process

Refer to Chapter 12.

Maintenance Process

Refer to Chapter 12.

Core Principle

Software validation takes place within the environment of an established software life cycle. The software life cycle contains software engineering tasks and documentation necessary to support the software validation effort. In addition, the software life cycle contains specific verification and validation tasks that are appropriate for the intended use of the software. This guidance does not recommend any particular life cycle models – only that they should be selected and used for a software development project.

(FDA, General Principles of Software Validation; Guidance for Industry and FDA Staff. [January 11, 2002], www.fda.gov/cdrh/comp/guidance/938.html)

Appendix I: Glossary of Terms

For additional terms, refer to the *Glossary of Computerized System and Software Development Terminology*;* "A Globally Harmonized Glossary of Terms for Communicating Computer Validation Key Practices",† EudraLex, "Good Manufacturing Practice (GMP) Guidelines – Glossary" (Volume 4),‡ and the *MHRA GMP Data Integrity Definitions and Guidance for Industry* (March 2018).

For the purpose of this glossary, the terms and definitions given in 9000-3 and ISO 12207 are applicable. In the event of a conflict in terms and definitions, the terms and definitions specified in this glossary and the references in the first paragraph above apply.

Abstraction: This is a basic principle of software engineering, and enables understanding of the application and its design, and the management of complexity.

Acceptance criteria: The criteria that a system or component must satisfy to be accepted by a user, customer, or other authorized entity. (IEEE)

Acceptance test: Testing conducted to determine whether a system satisfies its acceptance criteria and to enable the customer to determine whether to accept the system. (IEEE)

Access: The ability or opportunity to gain knowledge of stored information. (DOD 5015.2-STD)

* FDA. *Glossary of Computerized System and Software Development Terminology*, Division of Field Investigations, Office of Regional Operations, Office of Regulatory Affairs, August 1995.

† Herr, R. R. and Wyrick, M. L. "A Globally Harmonized Glossary of Terms for Communicating Computer Validation Key Practices." *PDA Journal of Pharmaceutical Science and Technology*, 53(2) 1999; 97–103.

‡ http: //ec.europa.eu/health/files/eudralex/vol-4/pdfs-en/glos4en200408_en.pdf.

Accuracy: It refers to whether the data values stored for an object are the correct values. To be correct, a data values must be the right value and must be represented in a consistent and unambiguous form.

Acquirer: An organization that acquires or procures a system, software product or software service from a supplier. (ISO 12207: 1995*)

Application: Software installed on a defined platform/hardware providing specific functionality. (EMA Annex 11)

Application developer: See Software developer.

Approver(s): In the context of configuration management, the approver is the person(s) responsible for evaluating the recommendations of the reviewers of deliverable documentation, and for rendering a decision on whether to proceed with a proposed change and initiating the implementation of a change request.

Archive: Long-term, permanent retention of completed data and relevant metadata in its final form for the purposes of reconstruction of the process or activity.

Assessment: Investigation of processes, systems, or platforms by a subject matter expert or by IT quality and compliance. An assessment does not need to be independent in contrast to audit.

Audit: An independent examination of a software product, software process, or set of software processes to assess compliance with specifications, standards, contractual agreements, or other criteria. (IEEE)

Auditor: In the context of configuration management, the auditor is the person responsible for reviewing the steps taken during a development or change management process to ensure that the appropriate procedures have been followed.

Audit trail: (1) An electronic means of auditing the interactions with records within an electronic system so that any access to the system can be documented as it occurs for identifying unauthorized actions in relation to the records, e.g. modification, deletion, or addition. (DOD 5015.2-STD) (2) GMP audit trails are metadata that are a record of GMP critical information (for example the change or deletion of GMP relevant data). (MHRA)

Authentication: Verifying the identity of a user, process, or device, often as a prerequisite to allowing access to resources in an information system. (NIST Special Publication 800-18)

* Note: The 1995 revision is not the most recent version.

Authenticity: The property of being genuine and being able to be verified and trusted; confidence in the validity of a transmission, a message, or message originator. See authentication. (NIST Special Publication 800-18)

Automated systems: A broad range of systems including, but not limited to, automated manufacturing equipment, automated laboratory equipment, process control, manufacturing execution, clinical trials data management, and document management systems. The automated system consists of the hardware, software, and network components, together with the controlled functions and associated documentation. Automated systems are sometimes referred to as computerized systems. (PICS CSV PI 011-3*)

Availability: Ensuring timely and reliable access to and use of information. (44 U.S.C., SEC. 3542)

Backup: A copy of current (editable) data, metadata and system configuration settings (variable settings which relate to an analytical run) maintained for the purpose of disaster recovery. (MHRA)

Baseline: An agreed description of the attributes of a product, at a-point in-time, which serves as a basis for defining change. A "change" is a movement from this baseline state to a next state.

Bespoke computerized system: A computerized system individually designed to suit a specific business process. (EMA Annex 11)

Best practices: Practices established by experience and common sense.

Biometrics: Are methods of identifying a person's identify based on physical measurements of an individual's physical characteristics or repeatable actions. Some examples of biometrics include identifying a user based on a physical signature, fingerprints, and so on.

Business continuity plan: A plan describing how business processes will continue, respond or recover in the event of a disruption. The plan will include preparedness to meet and address emergencies and threats based on the business' prioritization of those business processes.

Calibration: Set of operations that establish, under specified conditions, the relationship between values of quantities indicated by a measuring instrument or measuring system, or values represented by a material measure or a reference material, and the corresponding values realized by standards. (PICS CSV PI 011-3)

---

* Pharmaceutical Inspection Cooperation Scheme (PIC/S). *Good Practices for Computerized Systems in "GxP" Regulated Environments*, PI 011-3, September 2007.

Certificate: Certificates are used to verify the identity of an individual, organization, web server, or hardware device. They are also used to ensure nonrepudiation in business transactions, as well as to enable confidentiality through the use of public-key encryption.

Certification authority: As part of a public-key infrastructure (PKI), an authority in a network that issues and manages from a certificate server security credentials and public-key for message encryption and decryption. (NARA)

Certified copy: (1) A copy of original information that has been verified, as indicated by a dated signature, as an exact copy having all of the same attributes and information as the original. (Source: FDA, "Electronic Source Data in Clinical Investigations", September 2013) (2) A copy of original information that has been verified as an exact (accurate and complete) copy having all of the same attributes and information as the original. The copy may be verified by a dated signature or by a validated electronic process. (Source: CDISC [Clinical Data Interchange Standards Consortium] "Clinical Research Glossary", Version 8.0, December 2009)

Change: Any variation or alteration in form, state or quality. It includes: additions, deletions, or modifications impacting the hardware or software components used that affect operational integrity, service level agreements, or the validated status of applications on the system.

Change control: A formal system by which qualified representatives of appropriate disciplines review proposed or actual changes that might affect the validated status of facilities, systems, equipment or processes. The intent is to determine the need for action that would ensure and document that the system is maintained in a validated state. (EMA Annex 15, Qualification and Validation)

Cipher: Series of transformations that converts plaintext to cipher text using the cipher key.

Cipher key: Secret cryptography key that is used by the key expansion routine to generate a set of round keys.

Cipher text: Data output from the cipher or input to the inverse cipher.

Clear printed: Printouts that apart from the values themselves, the units and the respective context can also be seen in the printout. ("Q&As on Annex 11", *Journal for GMP and Regulatory Affairs*, Issue 8, April/May 2012)

Cloud computing: It is the practice of using a network of remote servers hosted on the Internet to store, manage, and process data, rather than a local server or a personal computer.

Code audit: An independent review of source code by a person, team, or tool to verify compliance with software design documentation and programming standards. Correctness and efficiency may also be evaluated. (IEEE)

Code of Federal Regulations: The codification of the general and permanent rules published in the Federal Register by the executive departments and agencies of the US Federal Government.

Code inspection: A manual (formal) testing (error detection) technique where the programmer reads source code, statement by statement, to a group who ask questions analyzing the program logic, analyzing the code with respect to a checklist of historically common programming errors, and analyzing its compliance with coding standards. This technique can also be applied to other software and configuration items. (Myers/NBS)

Code review: A meeting at which software code is presented to project personnel, managers, users, customers, or other interested parties for comment or approval. (IEEE)

Code walkthrough: A manual testing (error detection) technique where program (source code) logic (structure) is traced manually (mentally) by a group with a small set of test cases, while the state of program variables is manually monitored, to analyze the programmer's logic and assumptions. (FDA *Glossary of Computerized System and Software Development Technology* [8/95])

Commercial of the shelf software: Software commercially available, whose fitness for use is demonstrated by a broad spectrum of users. (EMA Annex 11)

Commissioning: Refer to "Site acceptance testing". (SAT)

Competent: Having the necessary experience and/or training to adequately perform the job

Completeness: The property that all necessary parts of the entity in question are included. Completeness of a product is often used to express the fact that all requirements have been met by the product.

Complexity: In the context of this book, complexity means the degree to which a system or component has a design or implementation that is difficult to understand and verify.

Compliance: Compliance covers the adherence to application-related standards or conventions or regulations in laws and similar prescriptions. Fulfillment of regulatory requirements.

Compliant system: A system that meets applicable guidelines and predicate rule requirements.

Computer: (1) A functional unit that can perform substantial computations, including numerous arithmetic operations and logical operations without human intervention. (2) Hardware components and associated software design to perform specific functions.

Computer system: (1) A system including the input of data, electronic processing, and the output of information to be used either for reporting or automatic control. (PICS CSV PI 011-3) (2) A functional unit, consisting of one or more computers and associated peripheral input and output devices, and associated software, that uses common storage for all or part of a program and also for all or part of the data necessary for the execution of the program; executes user-written or user-designated programs; performs user-designated data manipulation, including arithmetic operations and logic operations; and that can execute programs that modify themselves during their execution. A computer system may be a stand-alone unit or may consist of several interconnected units. (ANSI)

Computer systems validation: (1) The formal assessment and reporting of quality and performance measures for all the life cycle stages of software and system development, its implementation, qualification and acceptance, operation, modification, re-qualification, maintenance, and retirement. This should enable both the regulated user and competent authority to have a high level of confidence in the integrity of both the processes executed within the controlling computer system(s) and in those processes controlled by and/or linked to the computer system(s), within the prescribed operating environment(s). (PICS CSV PI 011-3*) (2) Documented evidence which provides a high degree of assurance that a computerized system analyses, controls, and records data correctly and that data processing complies with predetermined specifications. (WHO)

Computerized process: A process where some or all of the actions are controlled by a computer.

Computerized system: (1) A system controlled partially or totally by a computer. (2) See "Automated systems".

---

* Pharmaceutical Inspection Cooperation Scheme (PIC/S). *Good Practices for Computerized Systems in "GxP" Regulated Environments*, PI 011-3, September 2007.

Computer validation: Refer to "Computer systems validation"*

Concurrent validation: In some cases, a drug product or medical device may be manufactured individually or on a one-time basis. The concept of prospective or retrospective validation as it relates to those situations may have limited applicability. The data obtained during the manufacturing and assembly process may be used in conjunction with product testing to demonstrate that the instant run yielded a finished product meeting all of its specifications and quality characteristics. (FDA)

Confidentiality: Preserving authorized restrictions on information access and disclosure, including means for protecting personal privacy and proprietary information. (44 U.S.C., SEC. 3542)

Configurable software: Application software, sometimes general purpose, written for a variety of industries or users in a manner that permits users to modify the program to meet their individual needs. (FDA)

Configuration item: Entity within a configuration that satisfies an end use function and that can be uniquely identified at a given reference point. (ISO 9000-3)

Contemporaneous e-records: Are e-records recorded at the time they are generated.

Control system: Included in this classification are supervisory control and data acquisition systems (SCADA), distributed control systems (DCS), statistical process control systems (SPC), programmable logic controllers (PLCs), intelligent electronic devices, and computer systems that control manufacturing equipment or receive data directly from manufacturing equipment PLCs.

Consistency: The property of logical coherency among constituent parts. Consistency may also be expressed as adherence to a given set of rules.

Correctness: The extent to which software is free from design and coding defects, i.e. fault free. It is also the extent to which software meets its specified requirements and user objectives.

Criticality: In the context of this book, criticality means the regulatory impact to a system or component. See "Critical systems".

Critical: Describes a process step, process condition, test requirement, or other relevant parameter or item that must be controlled within

* Pharmaceutical Inspection Cooperation Scheme (PIC/S). *Good Practices for Computerized Systems in "GxP" Regulated Environments*, PI 011-3, September 2007.

predetermined criteria to ensure that the product/process meets its specification.

Critical electronic records: In this book critical e-records are interpreted as meaning e-records with high risk to product quality or patient safety. (ISPE GAMP COP Annex 11 – Interpretation, July/August 2011).

Critical data: In this book critical data is interpreted as meaning data with high risk to product quality or patient safety. (ISPE GAMP COP Annex 11 – Interpretation, July/August 2011).

Critical process parameter: Process parameter whose variability has an impact on a critical quality attribute and therefore should be monitored or controlled to assure the process produces the desired product quality. (Q8R2)

Critical requirement: A requirement that, if not met, has an adverse impact on any of the following: patient safety, product quality, requirements satisfying health authority regulation, cGxP data integrity, or security.

Critical systems: Systems that directly or indirectly influence patient safety, product quality, and data integrity.

Cryptography or cryptology: It is the practice and study of techniques for secure communication in the presence of third parties called "adversaries".

Custom-built software: Also known as a bespoke system, custom-built software is software produced for a customer, specifically to order, to meet a defined set of user requirements. (GAMP)

Customized computerized system: See "Bespoke computerized system".

Data: The contents of the record, is the basic unit of information that has a unique meaning and can be transmitted.

Information derived or obtained from raw data (e.g. a reported analytical result). (MHRA)

Database: In electronic records, a set of data, consisting of at least one file or of a group of integrated files, usually stored in one location and made available to several users at the same time for various applications. (36 CFR 1234.2, reference (ii))

Database management system (DBMS): A software system used to access and retrieve data stored in a database. (36 CFR 1234.2, reference (ii))

Data collection: The process of gathering and measuring information on variables of interest.

Data governance: The sum of arrangements to ensure that data, irrespective of the format in which it is generated, are recorded, processed, retained, and used to ensure a complete, consistent, and accurate record throughout the data life cycle.

Data handling: The process of ensuring that data is stored, archived, or disposed in a safe and secure manner during the data life cycle.

Data migration: Data migration is the process of transferring data between storage types, formats, or computer systems. It is a key consideration for any system implementation, upgrade, or consolidation. (Wikipedia)

Data integrity: The property that data has not been altered in an unauthorized manner. Data integrity covers data in storage, during processing, and while in transit. (NIST SP 800-33) The extent to which all data are complete, consistent and accurate throughout the data lifecycle. (MHRA)

Data life cycle: All phases in the life of the data (including raw data) from initial generation and recording through processing (including transformation or migration), use, data retention, archive/retrieval, and destruction. (MHRA)

Data ownership: It refers to the possession of and responsibilities for information.

Data selection: The process of determining the appropriate data type and source, as well as suitable instruments to collect data.

Data source: Origin where data is collected.

Data warehousing: An architected, periodic and coordinated process of copying from numerous sources into an optimized environment capable of analytical and informational processing.

Decommissioning: A planned, systematic process to disassemble and retire from service a facility system and equipment without altering the integrity (validation state) of any other facility, system or equipment previously connected to the facility, system or equipment being decommissioned. The decommissioning is done via inspection, testing and documentation.

Decryption: The transformation of unintelligible data ("cipher text") into original data ("clear text").

Delete: The process of permanently removing, erasing, or obliterating recorded information from a medium, especially an electronic medium.

Deliverable: A tangible or intangible object produced as a result of project execution, as part of an obligation. In validation projects, deliverables are usually documents.

Design qualification: The documented verification that the proposed design of the facilities, systems and equipment is suitable for the intended purpose. Also known as "design verification". (EMA Annex 15, Validation and Qualification)

Derived data: Data that was originally supplied in one form, but was converted to another form using some automated process.

Developer: An organization that performs development activities (including requirements analysis, design, testing through acceptance) during the software life cycle process. In this book a "developer" can either be an external company or an in-house software development group.

Development: Software life cycle process that contains the activities of requirements analysis, design, coding, integration, testing, installation, and support for acceptance of software products. (ISO 9000-3)

Deviation: When a system does not act as expected.

Digital certificate: A digital certificate (a.k.a a public-key certificate or identity certificate) is a credential issued by a trusted authority. An entity can present a digital certificate to prove its identity or its right to access information. It links a public-key value to a set of information which identifies the entity associated with the use of the corresponding private key. Certificates are authenticated, issued, and managed by a trusted third party called a certification authority (CA). See also "Public-key certificates".

Digital signature standard (DSS): A National Institute of Standards and Technology (NIST) standard for digital signatures, used to authenticate both a message and the signer. DSS has a security level comparable to RSA (Rivest-Shamir-Adleman) cryptography, having 1,024-bit keys.

Disaster recovery: The activities required to restore one or more computer system to its valid state in response to a major hardware or software failure or destruction of facilities.

Disaster recovery plan: The written and approved plan associated with a disaster recovery.

Discrepancy: Any problem or entry into the problem reporting system. Includes all bugs and may also include design issues.

Destruction: In records management, the major type of disposal action. Methods of destroying records include selling or salvaging the record medium and burning, pulping, shredding, macerating, or discarding with other waste materials.

Disposition: Disposition means those actions taken regarding records after they are no longer in office space to conduct current business. (41 CFR 201-4 and RM Handbook, references (kk) and (w))

Documentation: (1) Manuals, written procedures or policies, records, or reports that provide information concerning the uses, maintenance, or validation of a process or system involving either hardware or software. This material may be presented from electronic media. Documents include, but are not limited to, standard operating procedures (SOPs), technical operating procedures (TOPs), manuals, logs, system development documents, test plans, scripts and results, plans, protocols, and reports. Refer to "Documentation" and "Documentation, level of" in the *Glossary of Computerized System and Software Development Terminology*, August 1995. (2) Any written or pictorial information describing, defining, specifying, reporting, or certifying activities, requirements, procedures, or results. (ANSI N45.2.10-1973)

Efficacy: The measurement of a medicine's desired effect under ideal conditions, such as in a clinical trial.

Electronic record (e-record): Information recorded in electronic form that requires a computer system to access or process. (SAG, "A Guide to Archiving of Electronic Records", February 2014).

In this book, based on the MHRA definitions, raw data and data are considered e-records. When referring to both, electronic raw data and data, the term "e-records" will be used.

Electronic record life cycle: All phases in the life of the electronic record from initial generation and recording through processing (including transformation or migration), use, electronic records retention, archive/retrieval, and destruction.

Electronic source data: Data initially recorded in electronic format. (FDA, "Electronic Source Data in Clinical Investigations", September 2013)

Electronic storage device: Hard drives and any form of fixed or portable storage media (e.g. network drives, CDs/DVDs, USB jump/flash drives, and other peripherals).

End-user: Personnel who use the validated computer system.

Emergency change: A change to a validated system that is determined to be necessary to eliminate an error condition that prevents the use of the system and interrupts the business function.

Emulation: Refers to the process of mimicking, in software, a piece of hardware or software so that other processes think that the original equipment/function is still available in its original form. Emulation is essentially a way of preserving the functionality of and access to digital information which might otherwise be lost due to technological obsolescence.

Encryption: (1) The process of converting information into a code or cipher so that people will be unable to read it. A secret key, or password, is required to decrypt (decode) the information. (2) Transformation of confidential plaintext into cipher text to protect it. An encryption algorithm combines plaintext with other values called keys, or ciphers, so the data becomes unintelligible. (45 CFR 142.304)

Entity: A software or hardware product which can be individually qualified or validated.

Establish: Establish is defined in this book as meaning to define, document, and implement.

Evaluation: A systematic determination of the extent to which an entity meets its specified criteria.

Expected result: What a system should do when a particular action is performed.

Factory acceptance test: An acceptance test in the supplier's factory, usually involving the customer. (IEEE)

Failure analysis: It is the process of collecting and analyzing data to determine the cause of a failure. One of the software-based fault location techniques is the automatic test pattern generation.

FDA guidance documents: FDA guidance documents represent the FDA's current thinking on a particular subject. These documents do not create or confer any rights for or on any person and do not operate to bind the FDA or the public. An alternative approach may be used if such an approach satisfies the requirements of the applicable statutes, regulations, or both.

Federal Register: A daily issuance of the US government which provides a uniform system for making available to the public regulations and legal notices issued by federal agencies.

Field devices: Hardware devices that are typically located in the field at or near the process, and which are needed to bring information to the computer or to implement a computer-driven control action. Devices include sensors, analytical instruments, transducers, and valves.

File: An arrangement of records. The term is used to denote papers, photographs, photographic copies, maps, machine-readable information, or other recorded information regardless of physical form or characteristics, accumulated or maintained in filing equipment, boxes, or machine-readable media, or on shelves, and occupying office or storage space. (41 CFR 201-4 and 36 CFR 1220.14, references [kk] and [11])

Final rule: The regulation finalized for implementation, published in the US Federal Register (preamble and codified), and codified in the Code of Federal Regulation (CFR).

Format: For electronic records, the format refers to the computer file format described by a formal standard or specification or vendor formal standard or specification. For non-electronic records, the format refers to its physical form, e.g. paper, microfilm, video, and so on.

Function: A set of specified, ordered actions that are part of a process.

Functional testing: Application of test data derived from the specified functional requirements without regard to the final program structure.

GMP (Good manufacturing practice): The part of quality assurance which ensures that products are consistently produced and controlled in accordance with the quality standards appropriate to their intended use. (Commission Directive 2003/94/EC)

Current Good Manufacturing Practice (CGMP) refers to requirements in the Federal Food, Drug, and Cosmetic Act (FD&C Act), Section 501(a)(2)(B), for all drugs and active pharmaceutical ingredients (APIs). For finished human and animal drugs, the term includes applicable requirements under 21 CFR parts 210 and 211. For biologics, the term includes additional applicable requirements under 21 CFR parts 600–680. (US FDA)

GMP controls: Set of controls that provide assurance of consistently continued process performance and product quality.

GMP regulated activities: The manufacturing-related activities established in the basic legislation compiled in Volume 1 and Volume 5 of the publication *The Rules Governing Medicinal Products in the European Union*, US FDA 21 CFR Part 211, *Current Good Manufacturing Practice in Manufacturing, Processing, Packing or Holding of Drugs; General and Current Good Manufacturing Practice for Finished Pharmaceuticals* or any predicate rule applicable to medicinal products for the referenced country.

Good documentation practices: Measures that collectively and individually ensure documentation, whether paper or electronic, is secure, attributable, legible, traceable, permanent, contemporaneously recorded, original, and accurate. (WHO)

Guidelines: A document providing guidance on the scientific or regulatory aspects of the development of medicines and applications for marketing authorization. Although guidelines are not legally binding, applicants need to provide justification for any deviations. (EMA)

Guidelines are departmental policy and recommended standards or statements that derive from legislation. They do not have the force of law or regulation.

GXP: A global abbreviation intended to cover GMP, GCP, GLP, and other regulated applications in context.

GxP application: Software entities which have a specific user defined business purpose that must meet the requirements of a GxP regulation.

GXP Computerized Systems: A computerized system which performs regulated operation which is required to be formally controlled under the Federal Food, Drug, and Cosmetic Act, the Public Health Service and/or applicable regulation.

GxP regulation: A global abbreviation intended to cover GMP, GCP, GLP, and other regulated applications in context.

The underlying international life science requirements such as those set forth in the US FD&C Act, US PHS Act, FDA regulations, EU Directives, Japanese MHL.W regulations, Australia TGA, or other applicable national legislation or regulations under which a company operates. (GAMP Good Practice Guide, IT Infrastructure Control and Compliance, ISPE 2005)

Human readable: An electronic record, data or signature that can be displayed in a viewable form, e.g. on paper or computer screen and has meaning (words in a written language).

Hybrid systems: Hybrid computer systems include combinations of paper records (or other non-electronic media) and electronic records, paper records and electronic signatures, or handwritten signatures executed to electronic records.

Information technology: Any equipment or interconnected system or subsystem of equipment that is used in the automatic acquisition, storage, manipulation, management, movement, control, display, switching, interchange, transmission, or reception of data or information by the executive agency. For purposes of the preceding sentence, equipment is used by an executive agency if the equipment is used by the executive agency directly or is used by a contractor under a contract with the executive agency which: (1) requires the use of such equipment; or (2) requires the use, to a significant extent, of such equipment in the performance of a service or the furnishing of a product. The term information technology includes computers, ancillary equipment, software, firmware and similar procedures, services (including support services), and related resources. (40 U.S.C., SEC. 1401)

Infrastructure: The hardware and software, such as networking software and operation systems, which makes it possible for the application to function. (EMA Annex 11)

Integrity: (1) Protection against unauthorized changes to information. (2) Condition existing when data is unchanged from its source and has not been accidentally or maliciously modified, altered, or destroyed. (National Information System Security [INFOSEC] Glossary) (3) The degree to which a system or component prevents unauthorized access to, or modification of, computer programs or data. (ANSI/IEEE)

Interface: A shared boundary. To interact or communicate with another system component. (ANSI/IEEE)

Impact of change: The impact of change is the effect of the change on the GxP computer system. The components by which the impact of change is evaluated may include, but not be limited to, business considerations; resource requirements and availability; application of appropriate regulatory agency requirements; and criticality of the system.

Inspection: (1) A manual testing technique in which program documents (specifications [requirements, design], source code or user's manuals) are examined in a very formal and disciplined manner to discover any errors, violations of standards or other problems. Checklists are typical vehicles used in accomplishing this process. (2) A visual examination of a software product to detect and identify software anomalies, including errors and deviations from standards and specifications. Inspections are peer examinations led by impartial facilitators who are trained in inspection techniques. Determination of remedial or investigative action for an anomaly is a mandatory element of a software inspection, although the solution should not be determined in the inspection meeting.

Installation qualification: Establishing confidence that process equipment and ancillary systems are capable of consistently operating within established limits and tolerances. (FDA)

Integration testing: Orderly progression of testing in which software elements, hardware elements, or both, are combined and tested, until all intermodule communication links have been integrated.

Integrity: Guarding against improper information modification or destruction and includes ensuring information non-repudiation and authenticity. (44 U.S.C., Sec. 3542)

Intended use: (1)Use of a product, process or service in accordance with the specifications, instructions, and information provided by the manufacturer. (ANSI/AAMI/ISO 14971) (2) Refer to the objective intent of the persons legally responsible for the labeling of devices. The intent is determined by such persons' expressions or may be shown by the circumstances surrounding the distribution of the article. This objective intent may, for example, be shown by labeling claims, advertising matter, or oral or written statements by such persons or their representatives. It may be shown by the circumstances that the article is, with the knowledge of such persons or their representatives, offered and used for a purpose for which it is neither labeled nor advertised. The intended uses of an article may change after it has been introduced into interstate commerce by its manufacturer. If, for example, a packer, distributor, or seller intends an article for different uses than those intended by the person from whom he received the devices. (US FDA Draft Guidance for Industry and Food and Drug Administration Staff – Mobile Medical Applications, July 2011)

IT infrastructure: The hardware and software such as networking software and operation systems, which makes it possible for the application to function. (EMA Annex 11)

Key practices: Processes essential for computer validation that consists of tools, workflow, and people. (PDA)

Legacy systems: (1) Production computer systems that are operating on older computer hardware or are based on older software applications. In some cases, the vendor may no longer support the hardware or software. (2) These are regarded as systems that have been established and in use for some considerable time. For a variety of reasons, they may be generally characterized by lack of adequate GMP compliance-related documentation and records pertaining to the development and commissioning stage of the system.

Additionally, because of their age there may be no records of a formal approach to validation of the system. (PICS CSV PI 011-3*)

Life cycle: All phases in the life of the system from initial requirements until retirement including design, specification, programming, testing, installation, operation, and maintenance. (EMA Annex 11)

Life cycle model: A framework containing the processes, activities, and tasks involved in the development, operation, and maintenance of a software product, spanning the life of the system from the definition of its requirements to the termination of its use. (ISO 9000-3)

Life cycle (record): The life span of a record from its creation to its final disposition is considered its life cycle. There are four stages in a record life cycle: creation, maintenance, retention management, and disposal.

Living document: A document (or collection of documents) revised as needed throughout the life of a computer system. Only the most recent version(s) is effective and supersedes prior versions.

Logically secure and controlled environment: A computing environment, controlled by policies, procedures, and technology, which deters direct or remote unauthorized access which could damage computer components, production applications and/or data.

Maintainer: An organization that performs maintenance activities. (ISO 12207: 1995†)

Major change: A change to a validated system that is determined by reviewers to require the execution of extensive validation activities.

Manufacture: All operations of purchase of materials and products, production, quality control, release, storage, and dispatch of medicinal products and the related controls.

Manufacturer: An entity that engages in CGMP activities, including implementation of oversight and controls over the manufacture of drugs to ensure quality.

Manufacturing: All operations of receipt of materials, production, packaging, repackaging, labeling, relabeling, quality control, release, storage, and distribution of medicinal products and the related controls.

Manufacturing systems: Elements of pharmaceutical and biopharmaceutical manufacturing capability, including manufacturing systems,

* Pharmaceutical Inspection Cooperation Scheme (PIC/S). *Good Practices for Computerized Systems in "GxP" Regulated Environments*, PI 011-3, September 2007.

† Note: The 1995 revision is not the most recent version.

facility equipment, process equipment, supporting utilities, associated process monitoring and control systems, and automation systems, that have the potential to affect product quality and patient safety. (ASTM E 2500-07)

May: This word, or the adjective "optional", mean that an item is truly optional. Statement using "may" for permissible actions.

Metadata: Data describing stored data: that is, data describing the structure, data elements, interrelationships, and other characteristics of electronic records. (DOD 5015.2-STD) Data that describe the attributes of other data, and provide context and meaning. Typically, these are data that describe the structure, data elements, interrelationships and other characteristics of data. It also permits data to be attributable to an individual. (MHRA)

Migration: The act of moving records from one system to another.

Minor change: A change to a validated system that is determined by reviewers to require the execution of only targeted qualification and validation activities.

Model: A model is an abstract representation of a given object.

Module testing: Refer to "Testing, Unit" in the *Glossary of Computerized System and Software Development Terminology,* August 1995.

NEMA enclosure: Hardware enclosures (usually cabinets) that provide different levels of mechanical and environmental protection to the devices installed within it.

Non-conformance: A departure from minimum requirements specified in a contract, specification, drawing, or other approved product description or service.

Non-custom purchased software package: A generally available, marketed software product which performs specific data collection, manipulation, output, or archiving functions. Refer to "Configurable, off-the-shelf software" in the *Glossary of Computerized System and Software Development Terminology,* August 1995.

Non-repudiation: Strong and substantial evidence of the identity of the signer of a message and of message integrity, sufficient to prevent a party from successfully denying the origin, submission or delivery of the message and the integrity of its contents.

Objective evidence: Qualitative or quantitative information, records or statements of fact pertaining to the quality of an item or service or to the existence of a quality system element, which is based on observation, measurement or test and which can be verified.

Operator: An organization that operates the system. (ISO 12207: 1995*)

Operating environment: All outside influences that interface with the computer system. (GAMP)

Ongoing evaluation: A term used to describe the dynamic process employed after a system's initial validation that can assist in maintaining a computer system in a validated state.

Operational testing: Refer to "Operational Qualification" in the *Glossary of Computerized System and Software Development Terminology,* August 1995.

Operating system: Software that controls the execution of programs and that provides services such as resource allocation, scheduling, input/output control, and data management. Usually, operating systems are predominantly software, but partial or complete hardware implementations are possible. (ISO)

Original record: Data as the file or format in which it was originally generated, preserving the integrity (accuracy, completeness, content and meaning) of the record, e.g. original paper record of manual observation, or electronic raw data file from a computerized system (MHRA)

Part 11 records: Records that are required to be maintained under predicate rule requirements and that are maintained in electronic format in place of paper format, or records that are required to be maintained under predicate rules, that are maintained in electronic format in addition to paper format, and that are relied on to perform regulated activities. Part 11 records include records submitted to the FDA, under predicate rules (even if such records are not specifically identified in Agency regulations) in electronic format (assuming the records have been identified in docket number 92S-0251 as the types of submissions the Agency accepts in electronic format). (FDA guidance: Part 11 Scope and Application)

Password: A character string used to authenticate an identity. Knowledge of the password that is associated with a user ID is considered proof of authorization to use the capabilities associated with that user ID. (CSC-STD-002-85)

Packaged software: Software provided and maintained by a vendor/supplier, which can provide general business functionality or system services. Refer to "Configurable, off-the-shelf software" in the *Glossary of Computerized System and Software Development Terminology*, August 1995.

---

* Note: The 1995 revision is not the most recent version.

Periodic review: A documented assessment of the documentation, procedures, records, and performance of a computer system to determine whether it is still in a validated state and what actions, if any, are necessary to restore its validated state. (PDA) The review is performed at regular intervals. The timing of intervals is left flexible.

Person: By "person", it refers to an individual or an organization with legal rights and duties.

Personal identification number: A PIN is an alphanumeric code or password used to authenticate the identity of an individual.

Physical environment: The physical environment of a computer system that comprises the physical location and the environmental parameters in which the system physically functions.

Planned change: An intentional change to a validated system for which an implementation and evaluation program is predetermined.

Policy: A directive which usually specifies what is to be accomplished.

Preamble: Analysis preceding a proposed or final rule that clarifies the intention of the rulemaking and any ambiguities regarding the rule. Responses to comments made on a proposed rule are published in the preamble preceding the final rule. Preambles are published only in the FR and do not have a binding effect.

Predicate regulations: The Federal Food, Drug, and Cosmetic Act, the Public Health Service Act or any FDA Regulation, with the exception of 21 CFR Part 11. Predicate regulations address the research, production, and control of FDA regulated articles.

Primary record: The record which takes primacy in cases where collected or retained concurrently by more than one method fail to concur. (MHRA)

Principles: A basic foundation of believes, truths, and so on, upon which others are based.

Procedural controls: (1) Written and approved procedures providing appropriate instructions for each aspect of the development, operations, maintenance, and security applicable to computer technologies. In the context of regulated operations, procedural controls should have QA/QC controls that are equivalent to the applicable predicate regulations. (2) A directive usually specifying how certain activities are to be accomplished. (PMA CSVC)

Process: (1) A set of specified, ordered actions required to achieve a defined result. (2) A set of interrelated or interacting activities that transform input into outputs. (ISO 9000-3)

Process owner: The person responsible for the business process. (EMA Annex 11)

Process system: The combination of the process equipment, support systems (such as utilities), and procedures used to execute a process.

Production environment: The operational environment in which the system is being used for its intended purpose, i.e. not in a test or development environment.

Production verification (PV): Documented verification that the integrated system performs as intended in its production environment. PV is the execution of selected performance qualification (PQ) tests in the production environment using production data.

Project: A project is an activity which achieves specific objectives through a set of defining tasks and effective use of resources.

Project management: Project management is the application of knowledge, skills, tools, and techniques to project activities to meet the project requirements. (ANSI)

Prospective validation: Validation conducted prior to the distribution of either a new product, or a product made under a revised manufacturing process, where the revisions may affect the product's characteristics. (FDA)

Public-key certificate: A public-key certificate (AKA a digital certificate or identity certificate) is an electronic representation of an identification or passport, issued by a certification authority (CA) to a public-key infrastructure (PKI) user, stating identification information, validity period, the holder's public-key, the identity and digital signature of the issuer, and the purpose for which it is issued. (GERM)

Qualification: (1) Action of proving that any equipment works correctly and actually leads to the expected results. The word validation is sometimes widened to incorporate the concept of qualification. (PIC/S) (2) Qualification is the process of demonstrating whether a computer system and associated controlled process/operation, procedural controls, and documentation are capable of fulfilling specified requirements. (3) The process of demonstrating whether an entity is capable of fulfilling specified requirements. (ISO 8402: 1994, 2.13.1)

Qualification protocol: A prospective experimental plan stating how qualification will be conducted, including test parameters, product characteristics, production equipment, and decision points on what constitutes an acceptable test. When executed, a protocol is intended to produce documented evidence that a system or subsystem performs as required.

Quality and technical records: Registered evidence about activities on the quality management system (QMS) and/or the process of performing tests (e.g. work sheets, logbooks, control graphs, documentation of equipment qualification, test requests, test reports, reports from audits, training records, records of corrective and preventive actions, and so on.). (OMLC – Management of Documents and Records [Rephrased])

Qualification reports: These are test reports which evaluate the conduct and results of the qualification carried out on a computer system.

Quality: The totality of features and characteristics of a product or service that bears on its ability to satisfy given needs.

Quality assurance: All planned and systematic activities implemented within the quality system and demonstrated as needed to provide adequate confidence that an entity will fulfill requirements for quality.

Quality management: All activities of the overall management function that determine the quality policy, objectives, and responsibilities, and implement them by such means as quality planning, quality control, quality assurance, and quality improvement within the quality system.

Raw data: All data on which quality decisions are based should be defined as raw data. It includes data which is used to generate other records. (Source: "EU Good Manufacturing Practice Medicinal Products for Human and Veterinary Use", Volume 4, Chapter 4: Documentation)

Original records and documentation, retained in the format in which they were originally generated (i.e. paper or electronic), or as a "true copy". Raw data must be contemporaneously and accurately recorded by permanent means. In the case of basic electronic equipment which does not store electronic data or provides only a printed data output (e.g. balance or pH meter), the printout constitutes the raw data. (MHRA)

Any laboratory worksheets, records, memoranda, notes, or exact copies thereof that are the result of original observations, and activities of a nonclinical laboratory study and are necessary for the reconstruction and evaluation of the report of that study. In the event that exact transcripts of raw data have been prepared (e.g. tapes which have been transcribed verbatim, dated, and verified accurate by signature), the exact copy or exact transcript may be substituted for the original source as raw data. Raw data may include photographs, microfilm or microfiche copies, computer printouts, magnetic media, including dictated observations, and recorded data from automated instruments. (Source: US FDA 21 CFR 58.3(k))

Record: Provide evidence of various actions taken to demonstrate compliance with instructions, e.g. activities, events, investigations, and, in the case of manufactured batches, a history of each batch of product, including its distribution. Records include the raw data which is used to generate other records. For electronic records regulated users should define which data are to be used as raw data. At least, all data on which quality decisions are based should be defined as raw data. (Eudralex, Volume 4, Chapter 4).

A record consists of information, regardless of medium, detailing the transaction of business. Records include all books, papers, maps, photographs, machine-readable materials, and other documentary materials, regardless of physical form or characteristics, made or received by an Agency of the United States Government under Federal law or in connection with the transaction of public business and preserved or appropriate for preservation by that Agency or its legitimate successor as evidence of the organization, functions, policies, decisions, procedures, operations, or other activities of the Government or because of the value of data in the record. (44 U.S.C. 3301, reference (bb))

Record owner: A person or organization who can determine the contents and use of the data collected, stored, processed, or disseminated by that party regardless of whether or not the data was acquired from another owner or collected directly from the provider.

Records management: The field of management responsible for the efficient and systematic control of the creation, receipt, maintenance, use and disposition of records, including the processes for capturing and maintaining evidence of and information about business activities and transactions in the form of records. (ISO 15489: 2001)

Record reliability: A reliable record is one whose contents can be trusted as a full and accurate representation of the transactions, activities, or facts to which they attest and can be depended upon in the course of subsequent transactions or activities. (NARA)

Record retention period: Length of time the electronic record is to be retained, as mandated by the requirement of the record type, based on regulations or documented policies.

Record Retention Schedule: A list of record types with the required storage conditions and defined retention periods. The time (retention) periods are established based upon regulatory, legal and tax compliance requirements as well as operational need and historical value.

Re-engineering: The process of examining and altering an existing system to reconstitute it in a new form. May include reverse engineering (analyzing a system and producing a representation at a higher level of abstraction, such as design from code), restructuring (transforming a system from one representation to another at the same level of abstraction), documentation (analyzing a system and producing user or support documentation), forward engineering (using software products derived from an existing system, together with new requirements, to produce a new system), retargeting (transforming a system to install it on a different target system), and translation (transforming source code from one language to another or from one version of a language to another). (DOD-STD-498)

Regulated data: Information used for a regulated purpose or to support a regulated process. (GAMP)

Regulated record: It is a record required to be maintained or submitted by GxP regulations.

Regulated electronic records: It is a regulated record maintained in electronic format.

Reports: Document the conduct of particular exercises, projects or investigations, together with results, conclusions and recommendations (Eudralex, Volume 4, Chapter 4). A report containing regulated data is considered a regulated record.

Repository for electronic records: A direct access device on which the electronic records and metadata are stored.

Retention period: The duration for which records are retained. Retention periods are defined in a retention schedule document. These retention schedules are based on business requirements, country-specific regulatory, and legal requirements.

Regression testing: Regression testing is the process of testing changes to computer programs to make sure that the older programming still works with the new changes. Regression testing is a normal part of the program development process and, in larger companies, is done by code testing specialists. Test department coders develop code test scenarios and exercises that will test new units of code after they have been written. These test cases form what becomes the "test bucket".

Before a new version of a software product is released, the old test cases are run against the new version to make sure that all the old capabilities still work. The reason they might not work is because changing or adding new code to a program can easily introduce errors into code that is not intended to be changed.

Regulated operations: Process/business operations carried out on a regulated agency product that is covered in a predicated rule.

Regulated user: The regulated "good practice" entity, that is responsible for the operation of a computerized system and the applications, files and data held thereon. (PIC/S PI 011-3) See also "User" and "Operator".

Regulatory authorities: Bodies having the statutory power to regulate. The expression "regulatory authorities" includes the authorities that review submitted products data and consult inspections. These bodies are sometimes referred to as competent authorities.

Regulatory requirements: Any part of a law, ordinance, decree, or other regulation which applies to the regulated article.

Release: Particular version of a configuration item that is made available for a specific purpose. (ISO 9000-3)

Reliability: The ability of a system or component to perform its required functions under stated conditions for a specified period of time. (ANSI/IEEE Std 610.12-1990, IEEE "Standard Glossary of Software Engineering Terminology")

Reliable records: Records that are a full and accurate representation of the transactions, activities or facts to which they attest and can be depended upon in the course of subsequent transactions or activities.

Remediate: In the context of this book, the software, hardware, and/or procedural changes employed to bring a system into compliance with the applicable GxP rule.

Remediation plan: A documented approach on bringing existing computer systems into compliance with the regulation/s.

Replacement: The implementation of a new compliant system after the retirement of an existing system.

Re-qualification: Repetition of the qualification process or a specific portion thereof.

Requirement: A condition or capability that must be met or possessed by a system or system component to satisfy a contract, standard, specification, or other formally imposed document. The set of all requirements forms the basis for subsequent development of the system or system component. (ANSI/IEEE)

Retention period: The duration for which records are retained.

Retirement phase: The period in the SLC in which plans are made and executed to decommission or remove a computer technology from operational use.

Retrospective evaluation: Establishing documented evidence that a system does what it purports to do based on an analysis of historical information. The process of evaluating a computer system, which is currently in operation, against standard validation practices and procedures. The evaluation determines the reliability, accuracy, and completeness of a system.

Retrospective validation: See "Retrospective evaluation".

Review: Checking of the suitability of a document.

Revision: Different versions of the same document. Can also be used in reference to software, firmware and hardware boards. Implies a fully tested, fully functional and released unit/component/document.

Risk: A measure of the extent to which an organization is threatened by a potential circumstance or event, and typically a function of the following:

a. The adverse impacts that would arise if the circumstance or event occurs.
b. The likelihood of occurrence. Likelihood is influenced by the ease of exploit(s) required and the frequency with which an exploit or like-objects are being attacked at present. (K. Dempsey, P. Eavy and G. Moore, *Automation Support for Security Control Assessments* Volume 1: Overview, Draft NISTIR 8011, February 2016.)

Risk assessment: A comprehensive evaluation of the risk and its associated impact.

Risk management: The tasks and plans that help avoid risk and helps minimize damage.

Review: A process or meeting during which a software product is presented to project personnel, managers, users, customers, user representatives, or other interested parties for comment or approval. (IEEE)

SAT (Site acceptance test): Inspection and/or dynamic testing of the systems or major system components to support the qualification of an equipment system conducted and documented at the manufacturing site. An Acceptance Test at the Customer's site, usually involving the Customer. (IEEE)

Secure repository: A repository or application that, in accordance with specific country laws and regulations, permits users to securely store records and limits the ability to edit and delete documents.

Security controls: The management, operational, and technical controls (i.e. safeguards or countermeasures) prescribed for an information system to protect the confidentiality, integrity, and availability of the system and its information.

Self-inspection: An audit carried out by people from within the organization to ensure compliance with GMP and regulatory requirements.

Segregation of duties: A process that divides roles and responsibilities so that a single individual cannot subvert a critical process.

Service provider: An organization supplying services to one or more internal or external customers. (ITIL Service Design, 2011 Edition)

Shall: Used to express a provision that is binding, per regulatory requirement. Statements that use "shall" can be traced to regulatory requirements and must be followed to comply with such requirements.

Should: Used to express a non-mandatory provision. Statements that use "should" are best practices, recommended activities, or options to perform activities to be considered in order to achieve quality project results. Other methods may be used if it can be demonstrated that they are equivalent.

SIPOC diagram: It is a tool used to identify all significant elements of a process. The representation of such process is a high-level process map.

Signature (handwritten): The scripted name or legal mark of an individual handwritten by that individual and executed or adopted with the present intention to authenticate a writing in a permanent form. (21 CFR 11.3[8])

Software developer: Person or organization that designs software and writes the programs. Software development includes the design of the user interface and the program architecture as well as programming the source code. (TechWeb Network, www.techweb.com/encyclopedia/)

Software development standards: Written policies or procedures that describe practices a programmer or software developer should follow in creating, debugging, and verifying software.

Software item: Identifiable part of a software product. (ISO 9000-3)

Software product: Set of computer programs, procedures, and possibly associated documentation and data. (ISO 9000-3)

Source code: The human readable version of the list of instructions (programs) that enable a computer to perform a task.

Source data: All information in original records and certified copies of original records of clinical findings, observations, or other activities in a clinical trial necessary for the reconstruction and evaluation of the trial. Source data are contained in source documents (original records or certified copies). (Source: EMA/INS/GCP/454280/2010 GCP Inspectors Working Group [GCP IWG]. Reflection paper on expectations for electronic source data and data transcribed to electronic data collection)

All information in original records and certified copies of original records of 120 clinical findings, observations, or other activities (in a clinical investigation) used for the 121 reconstruction and evaluation of the trial. Source data are contained in source documents 122 (original records or certified copies). (Source: FDA, "Electronic Source Data in Clinical Investigations", September 2013)

Specification: A document that specifies, in a complete, precise, verifiable manner, the requirements, design, behavior, or other characteristics of a system or component, and often, the procedures for determining whether these provisions have been satisfied. (IEEE)

Stakeholder: In this book, anyone who has a stake in the successful outcome of the project – system owner(s), business managers, regulated end-users, quality assurance, software engineers, support people, and so forth.

Static analysis: (1) Analysis of a program that is performed without executing the program. (NBS) (2) The process of evaluating a system or component based on its form, structure, content, documentation. (IEEE)

Standard instrument software: These are driven by non user-programmable firmware. They are configurable. (GAMP)

Standard operation procedures: See "Procedural controls"

Standard software packages: A complete and documented set of programs supplied to several users for a generic application or function. (ISO/IEC 2382-20: 1990)

Subject matter experts: Individuals with specific expertise and responsibility in a particular area or field. (ASTM E 2500-07, *Standard Guide for Specification, Design, and Verification of Pharmaceutical and Biopharmaceutical Manufacturing Systems and Equipment*)

Supplier: An organization that enters into a contract with the acquirer for the supply of a system, software product or software service under the terms of the contract. (ISO 12207: 1995*)

* Note: The 1995 revision is not the most recent version.

System: (1) People, machines, and methods organized to accomplish a set of specific functions. (ANSI) (2) A composite, at any level of complexity, of personnel, procedures, materials, tools, equipment, facilities, and software. The elements of this composite entity are used together in the intended operational or support environment to perform a given task or achieve a specific purpose, support, or mission requirement. (DOD). (3) A group of related objects designed to perform or control a set of specified actions.

System backup: The storage of data and programs on a separate media, and stored separately from the originating system.

System documentation: The collection of documents that describe the requirements, capabilities, limitations, design, operation, and maintenance of an information processing system. See: "Specification", "Test documentation", "User's guide". (ISO)

System integrity: The quality that a system has when it performs its intended function in an unimpaired manner, free from unauthorized manipulation. (NIST SP 800-33)

System life cycle: All phases in the life of the system from initial requirements until retirement including design, specification, programming, testing, installation, operation, and maintenance. (EMA Annex 11)

System owner: The person responsible for the availability, and maintenance of a computerized system and for the security of the data residing on that system. (EMA Annex 11)

System retirement: The removal of a system from operational usage. The system may be replaced by another system or may be removed without being replaced.

System software: See "Operating system".

System specification: In this book system specification corresponds to requirements, functional and/or design specifications. Refer to "Specification".

System test: Process of testing an integrated hardware and software system to verify that the system meets its specified requirements.

Technological controls: Are program-enforcing compliance rules.

Templates: Guidelines that outline the basic information for a specific set of equipment. (JETT)

Test report: Document that presents test results and other information relevant to a test. (ISO/IEC Guide 2, 2004)

Test script: A detailed set of instructions for execution of the test. This typically includes the following:

- Specific identification of the test
- Prerequisites or dependencies
- Test objective
- Test steps or actions
- Requirements or instructions for capturing data (e.g. screen prints, report printing)
- Pass/fail criteria for the entire script
- Instructions to follow in the event that a non-conformance is encountered
- Test execution date
- Person(s) executing the test
- Review date
- Person reviewing the test results

For each step of the test script, the item tested, the input to that step, and the expected result are indicated prior to execution of the test. The actual results obtained during the steps of the test are recorded on or attached to the test script. Test scripts and results may be managed through computer-based electronic tools. Refer to "Test case" in the *Glossary of Computerized System and Software Development Terminology*, August 1995.

Test non-conformance: A non-conformance occurs when the actual test result does not equal the expected result or an unexpected event (such as a loss of power) is encountered.

Testing: Examining the behavior of a program by executing the program on sample data sets.

Third party: Parties not directly managed by the holder of the manufacturing and/or import authorization.

Time stamp: A record mathematically linking a piece of data to a time and date.

Traceability: (1) The degree to which a relationship can be established between two or more products of the development process, especially products having a predecessor-successor or master-subordinate relationship to one another; e.g. the degree to which the requirements and design of a given software component match. (IEEE) (2) The degree to which each element in a software development product establishes its reason for existing; e.g. the degree to which each element in a bubble chart references the requirement that it satisfies.

Traceability analysis: The tracing of (1) software requirements specifications requirements to system requirements in concept documentation,

(2) software design descriptions to software requirements specifications and software requirements specifications to software design descriptions, (3) source code to corresponding design specifications and design specifications to source code. Analyze identified relationships for correctness, consistency, completeness, and accuracy. (IEEE)

Traceability matrix: A matrix that records the relationship between two or more products, e.g. a matrix that records the relationship between the requirements and the design of a given software component. (IEEE)

Training plan: Documentation describing the training required for an individual based on his or her job title or description.

Training record: Documentation (electronic or paper) of the training received by an individual that includes, but is not limited to, the individual's name or identifier; the type of training received; the date the training occurred; the trainer's name or identifier; and an indication of the effectiveness of the training (if applicable).

Transfer: The act or process of moving records from one location to another.

Transient memory: Memory that must have a constant supply of power or the stored data will be lost.

True copy record: (1) An exact copy of an original record, which may be retained in the same or different format in which it was originally generated, e.g. a paper copy of a paper record, an electronic scan of a paper record, or a paper record of electronically generated data. (MHRA) (2) Accurate reproduction of the original record regardless of the technology used to create the reproduction (for example, printing, scanning, photocopying, microfilm, or microfiche). A true copy of an electronic record must contain the entire record, including all associated metadata, audit trails, and signatures, as applicable, to preserve content and meaning.

Trust: In the network security context, trust refers to privacy (the data is not viewable by unauthorized people), integrity (the data stays in its true form), non-repudiation (the publisher cannot say they did not send it), and authentication (the publisher – and recipient – are who they say they are).

Trustworthy computer systems: Trustworthy computer systems consist of computer infrastructure, applications, and procedures that:

- Are reasonably suited to performing their intended functions.
- Provide a reasonably reliable level of availability, reliability and correct operation.

- Are reasonably secure from intrusion and misuse.
- Adhere to generally accepted security principles.

Trustworthy records: Reliability, authenticity, integrity, and usability are the characteristics used to describe trustworthy records from a record management perspective. (NARA)

Unplanned (emergency) change: An unanticipated necessary change to a validated system requiring rapid implementation.

Usable records: Records that can be located, retrieved, presented, and interpreted.

User: The company or group responsible for the operation of a system. (GAMP) (see also "Regulated User"). The GxP customer, or user organization, contracting a supplier to provide a product. In the context of this document it is, therefore, not intended to apply only to individuals who use the system and is synonymous with "customer". (EMA Annex 11)

User backup/alternative procedures: Procedure which describes the steps to be taken for the continued recording and control of the raw data in the event of a computer system interruption or failure.

Unit: A separately testable element specified in the design of a computer software element. Synonymous to component, module. (IEEE)

Unit test: Test of a module for typographic, syntactic, and logical errors, for correct implementation of its design, and for satisfaction of its requirements.

Users: People or processes accessing a computer system either by direct connections (i.e. via terminals) or indirect connections (i.e. prepare input data or receive output that is not reviewed for content or classification by a responsible individual).

User ID: A sequence of characters which is recognized by the computer and which uniquely identifies one person. The user ID is the first form of identification. User ID is also known as a PIN or identification code.

Walkthrough: A static analysis technique in which a designer or programmer leads members of the development team and other interested parties through a software product, and the participants ask questions and make comments about possible errors, violation of development standards, and other problems. (IEEE)

Workflows: The intended steps, sequencing, specifications, calculations or other processes through which a piece of work passes from initiation to completion, e.g. operational checks, authority checks, device checks, built-in checks, accuracy checks, and so on.

Validated: It is used to indicate a status to designate that a system or software complies with applicable Good Manufacturing Practice (GMP) requirements.

Validation: Action of proving, in accordance with the principles of GMP, that any procedure, process, equipment, material, activity, or system actually leads to the expected results (see also "Qualification"). (PIC/S)

Validation coordinator: A person or designee responsible for coordinating the validation activities for a specific project or task.

Validation protocol: A written plan stating how validation will be conducted, including test parameters, product characteristics, production equipment, and decision points on what constitutes acceptable test results. (FDA)

Validation plan: A multidisciplinary strategy from which each phase of a validation process is planned, implemented, and documented to ensure that a facility, process, equipment, or system does what it is designed to do. May also be known as a system or software quality plan.

Validation summary report: Documents confirming that the entire project's planned activities have been completed. On acceptance of the validation summary report, the user releases the system for use, possibly with a requirement that continuing monitoring should take place for a certain time. (GAMP)

Verification: (1) The process of determining whether or not the products of a given phase of the SLC fulfill the requirements established during the previous phase. (2) A systematic approach to verify that manufacturing systems, acting singly or in combination, are fit for intended use, have been properly installed, and are operating correctly. This is an umbrella term that encompasses all types of approaches to assuring systems are fit for use such as qualification, commissioning and qualification, verification, system validation, or other. (ASTM 5200) (3) Confirmation by examination and provision of objective evidence that specified requirements have been fulfilled. (FDA Medical Devices) (4) In design and development, verification concerns the process of examining the result of a given activity to determine conformity with the stated requirement for that activity.

Verification (validation) of data: The procedures carried out to ensure that the data contained in the final report match original observations. These procedures may apply to raw data, data in case report forms (in hard copy or electronic form), computer printouts and statistical analysis and tables. (WHO)

Virtual private network: Describes the use of encryption to provide some secure a secure telecommunications route between parties over an insecure or public network, such as the Internet.

Warehouse: A facility or location where things are stored.

Will: This word denotes a declaration of purpose or intent by one party, not a requirement.

Work products: The intended result of activities or processes. (PDA)

Worst case: A set of conditions encompassing upper and lower processing limits and circumstances, including those within standard operating procedures, which pose the greatest chance of process or product failure when compared to ideal conditions. Such conditions do not necessarily induce product or process failure. (FDA)

Written: In the context of electronic records the term "written" means "recorded, or documented on media, paper, electronic or other substrate" from which data may be rendered in a human readable form. (EMA GMP Chapter 4, 2011)

Appendix II: Abbreviations and/or Acronyms

ABA American Bar Association
ADP automated data processing
AGV automated guidance vehicle
a.k.a also known as
ANDAs abbreviated new drug applications
ANSI American National Standard Institute
API active pharmaceutical ingredients
ASEAN Association of Southeast Asian Nations
ASTM American Society for Testing and Materials
CA certification authority
CAPA corrective and preventive actions
CEFIC Conseil Européen des Fédérations de l'Industrie Chimique
CFDA China Food and Drug Administration
CFR Code of Federal Regulation
CGMP current good manufacturing practices
CMC chemistry, manufacturing, and controls
CPG Compliance Policy Guid (US FDA)
CRC cyclic redundancy check
CRL certificate revocation list
CROs contract research organizations
CSV computer systems validation
DCS distributed control system
DES data encryption standard
DQ design qualification
DRM device master record
DSA digital signature algorithm

DSHEA	Dietary Supplement Health and Education Act
DTS	digital time-stamping service
EC	European Commission
EDMS	electronic document management system
EEA	European Economic Area
EEC	European Economic Community
EFS	encrypting file system
EMA	European Medicines Agency
ERP	enterprise resource planning
EU	European Union
EVM	earned value management
FAT	factory acceptance test
FD&C Act	Food, Drug and Cosmetic Act (US)
FDA	Food and Drug Administration (US)
FR	Federal Register (US)
FTP	file transfer protocol
GAMP	good automated manufacturing practices
GDP	good documentation practices
GCP	good clinical practices
GEIP	good e-records integrity practices
GLP	good laboratory practices
GMPs	good manufacturing practices
GXP/GxP	a global abbreviation intended to cover GMP, GCP, GLP, and other regulated applications in context GXP can refer to one specific set of practices or to any combination of the three
HMA	Heads of Medicines Agencies
HMI	human–machine interface
IaaS	infrastructure as a service
ICH	International Conference for Harmonization of Technical Requirements for Registration of Pharmaceuticals for Human Use
ICS	industrial control system
I/Os	inputs and outputs
IEC	International Electrotechnical Commission
IEEE	Institute of Electrical and Electronic Engineers
IIS	internet information services
IMDRF	International Medical Device Regulators Forum
IoT	Internet of Things
ISA	International Society of Automation
ISO	International Organization for Standardization

ISPE International Society for Pharmaceutical Engineering
IT information technologies
ITIL IT infrastructure library
ITSM IT service management
KMS key management service
LAN local area network
LIMS laboratory information management system
MA marketing authorization
MES manufacturing execution system
MHRA Medicines and Healthcare Products Regulatory Agency (UK)
MRA mutual recognition agreements
MTTR mean time to repair or mean time to recovery
MTBF mean time between failures
NARA National Archives and Records Administration
NBS National Bureau of Standards
NDAs new drug applications
NEMA National Electrical Manufacturers Association
NIST National Institutes of Standards and Technology
NTP network time protocol
OECD Organization for Economic Cooperation and Development
OMCL Official Medicines Control Laboratories
OLAs operational level agreements
OSHA Occupational Safety and Health Administration (US)
OTS off-the-shelf
P&ID process and instrumentation drawings
PaaS platform as a service
PAI pre-approval inspections
PAT process analytical tools
PDA Parenteral Drug Association
PIC/S Pharmaceutical Inspection Cooperation Scheme
PIN personal identification number
PKCS public-key cryptography standards
PKI public-key infrastructure
PLC programmable logic controller
PMDA Pharmaceuticals and Medical Devices Agency (Japan)
PQS pharmaceutical quality system
QA quality assurance
QbD quality by design
QC quality control

QMS	quality management system
QP	qualified person
R&D	research and development
RFP	request for proposal
RTU	remote terminal unit
SaaS	software as a service
SAP	systems, application and products
SAS	statistical analysis system licensed by the SAS Institute, Inc.
SAT	site acceptance test
SCADA	supervisory control and data acquisition
SDLC	software development life cycle
SHA-1	secure hash algorithm 1
SLA	service level agreement
SLC	system life cycle
SME	subject matter experts
SIPOC	suppliers, inputs, process, outputs, customers
SOPs	standard operating procedures
SPC	statistical process control
SQA	software quality assurance
SRS	System Requirements specifications
SQE	software quality engineering
SSA	Social Security Administration (US)
SSL	secure sockets layer
SWEBOK	software engineering body of knowledge
TGA	Therapeutic Goods Administration (Australia)
TLS	transport layer security
UCs	underpinning contracts
UPS	uninterruptable power supply
VPN	virtual privates network
WBS	work breakdown structure
WAN	wide area network
WL	warning letter
WLAN	wireless local area network
WHO	World Health Organization

Appendix III: Regulatory Cross Match

Table A3.1 Regulatory Cross Match

	References				
	Old Annex 11	*211*	*820*	*11*	*Others/Guidelines*
Principle					• GAMP 5 Management Appendix M3. • Data quality element: Accurate.
a. This annex applies to all forms of computerized systems used as part of a GMP regulated activities. A computerized system is a set of software and hardware components which together fulfill certain functionalities.		211.68[1]	820.70(i)	11.2(b)	• EU Directives 2017/1572 and 91/412/EEC. • PIC/S PI 011-3. • ISO 13485 7.5.2. • Article 1 draft Annex 2 CFDA GMP. • OECD Guidance Document, Section 1.1.1.
b. The application should be validated; IT infrastructure should be qualified.	11-3	211.68	820.70(i) 820.30(g) 820.170	11.10(a)	• Eudralex Volume 4, Glossary. • PIC/S PI 011-3. • ICH Q7A, Good Manufacturing Practice Guidance for Active Pharmaceutical Ingredients, Sections 5.40 and 5.41. • *WHO Technical Report Series*, No. 937, 2006. Annex 4. Appendix 5, Section 7.1 (Hardware). • ISO 13485 7.5.2; 7.3.6; 7.2; 7.2.1; 7.2.2. • Article 10 draft Annex 2 CFDA GMP. • GAMP GPG, IT Infrastructure Control and Compliance, 2005. • OECD Guidance Document, Section 1.1.2. • ICH E6 Guideline for GCP (June 1996), Section 5.5.3(a). • ANMAT (Argentina) 5.21. • US FDA, General Principles of Software Validation, Section 5.2.6. • Part II – Basic Requirements for Active Substances used as Starting Materials, Section 5.40.

(Continued)

Table A3.1 (Continued) Regulatory Cross Match

	References				
	Old Annex 11	*211*	*820*	*11*	*Others/Guidelines*
c. Where a computerized system replaces a manual operation, there should be no resultant decrease in product quality, process control or quality assurance. There should be no increase in the overall risk of the process.	Principle				• PIC/S PI 011-3. • US FDA CPG 7348.810 – Sponsors, CROs, and Monitors. • Brazilian GMPs Title VII Art 570. • Thailand CSV GMPs. • Article 2 draft Annex 2 CFDA GMP.
General					
1. **Risk Management** Risk management should be applied throughout the lifecycle of the computerized system taking into account patient safety, <u>data integrity</u>, and product quality. As part of a risk management system, decisions on the extent of validation and <u>data integrity controls</u> should be based on a justified and documented risk assessment of the computerized system.		211.68(b)[2]	820.30(g)		• 812.66[3]. • ICH Q9 Quality Risk Management. • ICH Q7 5.40. • ICH E6 (R2) 5.0.2. • ICH E6 (R2) 1.65. • NIST, Risk Management Guide for Information Technology Systems, Special Publication 800-30. • GHTF, Implementation of Risk Management Principles and Activities Within a Quality Management System. • ISO 14971:2007, Medical Devices – Application of Risk Management to Medical Devices. • GAMP Forum, Risk Assessment for Use of Automated Systems Supporting Manufacturing Process Risk to Record, Pharmaceutical Engineering, Nov/Dec 2002. • GAMP/ISPE, Risk Assessment for Use of Automated Systems Supporting Manufacturing Process – Functional Risk, Pharmaceutical Engineering, May/June 2003. • EU Annex 20. • US FDA, Guidance for the Content of Pre Market Submission for Software Contained in Medical Devices, May 2005. • Pressman, R. S. *Software Engineering – A Practitioner's Approach*, McGraw Hill.

(Continued)

Table A3.1 (Continued) Regulatory Cross Match

	References				
	Old Annex 11	*211*	*820*	*11*	*Others/Guidelines*
					• GAMP 5 Management Appendices M3 and M4; Operational Appendices O2, O6, O8, O9. • Brazilian GMPs Title VII Art 572. • ISO 13485 7.3.6. • *WHO Technical Report Series*, No. 281, 2013. • Health Canada API, C.02.05. • Interpretation #12. • Articles 3. 6, 12 draft Annex 2 CFDA GMP. • OECD Guidance Document, Section 1.2. • ANMAT (Argentina) 5.21. • US FDA, General Principles of Software Validation Section 4.8. • PIC/S Guidance PI 011-3, Sections 4.5 and 4.6. • Establishing Data Criticality and Inherent Integrity Risk, MHRA, March 2018). • Sections 5.3 and 5.4, PIC/S PI 041-1 (Draft 2). • Section 5.0, *WHO Technical Report Series*, No. 995, 2016.
2. **Personnel** There should be close cooperation between all relevant personnel such as process owner, system owner, qualified persons and IT. All personnel should have appropriate qualifications, level of access and defined responsibilities to carry out their assigned duties. (Data quality element: Attributable)	11-1	211.101(d) 211.122 211.186 211.188(b)(11)	820.20(b)(1) and (2), 820.25	11.10(i) 11.10(j) 11.100(b)	• EudraLex, *The Rule Governing Medicinal Products in the European Union*, Volume 4, EU Guidelines for Good Manufacturing Practices for Medicinal Products for Human and Veterinary Use, Part 1, Chapter 2 – Personnel, February 2014. • 21 CFR 110(c). • 21 CFR 606.160(b)(5)(v). • 21 CFR Part 312.53(a) and .53(d). • 21 CFR 58.29. • *WHO Technical Report Series*, No. 937, 2006. Annex 4, Section 13. • GAMP 5, 6.2.3.1, 6.2.3.3, 6.2.3.3. 6.2.3.5 and Operational Appendix O12. • Brazilian GMPs Title VII Art 571.

(*Continued*)

Table A3.1 (Continued) Regulatory Cross Match

	References				
	Old Annex 11	*211*	*820*	*11*	*Others/Guidelines*
					• ISO 13485 5.5; 5.5.1; 5.5.3; 6.2; 6.2.1; 6.2.2. • Japan CSV Guideline (Guideline on Management of Computerized Systems for Marketing Authorization Holder and Manufacturing of Drugs and Quasi-Drugs, October 2010), Section 6.8. • Thailand CSV GMPs, Clause 510. • Health Canada API, C.02.006. • OECD Guidance Document, Section 1.3. • Brazil API (RDC Resolution #69 Chapter VI Section VI Art. 258). • US FDA, Data Integrity (Draft) Guidance III.16. • Section 8.0, *WHO Technical Report Series*, No. 995, 2016.
3. Suppliers and Service Providers 3.1. When third parties (e.g. suppliers, service providers) are used e.g. to provide, install, configure, integrate, validate, maintain (e.g. via remote access), modify or retain a computerized system or related service or for data processing, formal agreements must exist between the manufacturer and any third parties, and these agreements should include clear statements of the responsibilities of the third party. IT-departments should be considered analogous. 3.2. The competence and reliability of a supplier are key factors when selecting a product or service provider. The need for an audit should be based on a risk assessment.	11-18	Sub Part B 211.34	820.20(b) (1) and (2), 820.50		• EudraLex, *Rules Governing Medicinal Products in the European Union*, Volume 4, Good Manufacturing Practice, Medicinal Products for Human and Veterinary Use, Chapter 7: Outsourced Activities, January 2013. • 21 CFR 110(c). • ICH Q7, Good Manufacturing Practice Guidance for Active Pharmaceutical Ingredients. • ICH Q10 Section 2.7 Management of Outsourced Activities and Purchased Materials. • *WHO Technical Report Series*, No. 937, 2006. Annex 4. Appendix 5, Section 6.2. • GAMP 5 Section 6.1.4. • GAMP 5 Management Appendices M2 and M6. • Brazilian GMPs Title VII Art 589. • ISO 13485 5.5; 5.5.1; 5.5.3; 6.2; 6.2.1; 6.2.2' 7.4; 7.4.1. • China GMPs, Section 7. • Thailand CSV GMPs, Clause 527.

(*Continued*)

Table A3.1 (Continued) Regulatory Cross Match

	References				
	Old Annex 11	*211*	*820*	*11*	*Others/Guidelines*
3.3. Documentation supplied with commercial off-the-shelf products should be reviewed by regulated users to check that user requirements are fulfilled. 3.4. Quality system and audit information relating to suppliers or developers of software and implemented systems should be made available to inspectors on request. 3.5. The supplier should be assessed appropriately.					• PDA, Technical Report No. 32 Auditing of Supplier Providing Computer Products and Services for Regulated Pharmaceutical Operations, *PDA Journal of Pharmaceutical Science and Technology*, Sep/Oct 2004, Release 2.0, 58(5). • CEFIC CSV Guide, Section 7.4.6. • Article 4 draft Annex 2 CFDA GMP. • OECD Guidance Document, Section 1.6. • PIC/S Guidance PI 011-3 Sections 5.1, 5.2, 11. • Section 6.20, MHRA, March 2018. • Section 10.0, PIC/S PI 041-1 (Draft 2). • Section 7.0, *WHO Technical Report Series*, No. 995, 2016.
Project Phase					• OECD Guidance Document, Section 2.
4. **Validation** 4.1. The validation documentation and reports should cover the relevant steps of the life cycle. Manufacturers should be able to justify their standards, protocols, acceptance criteria, procedures and records based on their risk assessment. 4.2. Validation documentation should include change control records (if applicable) and reports on any deviations observed during the validation process. 4.3. An up-to-date listing of all relevant systems and their GMP functionality (inventory) should be available. For critical systems an up-to-date system description detailing the physical and logical arrangements, data flows and interfaces with other systems or processes, any hardware and software prerequisites, and security measures should be available.	11-2 11-4 11-5 11-7	211.68 211.100(a), (b)	820.3(z) 803.17 820.40 820.170 820.30(g) 820.70(g) 820.70(i) 820.70(i) 820.30(c) 820.3(z) and (aa) 820.30(f) and (g) 820.30 820.50	11.10(a) 11.10(k) 11.10(h) 11.300(e)	• EU Directives 2017/1572, Article 9 Section 2. • ISO 90003:2004, Sections 7.3.2 through 7.3.5; 7.3.6.2a through 7.3.6.2.c; 7.5.1.5 and 7.5.1.6; 7.3.6.2d; 7.3.7; 7.5.3.2. • ISO-27000, Sections 12.1 and 12.2. • Medicines and Healthcare Products Regulatory Agency (MHRA) (UK). • IEEE. • PIC/S PI 011-3 Sections 6.3, 7, 9, 10, 13.2, 14.3, 23.8, 23.10, • 21 CFR 606.160(b)(5)(ii) and 606.100(b)(15). • ICH Q7, Good Manufacturing Practice Guidance for Active Pharmaceutical Ingredients, Sections5.41, 12.2. • ICH Q9, Quality Risk Management. • 11-1. • 21 CFR 58.61; 63(a) and (c); 58.81(c) and (d); 58.33. • 21 CFR 59.190. • Blood Establishment Computer System Validation in the User's Facility, April 2013. • US FDA, General Principles of Software Validation.

(*Continued*)

Table A3.1 (Continued) Regulatory Cross Match

	References				
	Old Annex 11	*211*	*820*	*11*	*Others/Guidelines*
4.4. User requirements specifications should describe the required functions of the computerized system and be based on documented risk assessment and GMP impact. User requirements should be traceable throughout the life cycle[4]. 4.5. The regulated user should take all reasonable steps, to ensure that the system has been developed in accordance with an appropriate quality management system. The supplier should be assessed appropriately. 4.6. For the validation of bespoke or customized computerized systems there should be a process in place that ensures the formal assessment and reporting of quality and performance measures for all the life cycle stages of the system formal assessment and reporting of quality and performance measures for all the life cycle stages of the system. 4.7. Evidence of appropriate test methods[5] and test scenarios should be demonstrated. <u>Particularly, system (process) parameter limits, data limits and error handling should be considered</u>[6]. Automated testing tools and test environments should have documented assessments for their adequacy.					• *WHO Technical Report Series*, No. 937, 2006. Annex 4. Appendix 5. • GAMP 5, Sections 4.2.1, 4.2.3, 4.2.4, 5.2.3, 5.2.5, 6.1.5, 6.1.6, 6.2.6, 6.2.8, 6.2.9, 6.2.10. • GAMP 5, Development Appendices: D1 – D7; Management Appendices M1 – M10; Operational Appendix O1. • 21 CFR 1271.160(d). • 21 CFR 803.17; 21 CFR 803.18. • EU Annex 15. • Brazilian GMPs Title VII Art 573, 574, 575, 576, 578. • Brazilian Medical Devices (RDC No 16), Sections 1.2.4, 4.1.8, 4.2.1.1, 5.4.6, 5.5.2 and 5.5.3, 5.6. • ISO 13485 2.3; 7.2; 7.2.1; 7.2.2; 7.5.1.2.2; 7.3.6; 6.3; 7.5.2. • ISO/TR 14969:2004 7.5.2. • ISO 27000 Section 7.1. • Japan CSV Guideline (Guideline on Management of Computerized Systems for Marketing Authorization Holder and Manufacturing of Drugs and Quasi-Drugs, October 2010), Sections 4, 5 and 9. • China GMPs Article 109. • Thailand CSV GMPs, Clauses 511, 512, 513, 514, 516. • Health Canada API, C.02.05 Interpretation #12; #13; #14; 17. C.02.015 Interpretation #3; #13.5. • Articles 5, 7, 8, 9, 11, 13 draft Annex 2 CFDA GMP. • OECD Guidance Document, Sections 1.5., 1.7, 1.9, 2.1, 2.3 through 2.8. • ANMAT (Argentina) 5.25. • US FDA, General Principles of Software Validation 4.1, 4.5, 5.1, 5.2, 5.2.1, 5.2.2, 5.2.3, 5.2.4, 5.2.5, 5.2.6, 23.10. • Brazil API (RDC Resolution #69 Chapter VI Section VI). • *WHO Technical Report Series*, No. 986, Annex 2 (Section 15.9). • ITIL, Service Design (Section 5.2.8).

(Continued)

Table A3.1 (Continued) Regulatory Cross Match

	References				
	Old Annex 11	*211*	*820*	*11*	*Others/Guidelines*
4.8. <u>If data are transferred to another data format or system, validation should include checks that data are not altered in value and/or meaning during this migration process</u>[7].					• US FDA, Data Integrity (Draft) Guidance III.3. • Part II, Basic Requirements for Active Substances used as Starting Materials, Section 5.41 and 5.42. • Sections 5, 6.8, 6.11, 6.17.1, 6.19 and 5, MHRA March 2018. • Section 9.0, *WHO Technical Report Series*, No. 995, 2016. • NSF 363-14 Section 6.3.2.3 (a) and (c). • OMCL 7.3.
Operational Phase					• GAMP 5, Operational Appendix O12. • OECD Guidance, Section 3. • ANMAT (Argentina) 5.22 and 5.23. • Part II, Basic Requirements for Active Substances used as Starting Materials, Section 5.44.
5. Data Computerized systems exchanging data electronically with other systems should include appropriate built-in checks for the correct and secure entry and processing of data, in order to minimize the risks.[8] (Data quality element: Accurate)	11-6	211.68(b) 211.88 211.194(d)	806.1 820.25 820.70(a) 820.180 820.184	11.10(a) 11.10(b) 11.10(e) 11.10(f) 11.10(g) 11.10(h) 11.30	• US FDA, 425.400; 803.1; 803.10; 803.14; 806.10; 806.30; 58.15; 58.33; 58.35; 59.190. • EudraLex, Volume 4 Good Manufacturing Practice (GMP) Guidelines, Part I – Basic Requirements for Medicinal Products, Chapter 4 – Documentation. • EU Directives 2017/1572, Chapter 9, Article 2. • GAMP 5, Operational Appendix O9. • Brazilian GMPs Title VII Art 577. • ISO 134854 6.2; 6.2.1; 6.2.2 • 7.5; 7.5.1; 7.5.1.1; 4.2.4; 7.5.1. • Thailand CSV GMPs, Clause 515. • OECD Guidance, Section 2.9. • ICH Q7, Section 5.45. • ITIL, Service Design (Chapter 5.2.10). • Section 9.2.1 (Data transfer between systems) and 9.5, PIC/S PI 041-1 (Draft). • Section 6.7, MHRA March 2018.

(Continued)

Table A3.1 (Continued) Regulatory Cross Match

	References				
	Old Annex 11	*211*	*820*	*11*	*Others/Guidelines*
6. **Accuracy Checks** For critical data[9] entered manually, there should be an additional check on the accuracy of the data. This check may be done by a second operator or by validated electronic means. The criticality and the potential consequences of erroneous or incorrectly entered data to a system should be covered by risk management.[10] (Data quality element: Accurate)	11-9	211.68(c)	820.25 820.70	11.10(f)	• The APV Guideline, Computerized Systems, based on Annex 11 of the EU-GMP Guideline. • EudraLex, Volume 4 Good Manufacturing Practice (GMP) Guidelines, Part I – Basic Requirements for Medicinal Products, Chapter 4 – Documentation. • PIC/S PI 011-3. • EU Annex 11-1. • *WHO Technical Report Series*, No. 937, 2006. Annex 4. Appendix 5, Section 4.5. • Brazilian GMPs Title VII Art 577, 580. • ISO 13485 6.2; 6.2.1; 6.2.2; 7.5. • Thailand CSV GMPs, Clause 518. • Health Canada API, C.02.015 Interpretation #18. • Article 15 draft Annex 2 CFDA GMP. • OECD Guidance, Section 3.1. • ANMAT (Argentina) 5.26 and 5.30. • Brazil API (RDC Resolution #69 Chapter VI Section VI Article 265). • ITIL, Service Design (Chapter 5.2.10). • Part II, Basic Requirements for Active Substances used as Starting Materials, Sections 5.45 and 5.49. • QMC 7.3 • Section 6.11.1, MHRA March 2018.
7. **Data Storage** 7.1. Data should be secured by both physical and electronic means against damage. Stored data should be checked for accessibility, readability and accuracy. Access to data should be ensured throughout the retention period. (Data quality element: Legible)	11-13 11-14	211.68(b) 211.180(e)	803.1 820.20 820.40 820.180 806.1	11.10(c) 11.10(d) 11.10(e) 11.10(g) 11.10(h) 11.30	• 812.38. • EU Directives 2017/1572, Article 9 Section 2. • PIC/S PI 011-3. • EudraLex, Volume 4 Good Manufacturing Practice (GMP) Guidelines, Part I – Basic Requirements for Medicinal Products, Chapter 4 – Documentation. • ICH E6 GCP (2) 5.5.3(f). • ICH Q7 5.48.

(Continued)

Table A3.1 (Continued) Regulatory Cross Match

	References				
	Old Annex 11	*211*	*820*	*11*	*Others/Guidelines*
7.2. Regular backups of all relevant data should be done. Integrity and accuracy of backup data and the ability to restore the data should be checked during validation and monitored periodically.[11]					• 21 CFR 58.33; .190(d); .35; .195 • Specific records retention requirements are found in applicable predicate rule. For example 21 CFR 211.180(c), (d), 108.25(g), and 108.35(h), and 58.195. • 812.140(a) and (b). • *WHO Technical Report Series*, No. 937, 2006. Annex 4. Appendix 5, Sections 5 and 7.2.2. • 21 CFR 123.9(f) • GAMP Appendix O9 and O11. • Brazilian GMPs Title VII Art 585. • ISO 13485 6.2; 6.2.1; 6.2.2; 7.5. • Japan CSV Guideline (Guideline on Management of Computerized Systems for Marketing Authorization Holder and Manufacturing of Drugs and Quasi-Drugs, October 2010), Section 6.3. • Japan's Pharmaceutical and Food Safety Bureau, Using Electromagnetic Records and Electronic Signatures for Application for Approval or Licensing of Drugs, Section 3, April 2005. • Thailand CSV GMPs, Clause 517, 522, 523. • Health Canada API, C.02.05, Interpretation #16. • Article 19 draft Annex 2 CFDA GMP. • OECD Guidance, Section 3.2, 3.11. • GAMP 5, Section 4.3.6.1. • ISO 27000, Section 10.5. • Brasil API (RDC Resolution #69 Chapter VI Section VI Article 269). • *WHO Technical Report Series*, No. 986 Annex 2 (Section 15.9). • ITIL, Service Design (Chapter 5.2.11). • US FDA, Data Integrity (Draft) Guidance III.1.e. • 211.68(b); 211.188; 211.194.

(*Continued*)

Table A3.1 (Continued) Regulatory Cross Match

	References				
	Old Annex 11	*211*	*820*	*11*	*Others/Guidelines*
					• Part II, Basic Requirements for Active Substances used as Starting Materials, Section 5.48. • Sections 6.16 and 6.17.2, MHRA March 2018. • Section 9.7, PIC/S PI 041-1 (Draft 2). • OMLC 7.3 and 7.4.
8. Printouts 8.1. It should be possible to obtain clear printed copies of electronically stored e-records. 8.2. For records supporting batch release it should be possible to generate printouts indicating if any of the e-record has been changed since the original entry.[12] (Data quality element: Original)	11-12	211.180(c) 211.194(a)	43 FR 31508 July 21, 1978 803.1 803.10 803.14 806.30 820.40 820.180 806.1	11.10(b)	• 812.150, 58.15. • Directive 1999/93/EC of the European Parliament and of the Council of 13 December 1999 on a Community framework for electronic signatures. • PIC/S PI 011-3. • FDA, Guidance for Industry Part 11, Electronic Records; Electronic Signatures – Scope and Application, August 2003. • The APV Guideline, Computerized Systems, based on Annex 11 of the EU-GMP Guideline. • US FDA, CPG Sec. 130.400, Use of Microfiche and/or Microfilm for Method of Records Retention. • Brazilian GMPs Title VII Art 583. • ISO 13485 4.2.3; 4.2.4. • Thailand CSV GMPs, Clause 521. • OECD Guidance Document, Section 3.3. • Section 6.19, MHRA March 2018.
9. Audit Trails Consideration should be given, based on a risk assessment, to building into the system the creation of a record of all GMP-relevant changes and deletions (a system generated "audit trail"). For change or deletion of GMP-relevant data the reason should be documented. Audit trails need to be available and convertible to a generally intelligible form and regularly reviewed.[13]	11-10	211.180(e)	803.18 820.40	11.10(e) 11.10(k)(2) 11.50(a)(2)	• 1978 US CGMP rev. Comment paragraph 186. • FDA, Guidance for Industry Part 11, Electronic Records; Electronic Signatures – Scope and Application, August 2003. • The APV Guideline, Computerized Systems, based on Annex 11 of the EU-GMP Guideline. • PIC/S PI 011-3. • ICH Q7, Good Manufacturing Practice Guidance for Active Pharmaceutical Ingredients. • ICH E6 GCP (R2) 4.9.0, 5.5.3(c), 5.5.4.

(Continued)

Table A3.1 (Continued) Regulatory Cross Match

	References				
	Old Annex 11	*211*	*820*	*11*	*Others/Guidelines*
(Data quality elements: Legible and Original) Note: In addition to the system generated audit trail, some implementation included the documentation that allows reconstruction of the course of events. Implicitly, this approach does not required a computer system generated audit trail.					• 21 CFR 58.130(d); 211.160(a); 211.194; 212.110(b). • Glossary of the Note for Guidance on Good Clinical Practice (CPMP/ICH/135/95). • Brazilian GMPs Title VII Art 581. • ISO 13485 4.2.3. • Thailand CSV GMPs, Clause 519. • Health Canada API, C.02.05, Interpretation #15. • OECD Guidance Document, Section 3.4. • *WHO Technical Report Series*, No. 986 Annex 2 (Section 15.9). • US FDA, Data Integrity (Draft) Guidance III.1.c; 7 & 8. • Part II, Basic Requirements for Active Substances used as Starting Materials, Section 5.43. • Section 9.4, PIC/S PI 041-1 (Draft 2). • EU Directives 2017/1572, Article 9 Section 2. • Section 6.13, MHRA March 2018.
10. Change and Configuration Management Any changes to a computerized system including system configurations should only be made in a controlled manner in accordance with a defined procedure. (Data quality elements: Legible and Accurate)	11-11	211.68 211.180(e)	820.30(i) 820.70(i) 820.40	11.10(d) 11.10(e)	• ISO 90003, 2004, Sections 7.3.7 and 7.5.3.2. • PIC/S PI 011-3. • The APV Guideline, Computerized Systems, based on Annex 11 of the EU-GMP Guideline. • *WHO Technical Report Series*, No. 937, 2006. Annex 4. Section 12. • Pressman, R. S. *Software Engineering – A Practitioner's Approach*, McGraw Hill. • GAMP 5 Management Appendix M3; GAMP 5 – Operational Appendices O6 and O7. • GAMP 5, Section 4.3.4.1. • Brazilian GMPs Title VII Art 582. • ISO 13485 7.3.7; 7.5.2; 4.2.3. • Japan CSV Guideline (Guideline on Management of Computerized Systems for Marketing Authorization Holder and Manufacturing of Drugs and Quasi-Drugs, October 2010), Section 6.6.

(Continued)

Table A3.1 (Continued) Regulatory Cross Match

	References				
	Old Annex 11	*211*	*820*	*11*	*Others/Guidelines*
					• China GMP, Articles 240–246. • Thailand CSV GMPs, Clause 520. • Health Canada API, C.02.015 Interpretation #20. • Article 17 draft Annex 2 CFDA GMP. • OECD Guidance Document, Sections 1.8, 2.2, 3.5, 4. • ANMAT (Argentina) 5.28. • ICH E6 (R2), Section 5.5.4(h). • ICH Q7, Section 5.47. • General Principles of Software Validation Sections 4.7 and 5.2.7. • Part II – Basic Requirements for Active Substances used as Starting Materials, Section 5.47. • NSF 363-14 Section 6.3.2.3 (e). • Section 6.20, MHRA March 2018.
11. **Periodic evaluation** Computerized systems should be periodically evaluated to confirm that they remain in a valid state and are compliant with GMP. Such evaluations should include, where appropriate, the current range of functionality, deviation records, incidents, problems, upgrade history, performance, reliability, security, and validation status report(s). (Data quality element: Accurate)		211.68 211.180(e)	820.20(c)	11.10(k) 11.300(b) and (e)	• US FDA CPG 7132a.07, Computerized Drug Processing; Input/Output Checking. • ICH Q7, 12.60. • *WHO Technical Report Series*, No. 937, 2006. Annex 4. Appendix 5, Section 1.5 • GAMP 5, Section 4.3.5. • GAMP 5 Management Appendix M3; GAMP 5, Operational Appendices O3 and O8 • 58.35; 58.190; 58.195. • Annex 15 clauses 23 and 45. • ISO 13485 5.6; 5.6.1; 5.6.2; 5.6.3; 8.2.2; 8.5; 8.5.1. • China GMPs Section 8. • OECD Guidance Document, Section 3.6. • ITIL, Service Design (Chapter 5.2.13). • Sections 3.5 and 6.15, MHRA March 2018.

(Continued)

Table A3.1 (Continued) Regulatory Cross Match

	References				
	Old Annex 11	*211*	*820*	*11*	*Others/Guidelines*
12. Security 12.1. Physical and/or logical controls should be in place to restrict access to computerized systems to authorized persons. Suitable methods of preventing unauthorized entry to the system may include the use of keys, pass cards, personal codes with passwords, biometrics, restricted access to computer equipment, and data storage areas. 12.2. The extent of security controls depends on the criticality of the computerized system. 12.3. Creation, change, and cancellation of access authorizations should be recorded. 12.4. Management systems for data and for documents should be designed to record the identity of operators entering, changing, confirming, or deleting data including date and time.[14] (Data quality elements: Attributable [12.4] and Contemporaneous [12.4])	11-8	211.68(b) 211.160(a)		11.10(b) 11.10(c) 11.10(d) 11.10(g) 11.300	• PIC/S PI 011-3, Sections 19.2; 19.3. • ICH E6 GCP (R2) 5.5.3 (d), (e). • ICH Q7, Section 5.43. • 21 CFR Part 58.51; 58.190(d); 211.68(b). • *WHO Technical Report Series*, No. 937, 2006. Annex 4. Appendix 5 Section 4. • GAMP 5, Section 4.3.7.1. • GAMP 5 Management Appendix M9; GAMP 5 – Operational Appendix O11. • Brazilian GMPs Title VII Art 579. • Japan CSV Guideline (Guideline on Management of Computerized Systems for Marketing Authorization Holder and Manufacturing of Drugs and Quasi-Drugs, October 2010), Section 6.4. • Thailand CSV GMPs, Clause 517. • Health Canada API, C.02.05, Interpretation #15. • Articles 14, 16 draft Annex 2 CFDA GMP. • OECD Guidance Document, Section 3.7. • ANMAT (Argentina) 5.24. • ISO-27000, Sections 12.1 and 11.2. • Brazil API (RDC Resolution #69 Chapter VI Art. 106 Paragraph 2). • WHO, Technical Report 986 Annex 2 (Section 15.9). • ITIL, Service Design (Chapter 5.2.13). • EU Directives 2017/1572, Article 9 Section 2. • US FDA, Data Integrity (Draft) Guidance III.4 & .5. • Part II – Basic Requirements for Active Substances used as Starting Materials, Section 5.43. • Section 6.20, MHRA March 2018. • Section 9.3, PIC/S PI 041-1 (Draft 2). • NSF 363-14 Section 6.3.2.3 (b). • OMCL Section 7.1.

(Continued)

Table A3.1 (Continued) Regulatory Cross Match

	References				
	Old Annex 11	*211*	*820*	*11*	*Others/Guidelines*
13. Incident Management All incidents, not only system failures and data errors, should be reported and assessed. The root cause of a critical incident should be identified and should form the basis of corrective and preventive actions.	11-17	211.100(b)	820.100		• ICH Q7A, Good Manufacturing Practice Guidance for Active Pharmaceutical Ingredients, Section 5.46. • ICH E6, Section 5.1.3. • GAMP 5 Operational Appendices O4. O5, and O7. • Brazilian GMPs Title VII Art 588. • ISO 13485 8.5; 8.5.1; 8.5.2; 8.5.3. • Japan CSV Guideline (Guideline on Management of Computerized Systems for Marketing Authorization Holder and Manufacturing of Drugs and Quasi-Drugs, October 2010), Sections 6.7 and 7.2. • China GMPs, Sections 5 and 6. • Thailand CSV GMPs, Clause 526. • Health Canada API, C.02.015 Interpretation #19. • Articles 20 and 21 draft Annex 2 CFDA GMP. • OECD Guidance Document, Section 3.8. • ANMAT (Argentina) 5.27. • US FDA, General Principles of Software Validation, Section 5.2.7. • Part II – Basic Requirements for Active Substances used as Starting Materials, Section 5.46. • Section 3.9, MHRA March 2018.
14. Electronic Signature Electronic records may be signed electronically. Electronic signatures are expected to: • have the same impact as handwritten signatures within • the boundaries of the company[15], • be permanently linked to their respective record,				11.3(b)(7); 11.10(e); 11.50; .70, .100, .200, .300	• EU GMP Chapter 4 Principle. • Annex 11-8.1, 9, 12.4, 17. • ICH Q7A, Good Manufacturing Practice Guidance for Active Pharmaceutical Ingredients, Section 5.43. • Electronic Signatures in Global and National Commerce (E-Sign), a US federal law. (available at: http://thomas.loc.gov/cgi-bin/query/z?c106:S.761:) • 21 CFR 58.33; .81; .35; .120; .185.

(Continued)

Table A3.1 (Continued) Regulatory Cross Match

	References				
	Old Annex 11	*211*	*820*	*11*	*Others/Guidelines*
• include the time and date that they were applied. (Data quality element: Contemporaneous)					• Japan's Pharmaceutical and Food Safety Bureau, Using Electromagnetic Records and Electronic Signatures for Application for Approval or Licensing of Drugs, Section 4, April 2005. • Article 22 draft Annex 2 CFDA GMP. • Guidance Document, Section .10. • US FDA, Data Integrity (Draft) Guidance III.11. • Section 6.14, MHRA March 2018. • Section 9.3 (Item #3), PIC/S PI 041-1 (Draft 2).
15. Batch Release When a computerized system is used for recording certification and batch release, the system should allow only qualified persons to certify the release of the batches and it should clearly identify and record the person releasing or certifying the batches. This should be performed using an electronic signature. (Data quality element: Attributable)	11-19	211.68 211.186 211.192 211.188(b)(11) 211.188(a)		11.70; Sub Part C	• 21 CFR 211.68. • The APV Guideline, Computerized Systems, based on Annex 11 of the EU-GMP Guideline. • 11-9; 11-14. • EC Directive 2001/83. • Brazilian GMPs Title VII Art 590. • Thailand CSV GMPs, Clause 528. • Article 21 draft Annex 2 CFDA GMP.
16. Business Continuity For the availability of computerized systems supporting critical processes, provisions should be made to ensure continuity of support for those processes in the event of a system breakdown (e.g. a manual or alternative system). The time required to bring the alternative arrangements into use should be based on risk and appropriate for a particular system and the business process it supports. These arrangements should be adequately documented and tested.[16]	11-15 11-16				• PIC/S PI 011-3. • GAMP 5, Sections 4.3.6.2 and 4.3.6.3. • GAMP 5 Operational Appendix O10. • Brazilian GMPs Title VII Art 586, 587. • Thailand CSV GMPs, Clause 524, 525. • OECD Guidance Document, Section 3.12. • ANMAT (Argentina) 5.29. • ICH Q7, Section 5.48. • Brazil API (RDC Resolution #69 Chapter VI Section VI Articles 271 and 272). • NSF 363-14 Section 6.3.2.3 (d). • 2001/83, Article 81. • Section 6.20, MHRA March 2018.

(*Continued*)

Table A3.1 (Continued) Regulatory Cross Match

	References				
	Old Annex 11	*211*	*820*	*11*	*Others/Guidelines*
17. Archiving Data may be archived. This data should be checked for accessibility, readability and integrity. If relevant changes are to be made to the system (e.g. computer equipment or programs), then the ability to retrieve the data should be ensured and tested. (Data integrity element: Legible)		211.68(b) 211.180(e)		11.10(c)	• Scientific Archivists Group, A Guide to Archiving of Electronic Records, 2014. www.sagroup.org.uk/images/documents/AGuidetoArchivingElectronicRecordsv1.pdf • DOD 5015.2-STD, *Design Criteria Standard for E-records Management Software Applications*. • GAMP 5 Operational Appendix O13. • GAMP GPG, Electronic Data Archiving, 2007. • Brazilian GMPs Title VII Art 584. • Draft OECD Guidance Document, Section 3.12. • Scientific Archivists Group, A Guide to Archiving of Electronic Records. • ITIL, Service Design (Chapter 5.2.13). • Sections 6.17.1, MHRA March 2018. • Section 9.7, PIC/S PI 041-1 (Draft 2). • EU Directives 2017/1572, Article 9 Section 2. • OMCL Section 6.9 and 7.4.

1 López, O. "A Historical View of 21 CFR Part 211.68." *Journal of GxP Compliance* 15(2) (Spring 2011).
2 Federal Register, Vol. 60 No. 13, 4087–4091, January 20, 1995.
3 All 21 CFR Part 812 regulations apply equally to both paper records and electronic records. The use of computer systems in clinical investigations does not exempt Investigational Device Exemption (IDE) from any 21 CFR 812 requirements.
4 López, O. "Requirements Management." *Journal of Validation Technology* 17(2) (Spring 2011).
5 Test methods – with the Black-Box Test, the test cases are derived solely from the description of the test object, the inner structure of the object is thus not considered when creating the test plan; With the White-Box Test, the test cases are derived solely from the structure of the test object. With the Source-Code Review, the source code is checked against the documentation describing the system by one or several professionals. The APV Guideline, Computerized Systems, based on Annex 11 of the EU-GMP Guideline, April 1996.
6 This sentence is related with the additional checks covered in Accuracy Checks (11-6).
7 Annex 11-4.8 is complemented with 11-7.1.
8 Annex 11-5 is fundamental in e-records integrity and it is related with Annex 11-4.7.
9 The term "critical data" in this context is interpreted as meaning data with high risk to product quality or patient safety. ISPE GAMP COP Annex 11 – Interpretation, July/August 2011.
10 Annex 11-6 is another fundamental section related with e-records integrity.

(Continued)

Table A3.1 (Continued) Regulatory Cross Match

[11] Annex 11-7 is another fundamental section related with e-records integrity.
[12] Annex 11-8 is another fundamental section related with e-records integrity.
[13] Annex 11-9 is another fundamental section related with e-records integrity.
[14] Annex 11-12 is another fundamental section related with e-records integrity.
[15] The phrase "within the boundaries of the company" clarifies that such signatures applied to records maintained by the regulated company are not subject to Directive 1999/93/EC on a company framework for e-signatures, nor the 2000/31/EC Directive on electronic commerce, nor any associated national regulations of EU Member States on such topics.
[16] Annex 11-16 is another fundamental section related with e-records integrity.

Revision History

Table A3.2 The History of the Changes

Date	*Update Reason*
02-FEB-2011	Creation of the Annex 11 matrix.
21-FEB-2011	Updated format of matrix and updated based on various references.
08-MAR-2011	Updated various 21 CFR 820 references based on the US FDA General Principles of Software Validation, January 2002, CDRH and CBER.
13-MAR-2011	Updated various 21 CFR 211 references based on the US FDA Guide to Inspection of Computerized Systems in Drug Processing, February 1983.
22-MAR-2011	Updated various 21 CFR 11 references based on regulation. Added raw data references. Updated periodic review based on comments by Jeffrey Torres.
31-MAR-2011	Updated "Principle" reference based on US FDA CPG 7348.810 – Sponsors, CROs, and Monitors. Updated various 21 CFR 820 references based on another matrix correlating various regulatory requirements. Updated various references based on ICH E6 GCP, 21 CFR 58, and 21 CFR 312.
09-APR-2011	Added ISO 14971 as a reference. Updated 11-7 based on 21 CFR 820.
23-APR-2011	Updated various references based on various CFRs.
11-MAY-2011	Updated based on regulations for Computerized Systems Used in Medical Device Clinical Investigations, 21 CFR 812.
12-JUN-2011	Added 211.194(d) in Data Section; added reference on my recent article on Requirements Management, published by IVT; Section 4, added the Blood Establishment Computer System Validation in the User's Facility, October 2007 (Draft Guidance); added as a reference EMA/INS/GCP/454280/2010 GCP Inspectors Working Group (GCP IWG), *Reflection paper on expectations for electronic source data and data transcribed to electronic data collection tools in clinical trials*; updated various references based on 21 CFR 58.
03-AUG-2011	Added regulatory requirements about 820 based on the US FDA Medical Devices QS Manual: A small entity compliance guide, Chapter 7; added in periodic review reference of ICH Q7, 12.6; modifications to Old-New Annex 11 mappings.

(*Continued*)

Table A3.2 (Continued) The History of the Changes

Date	*Update Reason*
23-AUG-2011	Added *WHO Technical Report Series*, No. 937, 2006. Annex 4. Appendix 5. 2006
26-AUG-2011	Added Electronic Signatures in Global and National Commerce (E-Sign), a US federal law
25-SEP-2011	Added GAMP 5 Cross references (Yves Samson); added definition of Test Methods based APV guideline.
24-OCT-11	Added Tissues Reg 21 CFR 1271.160(d); Food 21 CFR 123.9(f)
17-MAR-2012	Updated based on NEMA Presentation, Part 11 Recommendations for Changes, June 2004.
21-OCT-12	Updated based on presentation FDA Public Meeting June 2004 (R. Eaton and R. Nabar)
15-NOV-2012	Updated various references based ICH Q10, ISPE GAMP COP Annex 11 – Interpretation, July/August 2011.
2-DEC-12	Updated based on Brazilian GMPs, Title VII Resolution of the Executive Board No. 17, Computerized Information Systems. This can be found on page 109 de 148, **www.in.gov.br/imprensa/visualiza/index.jsp?jornal=1&pagina=94&data=19/04/2010**
07-APR-13	Updated guideline Blood Establishment Computer System Validation in the User's Facility, from October 2007 (Draft Guidance) to April 2013 (Final Guidance).
24-AUG-13	Updated with ISO 134854.
24-OCT-13	Added Japanese CSV Guidelines (Guidelines on Management of Computerized Systems for Marketing Authorization Holders and Manufacturers of Drugs and Quasi-Drugs, October 2010) and Japan's Pharmaceutical and Food Safety Bureau, Using Electromagnetic Records and Electronic Signatures for Application for Approval or Licensing of Drugs, April 2005.
31-OCT-13	Added State Food and Drug Administration, P.R. China, March 2011 and Thailand CSV GMPs contained in the Prescription of Details Regarding and Procedures of Manufacture of Modern Medicinal Products in compliance with Drug Lawa B.E.2554.
08-FEB-14	Added 91/412/EEC; *WHO Technical Report Series*, No. 981 PDA, Technical Report No. 32; CEFIC CSV Guide Rev 2, December 2002. Health Canada GMP Guidelines for API (GUI-0104) Dec 2013.
08-FEB-14b	Corrected copy. Added couple of sections left out from the Health Canada GMP Guidelines for API.

(*Continued*)

Table A3.2 (Continued) The History of the Changes

Date	*Update Reason*
26-MAR-14	Updated application sections based on ICH E6 GCP.
09-JUL-14	Incorrect references in 21 CFR Part 58, Security. China Food & Drug Administration (CFDA) draft of GMP Annex 2 Computerized Systems.
12-SEP-14	Added reference GAMP GPG, Electronic Data Archiving, 2007 to Archiving; Added reference GAMP GPG, IT Infrastructure Control and Compliance, 2005 to Principle b. Added reference ISO/TR 14969:2004 Medical Devices – Quality Management Systems – Guidance on the Application of ISO 13485. Added EudraLex, *The Rules Governing Medicinal Products in the European Union,* Volume 4, Good Manufacturing Practice, Medicinal Products for Human and Veterinary Use, Chapter 7: Outsourced Activities, January 2013 to Suppliers and Service Providers.
23-SEP-14	Added Draft OECD Guidance Document – The Application of GLP Principles to Computerised Systems, September 2014. (Note: The entries related with this draft, were replaced with the final document. Refer 21-Feb-18 entry.)
10-OCT-14	Based on the definition by the NIST (SP 800-33), highlighted the data integrity-related items on Annex 11.
19-DEC-14	Added ISO 90003:2014 applicable sections related with Configuration Management and applicable development phase activities.
05-MAR-15	Added ICH E6, Guideline for GCP (Jun 1996). Added Administracion Nacional de Medicamentos, Alimentos y Tecnologia Medicas (ANMAT) (Argentina's Ministerio de Salud Presidencia de la Nacion). Added ISO/IEC 27000 Information Security Management Systems. Added US FDA General Principles of Software Validation. Fixed minor errors.
01-AUG-15	In 11-17 added Scientific Archivists Group, A Guide to Archiving of Electronic Records, as a reference. Added Brazil API Regulations (RDC Resolution #69)
14-NOV-15	Added WHO Guide regarding the Principles of GMP Technical Report 986, Annex 2 WHO Good Manufacturing Practices for Pharmaceutical Products: Main Principles. Added ITIL, Service Design, Chapter 5.2 – Management of Data and Information, 2011 Edition
22-APR-16	Added US FDA Guidance for Industry: Data Integrity and Compliance with CGMP (Draft)

(Continued)

Table A3.2 (Continued) The History of the Changes

Date	*Update Reason*
11-AUG-16	Added Part II – Basic Requirements for Active Substances Used as Starting Materials Added EMA Q&A: GMP Data Integrity, August 2016. Added *MHRA GxP Data Integrity Definitions and Guidance for Industry*, July 2016 (Draft)
	Added PIC/S, *Good Practices for Data Management and Integrity in Regulated GMP/GCP Environments*, PI 041-1 (Draft 2), August 2016. TGA intends to reference the PIC/S *Good Practices for Data Management and Integrity In Regulated GMP/GDP Environments*, PI 041-1 (Draft 2) Added WHO Guidance on Good Data and Record Management Practices, *Technical Report Series*, No. 966, Annex 5 WHO Expert Committee on Specifications for Pharmaceutical Preparations.
28-SEP-16	Added NSF/IPEC/ANSI 363 – 2014 Good Manufacturing Practices (GMP) for Pharmaceutical Excipients
24-SEP-17	ICH E6 (R2) GCP Guideline (2016); Updated articles in EU GMP Directive 2003/94/EC with applicable articles in the new Directive 2017/1572; OMCL Management of Documents and Records (January 2016).
04-NOV-17	Integration of Q13 in Added EMA Q&A: GMP Data Integrity, August 2016, with Added US FDA Guidance for Industry: Data Integrity and Compliance with CGMP (Draft).
21-FEB-18	Replaced "Data integrity element" with "Data quality element:"; replaced Draft OECD Guidance Document – The Application of GLP Principles to Computerised Systems, September 2014 with the final version April 2016.
04-APR-18	The entries related with MHRA GxP Data Integrity Definitions and Guidance for Industry, July 2016 (Draft) were replaced with the final document. Refer 11-Aug-16 entry. The final guidance document, *MHRA GxP Data Integrity Guidance and Definitions* was published on March 2018.

Note: Periodically the content in Appendix III is updated. Check site: https://drive.google.com/open?id=1EqeWvGAipuuwQJh2qf0v7ru50BiWzov- to verify the most recent revision.

Appendix IV: Additional Readings

1. Aide-mémoire of German ZLG regarding EU GMP Annex 1, September 2013.
2. Appel, K. "How far does annex 11 go beyond Part 11?" *Pharmaceutical Processing*, September 2011.
3. APV. The APV Guideline "Computerized Systems" based on Annex 11 of the EU-GMP Guideline, Version 1.0, April 1996.
4. Brown, A. "Selecting Storage Media for Long-Term Preservation." The National Archives, DPGN-02, August 2008.
5. Cappucci, W. et al. "Annex 11 interpretation." *Pharmaceutical Engineering*, 31(4) 2011; 90–96.
6. CEFIC, API Committee. "Computer Validation Guide." January 2003.
7. Center for Technology in Government University at Albany, SUNY. "Practical Tools for Electronic Records Management and Preservation." July 1999.
8. Churchward, D. "Good Manufacturing Practice (GMP) Data Integrity: A New Look at an Old Topic." Part 1, June 2015. https://mhrainspectorate.blog.gov.uk/?=goo-manufacturing-practice-gmp-data-a-new-look-at-an-old-topic-part-1.
9. Churchward, D. "Good Manufacturing Practice (GMP) Data Integrity: A New Look at an Old Topic." Part 2, July 2015. https://mhrainspectorate.blog.gov.uk/2015/07/14/good-manufacturing-practice-gmp-data-integrity-a-new-look-at-an-old-topic-part-2/.
10. Churchward, D. "Good Manufacturing Practice (GMP) Data Integrity: A New Look at an Old Topic." Part 3, August 2015. https://mhrainspectorate.blog.gov.uk/2015/08/27/good-manufacturing-practice-gmp-data-integrity-a-new-look-at-an-old-topic-part-3/.
11. Commission Directive 2003/94/EC Laying Down the Principles and Guidelines of Good Manufacturing Practice in Respect of Medicinal Products for Human Use and Investigational Medicinal Products for Human Use, October 1994.
12. Commission Directive 91/412/EEC Laying Down the Principles and Guidelines of Good Manufacturing Practice for Veterinary Medicinal Products. July 1991.
13. Commission Directive 95/46/EC of the European Parliament and of the Council of 24 October 1995. On the Protection of Individuals with Regard to the Processing of Personal Data and on the Free Movement of Such Data. http://eur-lex.europa.eu/LexUriServ/LexUriServ.do?uri=CELEX:31995L0046:en:HTML.

14. Commission Directive 2017/1572 Supplementing Directive 2001/83/EC of the European Parliament and of the Council as Regards the Principles and Guidelines of Good Manufacturing Practice for Medicinal Products for Human Use. September 2017.
15. Council of Europe. "Handbook on European Data Protection Law." December 2013.
16. EU Annex III to "Guidance for the Conduct of Good Clinical Practice Inspections Computer Systems." May 2008. http://ec.europa.eu/health/files/eudralex/vol-10/chap4/annex_iii_to_guidance_for_the_conduct_of_gcp_inspections_-_computer_systems_en.pdf.
17. EudraLex. "EU Guidelines to Good Manufacturing Practice, Medicinal Products for Human and Veterinary Use, Part 1, Annex 11 – Computerized Systems." *The Rules Governing Medicinal Products in the European Union*, Volume 4. June 2011. http://ec.europa.eu/health/files/eudralex/vol-4/annex11_01-2011_en.pdf.
18. EudraLex. "EU Guidelines to Good Manufacturing Practice, Medicinal Products for Human and Veterinary Use, Annex 15 – Validation and Qualification." *The Rules Governing Medicinal Products in the European Union*, Volume 4. October 2015.
19. EudraLex. "EU Guidelines to Good Manufacturing Practice, Medicinal Products for Human and Veterinary Use. Annex 16 – Certification by a Qualified Person and Batch Release." *The Rules Governing Medicinal Products in the European Union*, Volume 4. 2001.
20. EudraLex. "EU Guidelines to Good Manufacturing Practice, Medicinal Products for Human and Veterinary Use – Glossary." *The Rules Governing Medicinal Products in the European Union*, Volume 4. February 2013.
21. EudraLex. "EU Guidelines for Good Manufacturing Practices for Medicinal Products for Human and Veterinary Use, Part 1, Chapter 2 – Personnel." *The Rules Governing Medicinal Products in the European Union*, Volume 4. February 2014.
22. EudraLex. "Good Manufacturing Practice, Medicinal Products for Human and Veterinary Use, Chapter 3 – Premises and Equipment." *The Rules Governing Medicinal Products in the European Union*, Volume 4. 2007.
23. EudraLex. "Good Manufacturing Practice, Medicinal Products for Human and Veterinary Use, Chapter 7 – Outsourced Activities." *The Rules Governing Medicinal Products in the European Union*, Volume 4. January 2013.
24. EudraLex. "EU Good Manufacturing Practice (GMP) Medicinal Products for Human and Veterinary Use, Chapter 9 – Self Inspections." *The Rules Governing Medicinal Products in the European Union*, Volume 4. 2001.
25. EudraLex. "Good Manufacturing Practice, Medicinal Products for Human and Veterinary Use – Glossary." *The Rules Governing Medicinal Products in the European Union*, Volume 4. 2007.
26. European Commission (EC). "General Data Protection Regulation (GDPR)." January 2012 (Proposed regulation to replace EU Data Protection Directive 95/46/EC).

27. European Directorate for the Quality of Medicine and Healthcare. "OMCL Validation of Computerised Systems Core Documents." May 2009, www.edqm.eu/medias/fichiers/Validation_of_Computerised_Systems_Core_Document.pdf.
28. European Medicines Agency (EMA). "Reflection Paper on the Expectations for Electronic Source Documents Used in Clinical Trials." August 2010.
29. European Medicines Agency (EMA). "Q&A: Good Manufacturing Practices (GMP)." February 2011.
30. European Medicines Agency (EMA). "Questions and Answers: Good Manufacturing Practice, EU GMP Guide Annexes: Supplementary Requirements: Annex 11: Computerised Systems." August 2016, www.ema.europa.eu/ema/index.jsp?curl=pages/regulation/general/gmp_q_a.jsp&mid=WC0b01ac058006e06c#section8.
31. GAMP®. "Good Practice Guide: A Risk-Based Approach to Compliant Electronic Records and Signatures." 2005.
32. GAMP®. "Good Practice Guide: Electronic Data Archiving." 2007.
33. GAMP®. "Good Practice Guide: Global Information Systems Control and Compliance – Appendix 2 – Data Management Considerations." 2005.
34. GAMP®. *Good Practice Guide: IT Control and Compliance*. Tampa, FL: International Society of Pharmaceutical Engineering, 2005.
35. GAMP®. "Good Practice Guide: Risk Based Approach to Operation of GXP Computerized Systems." 2010.
36. GAMP®/ISPE. *A Risk-Based Approach to Compliant GxP Computerized Systems*. 5th ed. Tampa, FL: International Society for Pharmaceutical Engineering, February 2008.
37. GCP Inspectors Working Group (GCP IWG). "Reflection Paper on Expectations for Electronic Source Data and Data Transcribed to Electronic Data Collection Tools in Clinical Trials." EMA/INS/GCP/454280/2010. August 2010.
38. GMP Journal. "Q&As on Annex 11 (1-4) at the Computer Validation in Mannheim, Germany, in June 2011." Issue 7, October/November 2011.
39. GMP Journal. "Q&As on Annex 11 (5-11) at the Computer Validation in Mannheim, Germany, in June 2011." Issue 8, April/May 2012.
40. GMP Journal. "Q&As on Annex 11 (12-16) at the Computer Validation in Mannheim, Germany, in June 2011." Issue 9, October/November 2012.
41. ICH Harmonized Tripartite Guideline. "Quality Risk Management, Q9." November 2005.
42. ICH Harmonized Tripartite Guideline. "Good Clinical Practice, E6." Rev 2, June 2016.
43. IDA Programme of the European Commission. "Model Requirements for the Management of Electronic Records." October 2002, www.cornwell.co.uk/moreq.html
44. IEEE. "Guide to the Software Engineering Body of Knowledge." Rev 3.0. 2014.
45. ISO 11799: 2003(E). "Information and documentation – Document storage requirements for archive and library materials."
46. ISO/IEC 1799:2005. "Information technology – Security techniques – Code of practice for information security management."

47. ISO/IEC 27001: 2013. "Information technology – Security techniques – Information security management systems – Requirements."
48. ISPE GAMP Forum. "Risk assessment for use of automated systems supporting manufacturing processes – Part 2 – Risk to records." *Pharmaceutical Engineering*, 23(6) (2003).
49. ISPE (Dr. Kate McCormick). "Regulatory Framework – EMEA." 2009.
50. ISPE (Dr. Kate McCormick). "Regulatory Framework – PIC/S and ICH." 2009.
51. Journal for GMP and Regulatory Affairs. "Q&As on Annex 11." Issue 8, April/May 2012.
52. López, O. "Annex 11: Progress in EU Computer Systems Guidelines." *Pharmaceutical Technology Europe*, 23(6) 2011, www.pharmtech.com/pharmtech/article/articleDetail.jsp?id=725378.
53. López, O. "Annex 11 and 21 CFR Part 11: Comparisons for International Compliance." MasterControl, January 2012, www.mastercontrol.com/newsletter/annex-11-21-cfr-part-11-comparison.html.
54. López, O. *An Easy to Understand Guide to Annex 11.* Premier Validation: Cork, Ireland, 2011, https://learnaboutgmp.com/gmp/an-easy-to-understand-guide-to-annex-11/.
55. López, O. *Computer Infrastructure Qualification for FDA Regulated Industries.* River Grover, IL: PDA and DHI Publishing, LLC. 2006.
56. López, O. "Data Integrity and Your E-Recs During Processing." LinkedIn, July 2017, www.linkedin.com/pulse/data-integrity-your-e-recs-during-processing-orlando-lopez/.
57. López, O. "Data Integrity Expectations of EU GMP Inspectors." *Pharmaceutical Engineering Europe*, 29(7) 2017.
58. López, O. "Digital Date and Time Stamps." LinkedIn, June 2017, www.linkedin.com/pulse/digital-date-time-stamps-orlando-lopez/.
59. López, O. "Electronic records lifecycle." *Journal of GxP Compliance*, 19(4) 2015, www.ivtnetwork.com/article/electronic-records-lifecycle
60. López, O. "EMA Annex 11 – Changes to Computer Systems Guidelines in the EU." LinkedIn, August 2017, www.linkedin.com/pulse/ema-annex-11-changes-computer-systems-guidelines-eu-orlando-lopez/.
61. López, O. "Overview of Technologies Supporting Security Requirements in 21 CFR Part 11 – Part I." *Pharmaceutical Technology*, 2002a.
62. López, O. "Overview of Technologies Supporting Security Requirements in 21 CFR Part 11 – Part II." *Pharmaceutical Technology*, 2002b.
63. López, O. "Maintaining the Validated State in Computer Systems." *Journal of GxP Compliance*, 17(2) 2013.
64. López, O. "Requirements for Electronic Records Contained in 21 *CFR* 211." *Pharmaceutical Technology*, 36(7) 2008, www.pharmtech.com/requirements-electronic-records-contained-21-cfr-211.
65. López, O. "Technologies Supporting Electronic Records Integrity – Part I." *GXP Journal Articles*, 21(5) 2017a, www.ivtnetwork.com/article/technologies-supporting-electronic-records-integrity?lipi=urn%3Ali%3Apage%3Ad_flagship3_profile_view_base%3BA9Ou4QzOTt2C%2BdkrfpMCag%3D%3D.

66. López, O. "Technologies Supporting Electronic Records Integrity – Part II." *GXP Journal Articles*, 21(5) 2017b, www.ivtnetwork.com/article/technologies-supporting-electronic-records-integrity-part-2-0?lipi=urn%3Ali%3Apage%3Ad_flagship3_profile_view_base%3BA9Ou4QzOTt2C%2BdkrfpMCag%3D%3D.
67. López, O. "Trustworthy Computer Systems." *Journal of GxP Compliance*, 19(2) 2015.
68. McDowall, R. D. "Comparison of FDA and EU Regulations for Audit Trails." *Scientific Computing*, 2014a.
69. McDowall, R. D. "Computer Validation: Do All Roads Lead to Annex 11?" *Spectroscopy*, 29(12) 2014b.
70. McDowall, R. D. "Ensuring Data Integrity in a Regulated Environment." *Scientific Computing*, March/April 2011.
71. McDowall, R. D. "Maintaining Laboratory Computer Validation – How to Conduct Periodic Reviews?" European Compliance Academy (ECA), GMP News, April 2012, www.gmp-compliance.org/pa4.cgi?src=eca_new_news_print_data.htm&nr=3085.
72. McDowall, R. D. "The New GMP Annex 11 and Chapter 4 is Europe's Answer to Part 11." European Compliance Academy (ECA), GMP News, January 2011, www.gmp-compliance.org/eca_news_2381_6886,6885,6738,6739,6934.html.
73. Mell, P., and Grance, T. *The NIST Definition of Cloud Computing*. NIST Special Publication 800-145. National Institute of Standards and Technology, Gaithersburg, Maryland, 2011.
74. MHRA. "GMP/GDP Consultative Committee Note of Meeting." October 2015, www.gov.uk/government/uploads/system/uploads/attachment_data/file/483846/GMP-GDP_CC_minutes_Oct_2015_FINAL.pdf.
75. MHRA. "Good Laboratory Practice: Guidance on Archiving." March 2006.
76. MHRA. "MHRA Expectation Regarding Self Inspection and Data Integrity." May 2014.
77. MHRA. "MHRA GxP Data Integrity Guidance and Definitions." March 2018.
78. NIST. "Guide for Conducting Risk Assessments." 800-30 Rev 1, September 2012.
79. OECD. "The Application of GLP Principles to Computerized Systems." OECD Guidance Document (Draft), September 2014.
80. PDA. "Validation and qualification of computerized laboratory data acquisition systems. Technical Report No. 31." *PDA Journal of Pharmaceutical Science and Technology*, 53(4), 1999.
81. Pressman, R. S. *Software Engineering – A Practitioner's Approach*. New York: McGraw-Hill, 2010.
82. Roemer, M. "New Annex 11: Enabling Innovation." *Pharmaceutical Technology*, 2011.
83. Safe Harbor US–EU Agreement on Meeting Directive 95/46/EC, www.export.gov/safeharbor/index.asp.
84. Schmitt, S. "Data Integrity." *Pharmaceutical Technology*, 38(7) 2014.
85. Schmitt, S. "Data Integrity – FDA and Global Regulatory Guidance." IVT, October 2014.

86. Stenbraten, A. "Cost-effective Compliance: Practical Solutions for Computerised Systems." Paper presented at the ISPE Brussels Conference, GAMP – Cost Effective Compliance, 19–20 September 2011.
87. Stokes, D. "Compliant Cloud Computing – Managing the Risks." *Pharmaceutical Engineering*, 33(4) 2013; 1–11.
88. Stokes, T. "Management's View to Controlling Computer Systems." *GMP Review*, 10(2) 2011.
89. TGA. "Australian Code of Good Manufacturing Practice for Human Blood and Blood Components, Human Tissues and Human Cellular Therapy Products." Version 1.0, April 2013.
90. TGA. "Data Management and Data Integrity (DMDI)." April 2017, www.tga.gov.au/data-management-and-data-integrity-dmdi.
91. US FDA 21 CFR Part 11. "Electronic Records; Electronic Signatures; Final Rule." *Federal Register*, 62(54) 1997; 13429.
92. US FDA 21 CFR Part 58. "Good Laboratory Practice for Non-Clinical Laboratory Studies."
93. US FDA 21 CFR Part 110. "Current Good Manufacturing Practice in Manufacturing, Packing, or Holding Human Food."
94. US FDA 21 CFR Part 312. "Investigational New Drug Application."
95. US FDA 21 CFR Part 606. "Current Good Manufacturing Practice for Blood and Blood Components."
96. US FDA 21 CFR Part 803. "Medical Device Reporting."
97. US FDA 21 CFR 1271. "Human Cells, Tissues, and Cellular and Tissue-Based Products."
98. US FDA. "FDA PAI Compliance Program Guidance, CPG 7346.832, Compliance Program Manual." May 2010, www.ipqpubs.com/wp-content/uploads/2010/05/FDA_CPGM_7346.832.pdf.
99. US FDA. "Guidance for Industry: Blood Establishment Computer System Validation in the User's Facility." April 2013.
100. US FDA. "Guidance for Industry: Computerized Systems in Clinical Investigations." May 2007.
101. US FDA. "Guidance for Industry: Electronic Records; Electronic Signatures – Scope and Application." August 2003.
102. US FDA. "Guidance for Industry: Electronic Source Data in Clinical Investigations." September 2013.
103. Wechsler, J. "Data Integrity Key to GMP Compliance." *Pharmaceutical Technology*, 2014.
104. WHO. " Guidance on Good Data and Record Management Practices." QAS/15.624, September 2015 (Draft).
105. WHO. "Validation of Computerized Systems." *Technical Report Series*, No. 937, Annex 4, Appendix 5, 2006.
106. Wingate, G. *Validating Automated Manufacturing and Laboratory Applications: Putting Principles into Practice*. New York: Taylor & Francis, 1997.
107. Yves, S. "New Annex 11, Evolution and Consequences." January/February, 2012, www.pharma-mag.com.

Appendix V: Reference Papers on E-Records Integrity

1. Technologies Supporting Electronic Records Integrity (Part I). www.ivtnetwork.com/article/technologies-supporting-electronic-records-integrity?lipi=urn%3Ali%3Apage%3Ad_flagship3_profile_view_base%3BA9Ou4QzOTt2C%2BdkrfpMCag%3D%3D.
2. Technologies Supporting Electronic Records Integrity (Part II). www.ivtnetwork.com/article/technologies-supporting-electronic-records-integrity-part-2-0?lipi=urn%3Ali%3Apage%3Ad_flagship3_profile_view_base%3BA9Ou4QzOTt2C%2BdkrfpMCag%3D%3D.
3. Data Integrity Expectations of EU GMP Inspectors. www.pharmtech.com/data-integrity-expectations-eu-gmp-inspectors.
4. Data Integrity and Your E-Recs During Processing. www.linkedin.com/pulse/data-integrity-your-e-recs-during-processing-orlando-lopez/.
5. Digital Date and Time Stamps. www.linkedin.com/pulse/digital-date-time-stamps-orlando-lopez/?trk=v-feed&lipi=urn%3Ali%3Apage%3Ad_flagship3_profile_view_base_recent_activity_details_shares%3Bk16dlsMbz%2F85fa352AWirw%3D%3D.
6. Data Integrity and Your E-Records Storage Devices. www.ispe.org/ispeak/data-integrity-e-records-storage-devices.
7. Electronic Records Integrity in the Data Warehouse Environments. www.ivtnetwork.com/article/electronic-records-integrity-data-warehouse-environments.
8. Electronic Records Lifecycle. www.ivtnetwork.com/article/electronic-records-lifecycle.
9. Trustworthy Computer System. www.ivtnetwork.com/article/trustworthy-computer-systems.
10. A Computer Data Integrity Compliance Model. www.pemag-digital.org/pemag/mar_apr_2015?pg=79#pg79.
11. EU Annex 11 and the Integrity of E-Recs. www.ivtnetwork.com/article/eu-annex-11-and-integrity-erecs.
12. Requirements for Electronic Records Contained in 21 CFR 211. www.pharmtech.com/requirements-electronic-records-contained-21-cfr-211.

Appendix VI: Case Study – Cloud-Based SCADA

Introduction

Chapter 22 discusses areas under the scrutiny of the regulated user and regulatory agencies attention. Some of these areas such as Cloud Environments,* E-records Integrity, IoT, and SLAs are areas associated with cloud-based supervisory control and data acquisition (SCADA) systems.

IoT and Big Data† analytics (Figure 22.1) are key components of Pharma 4.0. The objective of this initiative is the interconnectivity, automation, and ability to gather data beyond the manufacturing facility. Supporting Pharma 4.0 are cloud-based data management and advanced analytics.

SCADA systems are used when data collection is needed. In a typical manufacturing environment, SCADA systems manage manufacturing data related with a CGMP regulated activity.

By moving to a cloud-based environment, the SCADA system owner reduces the costs and problems related with the hardware layer of IT infrastructure.

The typical SCADA configuration in the manufacturing environment has been discussed as a case study elsewhere.‡, § Refer to Figure A6.1.

---

* López, O. "Electronic Records and Cloud Computing" in *Data Integrity in Pharmaceutical and Medical Devices Regulation Operations*, 1st ed. Boca Raton, FL: CRC Press, 2017; 193–199.

† López, O. "Electronic Records Integrity in a Data Warehouse and Business Intelligence." *Journal of Validation Technology Compliance*, 22(2) 2016.

‡ López, O. "Case Study SCADA and Annex 11" in *EU Annex 11 Guide to Computer Validation Compliance for Worldwide Health Agency GMP*. Boca Raton, FL: CRC Press, 2015; 327–339.

§ López, O. "Qualifying SCADA Systems in Practice Acquisition" in *Validating Pharmaceutical Systems – Good Computer Practice in Life Science Manufacturing*, J. Andrews, ed. Boca Raton, FL: CRC Press, 2006; 399–420.

The scope of this Appendix is the upgrade of a typical SCADA architecture to a cloud-based SCADA application running in a software as a service (SaaS) environment. The cloud-based SCADA is remotely connected to the manufacturing site control network. This case study addresses the associated technologies, and the regulatory expectations.

Relevant operational procedural controls are discussed in Chapter 12. Project cost is not addressed.

SCADA Basics

Cell controllers are used for manufacturing control and/or data acquisition. In their most basic form, these systems process inputs and direct outputs. Everything else is simply an activity supporting inputs and outputs (I/Os).* The primary concern for cell controllers is working accurately in the intended process. This is dynamically verified during the qualification† of the cell controller and the integration with the process equipment.

Cell controllers, such as SCADA, are typically used when data collection is needed. Presently, can be used to relay logic and implement analog loops control.

Programmable logic controllers (PLCs), as depicted in Figure A6.1, are always linked to a process plant via a real-time link. To be able to record data, PLCs cannot exist in isolation. The PLC must be linked to a SCADA system.

In a typical manufacturing floor environment, the SCADA application is running on-site, directly connected to the PLC. Sensors, limit switches, and other control components send information to diagnostic systems and control-based monitoring systems, e.g. PLC. The PLC in turn, send the transient data to the SCADA where it can be stored and disseminated to the manufacturing execution system (MES).

The SCADA systems are responsible for processing, storage, and handling of manufacturing-related raw/source data but usually not their final storage.

SCADA software performs the assigned functionality by using serial communication links between master and remote locations. It is primarily

* Snyder, D. "Take Advantage of Control Options." *A-B Journal,* March 1997.

† Qualification is the process of demonstrating whether a computer system and associated controlled process/operation, procedural controls, and documentation are capable of fulfilling specified requirements.

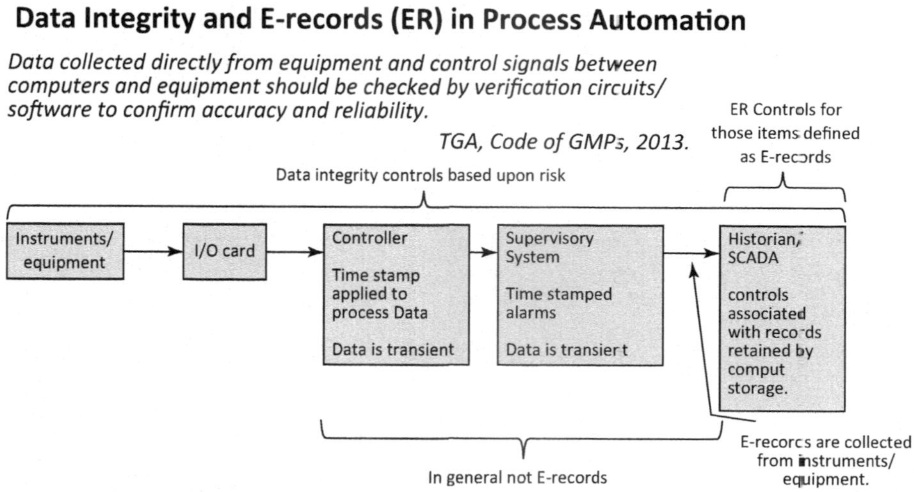

Figure A6.1 Typical data integrity configuration in manufacturing.

concerned with I/O monitoring and the passing of setpoints or open loop commands to remote controllers.

SCADA software, which is normally implemented by the SCADA system supplier, performs such functions as database management, scan I/O data from the remote terminal units (RTUs), log and report scheduling, display drivers, perform on-line calculations, mathematical subroutines, and protocol conversion.

These systems are responsible for the control of electronic records and their display. SCADA systems are supervisory in nature because they are not responsible for the primary control functions. They gather and send information to remote locations, interface with the primary controllers by sending setpoints or calculated values, and are capable of communicating over telephone lines, UHF/VHF radios, microwave systems, satellite systems, fiber optic cables, and via the internet.

In summary, SCADA systems:

- Collect and store historical data.
- Monitor the process and provide information to make decisions on products and processes.
- Provide supervisory control such as: analysis, yield reports, and product information.
- Provide a mechanism to access real-time data in PLCs.
- Detect system alarms.
- Report problems: displays, summaries, acknowledgments.
- Detect possible solutions.

For the purpose of this case study, the SCADA application runs entirely in a remote private cloud and remotely connected to the control network.

SCADA Related Cloud Environments

Cloud computing is the practice of using a network of remote servers hosted on the internet to store, manage, and process data, rather than a local server or a personal computer.

Cloud computing can support SCADA applications using two methods:

- The SCADA application is running on-site, directly connected to the control network and delivering information to the cloud where it can be stored and disseminated.

  The control functions of the SCADA application are entirely isolated to the control network. However, the SCADA application is connected to a service in the cloud that provides the SCADA raw data to a cloud data server. At the cloud data server, it is provided visualization, reporting, and access to remote users.
- The SCADA application is running entirely in the cloud and remotely connected to the control network.

  This is a common to distributed SCADA applications where a single, local SCADA deployment is not practical. The controllers are connected via WAN links to the SCADA application running entirely in the cloud. This is the architecture addressed in this case study.

The typical models in cloud environments and the impact to cloud-related SCADA environments are:

- Infrastructure as a service (IaaS): A virtual data center environment including servers, databases, network, storage, and so on, hosted at the cloud service provider's facility.

  IaaS enables service provider customers to deploy and run SCADA software as they wound on their own IT infrastructure. The consumers maintain control over operating systems, storage, deployed SCADA application, and selected networking components.
- Platform as a service (PaaS): A development environment for software application hosting by the cloud service provider who provide tools,

programming codes, interface modules, and so on, that allows IT professionals to develop software applications and integrate them together in the cloud infrastructure environment either hosted by the service provider or contracted to another provider.

PaaS is used by consumers who develop their own SCADA software and want a common development and runtime platform.

- Software as a service (SaaS): Software application hosted by the cloud service provider in order to perform functions or processes. In this model a regulated user uses a vendor's software application from a web browser or program interface. The regulated user does not manage or control the underlying cloud infrastructure; including the network, servers, operating systems, storage, or application capabilities; with the possible exception of application configuration settings.

  SaaS SCADA consumers don't manage or control the underlying cloud infrastructure. They pay a fee for use of the SCADA.
- Business process as a service (BPaaS): It is a new but popular model for cloud services where the cloud service provider takes full responsibility for not only the design, management, and control of its software application but also the operation of the business process on behalf of the client company.

Internet of Things

In the context of the SCADA systems, the IoT provides the connectivity which enables the remote exchange data between the PLC and MES.

One of the greatest challenges in developing SCADA in the cloud is the state of the internet itself as protocols and web browsers. These weren't designed for real-time data and control. Common complaints of internet-based SCADA system users included having to submit then wait, or pressing update or refresh buttons to show new data.

Many systems relied only on web-based technologies to deliver real-time data. Because the HyperText Transfer Protocol (HTTP)* was never designed for real-time control, these systems were always deficient responding in real time. This technical issue was resolved by giving each user an individual

* www.webopedia.com/TERM/H/HTTP.html.

virtual machine within the server cloud using a hypervisor.* All data is now kept safe and independent of other machines running in the cloud.

The hypervisors are highly available and portable, so in the event of a server failure, the virtual machine can be restarted on another hypervisor within minutes.

All the SCADA software runs within the virtual machine. Customers can connect directly to on-site controllers, and also make changes to controllers and troubleshoot process problems.

Service Level Agreements†

Where "cloud" services are used, attention should be paid to understanding the service provided, ownership, retrieval, retention, and security of e-records.

The physical location where the e-records is held, including the impact of any laws applicable to that geographic location, should be considered.

The responsibilities of the contract giver and acceptor should be defined in a service level agreement (SLA) or contract. This should ensure timely access to e-records, including metadata and audit trails, to the e-records owner and national competent authorities upon request. SLAs with providers should define responsibilities for archiving and continued readability of the e-records throughout the retention period.

Appropriate arrangements must exist for the restoration of the software/system as per its original validated state, including validation and change control information to permit this restoration.

Business continuity arrangements should be included in the contract and tested. The need for an audit of the service provider should be based upon risk.

Even the SLA provides the responsibility to execute the supporting activities by the contract acceptor; the contract giver continues to hold responsibility for the suitability and operability of the computer systems and the integrity of the e-records.

---

* https://en.wikipedia.org/wiki/Hypervisor.

† MHRA. *MHRA GxP Data Integrity Guidance and Definitions*, March 2018.

E-Records Integrity*

In the context of Annex 11, Figure A6.2 provides a pictorial view of the items that the contract giver/regulated user and the contract acceptor/supplier need to comply in a cloud environment. Note that during the operation of the system, the interface between the regulated user and the supplier are the periodic audits to the cloud computing supplier.

The regulated entity must perform periodic audits as part of their vendor assurance program. These audits must take into account the management of e-records integrity as part of the overall cloud service provider's E-records Integrity Governance.

As the reader may notice from above, no matter the selected model (traditional or cloud), the requirements for trustworthy and compliant computer systems performing regulated activities are the same. In addition, the responsibility of computer systems performing regulated activities always belongs to the regulated user.

From the point of view of the cloud service providers and the regulated users, the applicable e-records controls are contained in Chapters 14 through 16.

From the point of view of the regulated users, there are additional controls and requirements to consider.

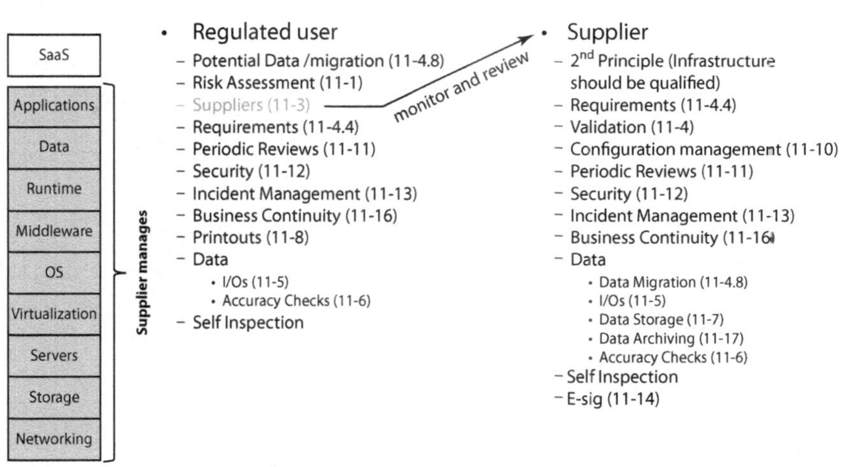

Figure A6.2 SaaS compliance.

* López, O. "Electronic Records and Cloud Computing" in *Data Integrity in Pharmaceutical and Medical Devices Regulation Operations*. Boca Raton, FL: CRC, 2017; 193–199.

E-records migration is the process of transferring e-records between storage types, formats, or computer systems. It is a key consideration for any system implementation, upgrade, or consolidation. E-records migration is usually performed programmatically to achieve an automated migration, freeing up human resources from tedious tasks. E-records migration occurs for a variety of reasons, including: server or storage equipment replacements or upgrades; website consolidation; server maintenance; and data center relocation.*

If e-records are transferred to another format or system, the verification of the e-records migration should include corroboration that e-records are not altered in value, meaning, structure, context and links (e.g. audit trails), and/or meaning during this migration process.

Accessibility and readability of the e-records (Annex 11 p7.1) are also applicable to the migration of e-records.

Of special interest between the regulated user and the cloud service provider is how the e-records will be accessed and, when necessary, sent to the regulated user. The controls associated with sending and receiving e-records are discussed in the Chapter 15. In general, e-records transfer is ensured by the commonly used network protocols.

The integrity of e-records stored in the cloud must be ensured by:

- proper assignment of access permissions by the cloud customer and cloud service provider based on "need to have", "need to know", "minimum possible access level" principles;
- the cloud service provider must run the technical infrastructure in line with good IT practices. The cloud environment must be properly secured and that includes professional patch management, malware protection, intrusion detection and prevention, and so on.

All critical elements important for the cloud customer have to be part of the SLA and understood by the cloud service provider. The cloud service provider must commit to compliance with these requirements.

References:

- Cloud Service Alliance, Cloud Control Matrix, Rev 3.0.1, July 2014.
- Cloud Service Alliance, Security Guidance for Critical Areas of Focus in Cloud Computing, Rev 3.0, November 2011.

* Janssen, C. "Data Migration." www.techopedia.com/definition/1180/data-migration (Retrieved 12 August 2013).

- ECA IT Compliance Working Group, Shared Platform and Cloud Services Implications for Information Governance and Records Management, www.it-compliance-group.org/icg_downloads html.

Other Considerations

Backup

In the cloud environment, if one of the cloud computing nodes fails, other nodes take over the function of the failed cloud computing node.

Data Recovery

The backup and recovery policies and procedures of a cloud service may be superior to those of a single company's IT infrastructure, and if copies are maintained in diverse geographic locations as with most cloud providers, may be more robust.

Private Cloud

Private cloud storage is a type of storage mechanism that stores an organization's data at in-house storage servers by implementing cloud computing and storage technology.

Private cloud storage is similar to public cloud storage in that it provides the usability, scalability, and flexibility of the storage architecture. But unlike public cloud storage, it is not publicly accessible and is owned by a single organization and its authorized external partners.

Private cloud storage is also known as internal cloud storage.

Redundancy Access

Access to user data in this infrastructure generally depends on the company's single internet provider. If the internet provider experiences an outage, then users don't have remote access to the SCADA application. Cloud computing providers have multiple, redundant internet connections. If users have internet access, they have access to the SCADA application.

Qualification of Cloud SCADA

Objectives and Benefits of the Upgrade

The objective of the SCADA qualification in the cloud environment is to demonstrate the intended use of the SCADA, response time, and the level of CGMP e-records integrity.

The following is a list of the benefits of this project:

- Doesn't involve the purchase, deployment, configuration of new servers and software, and cost of storage for e-records by the regulated user/entity.
- Reduced systems administrative costs and extension of the system life cycle.

In the context of key functionality, the expectations of the users must be equal or higher in the new architecture and environment. These expectations to consider are:

- Operator(s) actions traceability.
- E-records and system reliability.
- Ability to audit system generated e-records.
- File and system security.
- Access to production e-records, including alarms conditions, interface errors, and so on.
- Issuing of process command by operator(s).
- Monitoring of the process, including interfaces monitoring.
- E-records storage and archiving capabilities.
- Provide written report traceability to the file level.

When a typical SCADA architecture is replaced by a cloud-based SCADA architecture, there must be no resultant decrease in data quality, CGMP controls, and quality assurance. Consideration must be given to the risk of losing aspects of the previous system which could result from reducing the involvement of operators.

System Requirements

This section specifies all requirements for the SCADA system at the cloud. The SCADA application is to be running in the cloud and remotely connected to the manufacturing site control network.

Infrastructure (Hardware and Software)

1. Infrastructure must be run in line with good IT practices, including security, patch management, malware protection, intrusion detection, and prevention.
2. Infrastructure must be qualified.

Hardware Requirements

- *Infrastructure Hardware*
  1. An additional security server will be installed.
  2. Security server will provide the ability to archive data files to media that cannot be modified by ordinary means.
  3. Security server shall have the capability to recover from archival media.
  4. The SCADA server will maintain the capability to back up the system files and data.
  5. The SCADA and security servers will connect to the manufacturing site control network via the internet.
- *Operator Workstation Hardware*
  1. Operator workstation hardware will be located at the manufacturing area only.
  2. Login and run of the application is to be performed from the manufacturing area operated workstations. There will be no application executed outside the manufacturing area.
  3. Each operator workstation (computer hardware) may be modified (add larger hard drive, and so on) to allow the workstation to boot locally and host backup file(s).
  4. Each operator workstation shall have the capability to recover from controlled archived media.
- *PLC Hardware*

There will be no changes to the PLC hardware as a result of the upgrade project.

Interfaces

- *Operator Interface*
  1. The login process will be modified to make it compatible with requirement #2 in section "Operator Workstation Hardware," above.

2. Other than a revised login process, as listed above, the operator interface screens will not change as a result of the upgrade.
3. Interface between the operator interface and the SCADA must be encrypted (e.g. VPN).

- *Cloud SCADA Interfaces*
  1. Remote I/Os to/from the cloud SCADA must be encrypted.
  2. Computer systems exchanging e-records with the cloud SCADA (e.g. PLC, MES, remote/local workstations, and so on) must include appropriate built-in checks for the correct I/Os.

SCADA System Administrators Workstation

1. The system administrator workstation I/Os at the manufacturing site must be encrypted.
2. The system administrator workstation I/Os at the cloud SCADA site is to be connected via a secure local area network (LAN).
3. The system administrator workstation will not have access to the e-records and functionality associated with the operations, including e-records deletion, system configuration changes, and database modification.

Security Requirements*

1. Physical and/or logical controls should be in place to restrict access to computer system to unauthorized persons.
2. SCADA and security servers must be designed to record the identity of operators entering, changing, confirming or deleting data including server's clock.
3. The date/time stamp for the audit trail function shall be applied automatically by the digital time-stamping service and shall not be entered by the user.
4. The clock of the security server shall be synchronized to the digital time-stamping service once every five minutes.
5. The clock of each workstation shall be synchronized to the security server at a minimum of once every five minutes, or whenever a workstation is restarted.

---

* Cazemir, J., Overbeek, P., and Peters, L. *Security Management – The Key to Managing IT Services*. TSO, 2006.

6. Workstation clock can be used for time stamping those actions recorded on paper by the operator.
7. Operator level users will be prevented from accessing the operating system.
8. Only users with an access level of system administrator will have access to the operating system but will not have access to the e-records and functionality associated with the operations, including e-records deletion, system configuration changes, and database modification.
9. The upgrade will provide centralized password administration.
10. The system administrator(s) shall have the ability to add, modify, view, list, and perform maintenance on usernames and user rights.
11. The upgraded system will support at least six levels of access control security.
12. Users will be configured once and have different access levels on workstation-based access rights.
13. Passwords shall expire automatically. The password expiration period shall be a configurable parameter.
14. Password files shall be encrypted or otherwise secured so that passwords cannot be read by ordinary means.
15. The system shall ensure that usernames are unique and not reusable. The password selection ensures that the same user cannot re-use the last password.
16. Passwords will be masked as they are keyed in during login.
17. The system will provide the ability to enforce password length.
18. Failed login attempts shall be logged. The user shall be disabled after a configurable number of successive failed login attempts.
19. Any attempts of unauthorized use shall be reported to the system administrator.
20. All users will be subject to an automatic logout function based on user inactivity. The automatic logout time shall be a configurable parameter.
21. A record shall be maintained of all changes to user rights and access levels.
22. The access level rights shall be configurable by the system administrator.
23. Usernames shall not be capable of being physically deleted from the SCADA system.
24. When a user should no longer have access to the system, their account shall be disabled, but remain in the list of users.

E-Records Integrity Requirements

Data integrity must cover e-records in the cloud SCADA and security servers, during processing in the cloud SCADA, and while the e-records are in transit (e.g. interfaces). (NIST SP 800-33)

1. As applicable, e-records to be migrated to the cloud SCADA server must be verified. The objective of the verification is to ensure that the e-records are not altered in value and/or meaning during this migration process. The execution of the verification process must be documented in a protocol and the execution of the protocol must be recorded.
2. E-records shall have the ability to be archived to media that cannot be modified through ordinary means.
3. Historical data files, batch report data files, audit trail files, or archived versions of these files shall not be deleted or modified.
4. The system shall provide the ability to log system actions (with the associated date/time stamp) including:
   - Changes to usernames.
   - Successful and failed login attempts.
5. The system shall have the ability to log changes within the applications, as indicated by changes to address values containing process data. Process audit trail data includes:
   - Changes to recipe and set point values.
   - Changes to operating modes of controllers and devices.
   - Batch Commands (start/stop/pause/resume/abort, and so on).
   - Changes to alarm statuses and limits.
   - Events, warnings, alarms, and interlocks.
6. The system shall have the ability to load and view historical data files, archived data files, batch data files, trend data files and all other process data files that have been archived to removable storage media.
7. Changes to security levels shall be included in the audit trail.
8. An audit trail repository shall be created as part of the SCADA and the security administration servers.
9. The audit trail record shall include the operator name, time/date stamp, action, and reason in the audit trail file.
10. The audit trail function must be completely outside the access of users except for read-only access of the audit trail files.
11. The audit trail function shall not be capable of being disabled.

12. An electronic audit trail shall be collected by the systems and stored in the security server.
13. The audit trail function shall provide the ability to query entries or groups of entries based on date/time, batch number, and/or system tagname for a specified period of time.
14. Audit trail shall be able to be viewed, printed, and/or exported to a PC-based file in a commonly readable format.

Trending Requirements

1. There will be no changes to any of the functions or applications that use real-time trending as a result of this upgrade.

Reporting Requirements

1. It should be possible to obtain clear printed copies of electronically stored e-records, including audit trails, metadata, and e-signatures.
2. The system shall provide the ability to generate query-based historical reports in tabular form.
3. The system administrator will have the ability to print reports of users' IDs, security level and access rights.
4. The upgraded system shall have the ability to print archived process, alarm, batch, and trend data in a tabular format.
5. On those reports to be signed, the handwritten signatures shall be uniquely and non-repudiate linked to the electronic record(s).
6. When an e-record is linked with the paper-based report and the record is modified, the system should prompt the user for another handwritten signature.

Environmental Requirements

1. The security servers will be located in the secure computer rooms of both plants.
2. There will be no changes to the operating environment as a result of the upgrade.

Compatibility

1. All new hardware will be compatible with all existing system.
2. All changes to the system will not require modifications to the existing applications.

Performance

1. No additional system downtime shall be required as a result of the changes described in this document.
2. Any changes made to the operator workstation hardware shall not result in a degradation of the system performance (i.e. system transaction response times). If longer response times result, this must be identified, evaluated, and documented during system design.

Maintenance

1. No additional special tools shall be required to perform maintenance on the control system.
2. Periodically, server data will need to be moved from the process data servers to archive media in order to provide storage space for additional data.

Qualification Elements

The trustworthiness of electronic information is in part dependent on reliability and integrity of the computing technologies used for the e-records creation, use, maintenance, and storage. It is therefore, fitting that any emerging regulations for e-records be predicated on the use of computer technologies that are correct, reliable and suitable for their intended purpose. The qualification is the process to be followed to demonstrate that the technologies used supports the intended use of the cloud-based SCADA.

In this book, Chapters 4 through 6, 13, 14, and 17 provide a method to qualify a cloud-based SCADA.

In summary, the key elements to successfully execute qualification on a SCADA computer-related projects are:

- Selection of a development and maintenance methodology that best suits the nature of the system under development.
- Establish proper performance of the system:
  - Selection of hardware based on capacity and functionality.
  - Identification and testing of the operational data load limits to establish, if necessary, associated production procedures.

- Identification of operational functions associated with the users, sequencing, Part 11 remediation, company standards, and safety requirements.
- Identification and testing of "worst case" operational or production conditions.

- Documentation of the qualification process*
  - Written design specification that describes what the software is intended to do and how it is intended to do it;
  - A written test plan based on the design specification, including both structural and functional analysis.
  - Test results and an evaluation of how these results demonstrate that the predetermined design specification has been met.
  - Availability of procedural controls to maintain the qualification state of the computer system and its operating environment.
  - Any modification to a component of the system and it operating environment must be evaluated to determine the impact to the system. If required, qualification is to be re-executed totally or partially.

Because of the nature of the modifications, the operational qualification stressed about the input and outputs to/from the cloud-based SCADA server.

All work products (design specification, plan, test results, and so on) were considered project documentation. A subset of the project documentation is considered qualification documentation as well. Information was not duplicated to create a specific qualification-related document.

Summary

There were various factors to the success of this project:

- Clear interpretation of the regulation.
- Finding the technology based on analysis needs.
- The modifications and upgrades did not affect the applications or the performance of the servers.
- Providing requirements traceability to all project activities and work products.

---

* FDA. *Guidance for the Industry: Computerized Systems Used in Clinical Trials*, April 1999 (obsolete).

- Providing the documented evidence required by the regulations, without adding required project documentation.
- Controlling the cost and effectiveness of the project by finding the correct technology based on the context of the remediation plan.

Additional Readings

ASTM E 2500-07. *Standard Guide for Specification, Design, and Verification of Pharmaceutical and Biopharmaceutical Manufacturing Systems and Equipment*, 2013.

Cazemir, J., Overbeek, P., and Peters, L. *Security Management – The Key to Managing IT Services*. TSO, 2006.

EudraLex. "EU Guidelines to Good Manufacturing Practice, Medicinal Products for Human and Veterinary Use, Annex 15 – Qualification and Validation (Draft)." Volume 4, February 2014.

López, O. "Electronic Records and Cloud Computing" in *Data Integrity in Pharmaceutical and Medical Devices Regulation Operations*. Boca Raton, FL: CRC Press, 2017; 193–199.

López, O. *Qualification of SCADA Systems*. West Sussex, United Kingdom: Sue Horwood Publishing Limited, 2002.

Index